SOUTH ASIA:
From Freedom to Terrorism

It is better to reorganise that we are in darkness than to pretend that we can see the light.

Hedley Bull, The Anarchical Society (A Study of order in World Politics)

SOUTH ASIA:
From Freedom to Terrorism

SHASHI B. SAHAI

GYAN PUBLISHING HOUSE
New Delhi 110 002

SOUTH ASIA:
From Freedom to Terrorism
[*Politics, History, Current Affairs, International Relations*]

ISBN: 81-212-0580-8

Published in 1998 in India by
Gyan Publishing House
5, Ansari Road
New Delhi 110 002

Laser Typeset at Akshar, Delhi
Printed at Mehra Offset Press, New Delhi.

Dedicated to the memory of the half a million men, women and children who lost their lives during the partition riots in 1947 and those being killed everyday in terrorist violence and civil strife in India, Pakistan *and* Sri Lanka.

Contents

Preface

This book, virtually extracted from me by my publishers, is none the less a culmination of the exercise that began with the writing of my first book, *Politics of Corruption: The Goddess That Failed*. If my writing enterprise started as an act of shedding some painful burdens of the heart, the present book is an effort at shedding the last such burden. It says all that was left to be said about my country and countrymen.

In that sense *The Fifty Years: South Asia from Freedom to Violent Order* can be taken as the third and last volume of a series that began with *Politics of Corruption* and continued with *India: Twilight at Midday*. Taken together, the three books may be regarded as a triology with reasonable intellectual consistency. Although the three books focus on separate facets of Indian reality, they broadly complement each other and form a consistent whole. Already, those who had read *Politics of Corruption* were avid readers of *Twilight at Midday* and would, hopefully, seek for the third book too with the same degree of mental appetite and intellectual curiosity.

On the surface, though, *The Fifty Years: South Asia from Freedom to Violent Order* represents a departure from the earlier two books in respect of its canvas or scope. As the sub-title itself suggests, it covers not only India but Pakistan, Sri Lanka, Burma (Myanmar) and Bangladesh also in regard to its main theme—violent order. But that was unavoidable. For any study of 50 years of independence from colonial rule could not exclude Pakistan and Bangladesh which were part of one country at the time of independence Burma (Myanmar) which was so till a decade earlier and Sri Lanka which was nearly so. For one who was a young student at the time of independence and had seen the coming of it, how could the story of *The Fifty Years* begin without including the other four countries also? Specially when one has lived through every pulsating moment of that story intensely and shared its joys and sorrows.

For the post-independence generation, the current state of on-going, unceasing, relentless violence, terror and bloodshed within and among each of the four countries of South Asia is an accepted fact of life which does not cause any undue concern. It has also come to be accepted and acquiesced in just as easily that bomb blasts and killings in Kashmir, Punjab and the rest of India would be caused by Pak agencies and killings by masked gunmen in Karachi or bomb blasts in Lahore or Multan by Indian agents.

But those who have seen the whole sub-continent as one and lived through the marathon labyrinthian negotiations and settlements which brought about the birth of independent states of India and Pakistan, find it not so easy to stomach the contemporary situation of perennial strife and bloodshed. When the sub-continent was partitioned as a result of a political settlement between the Congress and the Muslim League brought about by the departing British, and not in consequence of a war between two fighting machines, no one had imagined that the two new states would be in a state of *permanent adversary relationship* even 50 years later. They find it difficult to reconcile to the colossal scale of human tragedy being perpetrated on either side of the territorial divide.

It hurts as much when 34 innocent passengers including 10 children, are killed in a powerful bomb explosion in a train near Bhatinda (India on 8 July 1997) as when unidentified gunmen indulge in targetted killings of people in Karachi (Pakistan) everyday almost ritually. It hurts more when one recalls the times of the Raj during which such macabre events happened only in fiction or some far away 'Timbuctoo' once in a blue moon. Unconsciously but compulsively, one starts looking back to the pre-independence time with a feeling of nostalgia, even though it hurts one's sense of patriotism.

The feeling is well summed up by a newspaper columnist commenting on India's 48th Independence Day celebrations in August 1995: " In 1947, good-Government was no substitute for self-Government. In 1995, self-Government is no substitute for good Government..... In our days of slavery, we had come to believe that Independence was the panacea for all our ills—social, economic and political .... The gleam of independence has dimmed except in the eyes of the hopelessly optimistic."*

Talk to any ordinary, politically non-committed person who has not directly or indirectly benefited from the post-independence boom in political corruption, a village old man, an old woman, a retired government employee or any other survivor of the pre-independence days, and he or she will echo the same feeling today. Talk to anyone other than the power-grabbers and their tribe, who was around at the dawn of independence, and India at 50 is a *shattered dream*.

A few years back, the late President of Sri Lanka, R. Premadasa and his wife came on a pilgrimage to Bodh Gaya in Bihar, India, the holy place of Lord Buddha's enlightenment. The distinguished couple were appalled at the utterly poor living conditions of the people in the neighbourhood of Buddha temple. They visited some of the hovels and tenements of the poor, offered them some instant assistance and promised to launch a scheme for the betterment of their living conditions. After their departure, an old woman said: "It is for the first time since the end of the British Raj that some one has been so protective and caring for a poor woman like me."

There are innumerable old men and women across the country, articulate and not so articulate survivors of the Raj period, who tell you the same thing in one way or the other. Particularly when it comes to talking about the state of violence and terror in India today, they mince no words in blaming it on the crooks and ignoramuses who are misgoverning the country, and harking back to the peace and security provided by the Raj. How come the dream of independence has soured so completely in 50 years?

The book tries to find an answer to that nagging question in regard to one vital concern of our life today— violence and terror in the sub-continent. Talking about the state of corruption in India, B.K. Nehru in his bare — all memoirs says, "Thanks God I no longer travel abroad. I feel ashamed to be a member of one of the

* "State of the Nation" by Poonam I. Kaushik in *The Hitwada*, dated 18 August 1995.

most corrupt societies in the world." He goes on to add that "this is not the India we worked for at all."* His exasperation at the abysmal depths of corruption the Indian society has sunk into is quite understandable. For today's India is of those who "come to tend your cattle and walk away with the fodder." It is India of those who brazenfacedly mock at moral standards by saying they had heard of football ground, cricket ground but not of moral ground. It is India of thugs and gangsters who have usurped power at least in some areas on flagrantly casteist and clanish support and are hardly distinguishable from mafia dons.

I had a similar feeling of alienation and desperation while writing *Politics of Corruption*. But you can at least physically exist in a corrupt society, howsoever corrupt it may be. In a wildly violent society that the whole of the sub-continent has come to be today, your very physical existence is at stake. You may be shot dead in your home, street or village pathway if you are in Kashmir, North-East or Bihar or blown to pieces while travelling in a bus or train anywhere in India. Karachi in Pakistan and parts of Sri Lanka are in similar plight. How is it that a whole sub-continent which was a model of peace and security under British rule for nearly two centuries has turned into one of the most dangerous places in the world to live in? What went wrong?

In exploring for an adequate answer to the question staring every South Asian in his face, I had to mentally reconstruct a series of the most corrosive heart-felt experiences of the last half century. Going down the memory lane step by step through all the horrors of the last 50 or 51 years, beginning the 'Great Calcutta Killing' and the partition riots, has been like wading through rivers of blood or orgy of fire, enough to mentally exhaust or 'burn out' any normal, sane human being completely. In the bargain, I have not only burnt my fingers but burnt myself out as far as the affairs of my country are concerned. No more of any further forays into the realm of Indian reality for me. The affair with India in my writing exercise ends with this book, which is kind of a valedictory presentation to my country. I have unburdened myself of my last load.

---

* *Nice Guys Finish Second*, B.K. Nehru, 1997.

But writing, as I now realise, is like reading an addition of sorts. Once you taste the pains and pleasures of writing, even though as a release or something, it is difficult, if not impossible, to give up writing altogether. I have not been a literati nor I am spiritually inclined so I could roam in the realms of fancy or spirituality. I am a very mundane person, very much this— worldly, constantly tossed about and utterly vulnerable mentally to the happenings around the world. In the circumstances, the only course open for me is to adjust my antenna outwardly, to the wider world outside the frontiers of my country. For at least in regard to one vital area of human concern—international violence or war—the world scene is as refreshing as the South Asian is depressing. While in South Asia new fronts of historical hatreds and animosities are opening every third day or month in the Habbesian 'War of each against all', long standing strifes and conflicts are ending in other parts of the world with remarkable ease.

And it is happening with a speed which was unimaginable even ten years ago. In less than a decade, seemingly interminable Civil wars and strifes in many troubled parts of the globe coming on since the end of the Second World War or so have ended astoundingly tamely, as if by a magic of history or miracle of providence. It happened in Nicaragua, El Salvador, Angola, Cambodia and the Middle East. The latest to come under the spell of this miracle is Guatemala in Latin America. A 36-year-old-civil war in that country in which 130,000 people, mostly non-combatant civilians, had been killed, came to a smooth end towards the end of December 1996. War weary guerrilla and government leaders signed an accord on 29 December, 1996 to bring central America's longest and most savage civil war to a close.

But that is only a relatively minor aspect of the peace drama unfolding itself on the world stage. My almost pathological sensitivity to anything wantonly destructive of human life, like war, in any corner of the globe had always gripped me with some kind of an unknown fear of a world holocaust. The psychic effect of having grown up in the midst of the most devastating world war of human history and lived through the threat of the final, nuclear destruction of humanity, has lingered. The threat looked like coming true in that grim autumn of 1962 when a dreadful confrontation— direct and nuclear— between the U.S. and Soviet Union over Cuba and the resultant nuclear holocaust appeared imminent. The indelible imprint of the Cuban nuclear crisis, which came close to making my unknown fear come true, has led me on to a ceaseless exploration of the Frankestein of war, which has been the most lethal man-made killer phenomenon in human history. In the process, I have stumbled upon some inexorable trends of social development which, for the first time in human history, point to the vista of permanent world peace that has been eluding mankind since the time the Greek Aryans conquered and destroyed Knossos, the capital of Minoans, in the Augean basin after 15th century B.C.

Keeping a tab on the happenings around the world, with the spectre of October 1962 deeply imbedded in a corner of the mind, I recorded as follows in my diary in 1989: "What has happened to the world? The outgoing hawkish US President Reagan, who started his regime by describing Soviet Union as the 'evil empire' has ended by certifying that Gorbachov was the best hope for peace in the world. The PLO leader Yasser Arafat, to whom the US was the arch enemy till the other day, has started regarding it as an honest broker, if not a warm friend, in Palestinian— Israeli dispute. The last two years encapsuled events which have undone conflict situations across the world coming on since 1914. Oh God, what a change? It has sent structures of war built for over 40 years tumbling down like nine pins."

In late 1989, Peter Millar, a newspaper columnist, put it thus, "only now is the Second World War ending ...... In 200 years from now, the 20th century may be seen as the era of the Great 75-year war which began in 1914 and ended in 1989."

My explorations are leading towards periods thousands of years before 1914 when the concept of world conquest seized mankind and soaked every page of known history and conjured up or constructed pre-history in human blood. The Greeks, Romans, Arabs, Mongols, and Turks were all world conquerors in the sense that they set about to conquer the *known world* or the *world that mattered* to them. After the birth of nation states in modern times, the nationalists took over from where the earlier world conquerors had left, plunging the world into a series of nationalist wars culminating into the two mega wars of the 20th century. What ended in 1989 was not what began in 1914, as Peter Millar says, but what began with the sacking of Knossos after 15th century B.C.

There will be few takers of what appears to me the inexorable logic of the evolution of human society. May be I am in the company of those who conceive of a time when "nuclear weapons will be nothing but memory." The idea of a warless world may appear too good, nebulous, generalised and sweeping today, but perhaps not so two hundred years from now. Even if it is a grand illusion, I would rather live with it until it proves to be so, if ever. It is better to live hugging an illusion about the future of the world than being torn apart everyday with one's country's reality. In any case, it is good enough to keep me engaged for the rest of my reading and writing life.

It has been a feat of sorts to complete this book in an incredibly short time, in the midst of various unavoidable distractions, to keep to the deadline of the 50th anniversary of South Asia's independence. It has been possible because one has emotionally lived through every momentous event in the story of these last 50 years. Unforgettable images stored in mind's vault, layers and layers of them, constituted the richest resource base of the writing. It was like writing one's memoirs without bringing in oneself, ostensibly or even in assessing events and passing judgements, which severely restricted the freedom associated with writing one's life story. That made the task more arduous.

But in spite of all my wish, and my publishers' anxiety, I couldn't have done the job but for exhaustive notes on South Asia prepared and books and materials collected by my younger son, Shikhar Sahai, for his Ph.D thesis before he joined one of the central services. It was just a chance that the topic of his thesis happened to be "India as a Major Power in the Eyes of her Neighbours." The basic facts about South Asia collected by him for preparation of his thesis, which I stumbled upon in course of the writing, came in very handy as valuable source material for the book.

15th August 1997

SHASHI B. SAHAI
'Sanctuary'
Hari Shankar Verma Lane
New Patliputra, Patna - 800 013

Acknowledgements

Reconstructing the scene of the tumultuous events immediately preceding the grant of independence and telling the story of the succeeding 50 years studded with equally, if not more, stormy happenings was a tough job by any reckoning. It would not have been possible without sincere help and cooperation from many friends as well as resource persons associated with several libraries. Particularly in view of the limited time span in which it had to be done.

One of the foremost among them is Lt. General S.K. Sinha PVSM (Retd.) a former Vice-Chief of the Army Staff, and now the Governor of Assam, who had served as a staff officer to Lt. General Sir Dudley Russall, Commander of the Delhi and East Punjab command set up to restore peace in riot-torn East Punjab in September 1947. From September to November 1947, he remained virtually confined to his command train escorting huge refugee columns to Pakistan border amidst attacks on them in the way and such other unfortunate scenes. He not only shared his traumatic experience of those times, giving an insight into the tempo of events, but also helped me with extracts from his book *Operation Rescue* relevant to that period.

I am equally grateful to my senior colleague, Fazal Ahmad I.P.S. (Retd.), a former Police Chief of Bihar, with whom I had frequent discussions in course of the writing. As Amir of Ahmadi sect in Bihar, he gave me full account of the fate of Ahmadis in Pakistan since its creation up to date. He also made available to me the official Report of the Court of Enquiry into anti-Ahmadi disturbances and violence in Pakistan in 1953 headed by Justice Muhammad Munir, who rose to be the Chief Justice of Pakistan. It is a classic 387-page report which provides a rare insight into the beginning of sectarianism in Pakistan in those early post-independence years, which has assumed such alarming proportions now. (Incidentally, Justice Munir has mentioned in his book *From Jinhah To Zia* published in 1981 that he himself was not in possession of a copy of that famous report.)

My most sincere thanks go to Dr. S. Narain and Dr. S.F. Rub of A.N.S. Institute of Social Sciences, Patna, but for whose active and continuous cooperation, I could not have done the job. I rushed to them whenever in need of any missing facts and links in the story and they placed the resources of the rich library of the A.N.S. Institute at my disposal. Dr. Rub also helped me to have access to the great central Khudabaksh Library known all over the country for its treasure of books on Muslim history, culture and politics. They also helped in sorting my thoughts out in course of several rounds of discussions with them.

My thanks are also due to the officers in charge of Sachchidanand Sinha Central Library, Patna, which is a storehouse of books on politics and political developments since pre-independence days, Bihar State Police Library, Patna, and library of the Bureau of Police Research and Development, Government of India, Delhi.

Finally, the list cannot be complete without bringing in Shashi Prabha, my life partner and companion, but for whose self-effacing support and help this book, as the earlier ones too, could not have come up. As a model aide, she adroitly fended me off from innumerable telephone calls and visitors during the period of writing, besides participating in and contributing to in-house discussions on the theme of the book along with my elder son, Sanjay Sahai.

16th August 1997 **SHASHI B. SAHAI**

SECTION I

SOUTH ASIAN DRAMA

1

The Coming of Freedom

End of Empire

It all began in mid 1945. Victory of Allied Powers in World War II was not only the moment of glory but also the moment of truth for the victorious Empire countries of western Europe. In just over a decade or so beginning 1945, they had to shed their imperial hold over the following countries, which had been colonial or semi-colonial territories for a century or more : India, Pakistan, Burma (now Myanmar), Ceylon (now Sri Lanka), East Indies (Indonesia), Malaya (Malaysia), Singapore, the Philippines, Laos, Cambodia, Vietnam, Syria, Iraq, Lebanon, Israel, Egypt, Libia, Cyprus, Tunisia, Morocco, Algeria Mauretania, Sudan, Gabon, Ivory Coast, Madagascar, Chad, Niger, Upper Volta, Dahomey, Togoland, Cameroons, Mali, Senegal, Guinea, Congo, Ghana, Nigeria, Sierra Leone, Tanganyka, Uganda, Rwanda, Burundi, Trinidad, Jamaica, etc.

They had all been colonies or otherwise less than fully self-governing under the tutelage of western metropolitan powers before the war. They all achieved full independence from the Empire countries within a remarkably short time-span after the war with remarkable ease. Some Empire countries like Holland and France might have dragged their feet in South East Asia for some time due to their lingering infatuation with the imperial idea, but they had to fold up and withdraw sooner than later. The countries liberated in this momentous sweep of history were as different from one another in their size, racial composition, strategic location, natural resources, etc. as, say, Indonesia and Cameroons. Many of the erstwhile colonial countries, particularly of the African continent, could not even boast of strong nationalist movements for independence before they got it as a bonus. Surely such a pervasive world-wide wind of liberation that swept the colonial countries across the board could not have been an accident of history. For history may move by fits and starts but not by accidents.

There was as much of a pattern in the liquidation of colonial empires after the Second World War as in their acquisition by imperial powers in earlier centuries. This momentous historical development needs fuller analysis and will be dealt with in another chapter. It may be of interest here to briefly touch upon the hiccups in the process symbolized by the acts of some at least of the imperial countries to delay the inevitable.

Holland and France were two such countries which refused to see the writings on the wall and hand over power gracefully to their erstwhile colonies in South East Asia. The Dutch and the French chose in stead to fight it out in East Indies (Indonesia) and Indo-China respectively, with intermittent negotiations thrown in between bouts of fighting, just to retain vestiges of authority and control in their erstwhile colonies. Of course, the situation in their colonies in South East Asia was a little complicated because these had been occupied by the Japanese during World War II and had to be first liberated by the Allied forces. But in stead of handing over in good grace to nationalist forces after the Japanese surrender in August 1945, they toyed with the idea of establishing some kind or the other of their pre-war imperial control over their former colonies.

The Dutch in East Indies (Indonesia)

The Dutch had actually organized the Netherlands Indies Civil Administration (NICA) to take over and govern the East Indies islands on recapture from the Japanese by the Allied forces. After the Japanese surrender, the Dutch re-established their rule through NICA over the islands of the Indies except for substantial areas of Java and Sumatra. These areas eluded them because the Indonesian Republic headed by the nationalist leader Sukarno had already established its authority in this region before the arrival of Allied forces in September 1945. Since then, it was a continuous state of fighting and negotiations simultaneously between the nationalist Republic and the Dutch seeking to retain some hold. In July 1947, the Dutch actually resorted to extensive military action against the Republic reducing its control to a small district in the neighbourhood of its capital Jakarta. The Indonesian question had to be taken up by the U.N. Security Council at this stage.

The Security Council imposed immediate cease-fire, the first of its career, which was accepted and yet violated by both parties. Protracted negotiations between the Dutch and Nationalist Republic under U.N. auspices, ensued, punctuated with truce agreements which were frequently violated. The last truce was terminated in December 1948 and the Dutch reverted to armed action against the nationalists. Dutch armed forces over-ran the Republican territory and captured leading members of the nationalist Republican government. It was only after effective U.N. Security Council intervention that the Dutch agreed to resume negotiations and, as a necessary pre-condition, to release the captured nationalist leaders. A truce was finally agreed upon and came into effect in August 1949.

A Round Table Conference was convened at the Hague and prolonged negotiations followed to hammer out a settlement. The conference continued in session until an agreement was reached and signed in November 1949. The agreement envisaged the establishment of a "Cooperative Union" of Holland and independent Indonesian state as equal partners. It was on this basis that sovereignty was finally transferred by the Dutch to Indonesia under intense international pressure on 27 December, 1949. Even the tenuous link between Holland and Indonesia through the so-called "Cooperative Union" could not last and was terminated in 1954. And in August 1956, Indonesia unilaterally repudiated its debts to Holland estimated by the latter at 170 million dollars. The rupture between the erstwhile empire country Holland and the independent Republic of Indonesia was complete, thanks to the obduracy of the Dutch to hold on to the shadow of the empire during the initial years after Japan's defeat.

The French in Indo-China

The French persistence with their imperial infatuation in Indo-China had a disastrous impact on South East Asia. Unlike in other occupied areas in that region, the Japanese had not totally displaced the authority of the French colonial power in Indo-China during the war. The reason was that France itself had surrendered before Germany earlier and under the Vichy regime collaborated with the Axis powers during the war. Japan therefore, after occupying

Indo-China entered into an agreement with the French government in August 1940 in terms of which it got all it needed in that region without formally replacing the French. It got the right of passage through French Indo-China in pursuit of its pacific war objectives as well as recognition of its dominant position economically and politically in that area. In return, it allowed the French governor Decoux to nominally rule over Indo-China states during the war.

In March 1945, however, when defeat in the war appeared a certainty, the Japanese withdrew support from the French governor and installed Emperor Bao Dai of Annam as the head of a puppet regime. But this regime was hotly resisted by the nationalists organized as Vietnam Independence League or "Viet Minh "under the radical leadership of Ho Chi Minh. And when the Japanese capitulated in August 1945, the nationalists took over control and Bao Dai fled over to France. On September 2,1945, the nationalists declared the establishment of independent Republic of Vietnam.

That was the moment of truth for France when it could have acted with statesmanship and accepted the inevitable. But it did not because it had no intention of withdrawing from Indo-China. Instead, the French government drafted fresh plans for a new colonial regime in Indo-China. The scheme envisaged transformation of the French Empire into a French Union comprising metropolitan France and four protectorates and a colony in Indo-China. This scheme fell far short of independence and even a meaningful autonomy. This could hardly be acceptable to the nationalists under Ho Chi Minh who had been waging underground resistance against both Japan and the French colonial regime during the war. They further consolidated their position in the northern half of Vietnam (north of the 16th parallel) where the Chinese did the job of receiving Japanese surrender. The Chinese allowed the nationalist Vietnam government to function, hold elections and establish a Parliament. In return, they extorted several concessions for China's nationals, trade and commerce.

Although the nationalists, entrenched in the north, could not dislodge the French from Saigon, other cities and coastal areas , a bitter civil war ensued in the region. Initially the U.S was unwilling to support French colonial interests against Vietnamese nationalism, but the situation drastically changed after 1950. With the outbreak of the Korean war, America started regarding the war in Indo-China as a part of its over-all fight against Soviet communism. Ho Chi Minh, it may be remembered, was not only a nationalist but also a great Marxist, and his regime by all accounts a communist regime. Once Vietnam got caught in the vortex of the cold war, it had to live through one of the longest and most savage wars of recent world history. And French imperial ambitions in Indo-China at the end of the war in 1945 had something to do with it, although it would be too simplistic to blame France alone for all that followed.

The British in Burma and Malaya (Malaysia)

The British too had the problem of war period, Japanese occupation in respect of two colonial countries in South East Asia—Burma and Malaya—at the end of the war in 1945. And in case of Malaya at least, they had to reckon with tenacious and prolonged communist guerrilla activities also. But they managed to avoid the kind of clumsy situation in which the Dutch in Indonesia and the French in Indo-China landed themselves at the end of the war. This was largely because they were clever enough to shed their imperial ambitions at the appropriate moment. It was the lingering desire of Holland and France to re-establish some sort of control over their erstwhile colonies which resulted in their armies being bogged down in unnecessary wars against the forces of nationalism in South East Asia which they were bound to lose. The British showed no signs of such a desire and if they had any, they gave it up in time.

Before the war, the Burmese had enjoyed a limited degree of self-government under the government of Burma Act of 1935 which came into effect in 1937. Sections of Burmese nationalists pressing for complete independence initially assisted and welcomed Japanese occupation as liberation from British rule, but soon got disillusioned. Diverse Burmese resistance groups sprang up in opposition to Japanese occupation, the most important of which was the Burma Defence Army commanded by Major General Aung San. By August 1944, the main resistance groups combined to form the Anti-Fascist Peoples Freedom League (AFPFL) under the leadership of Aung San to fight for driving the Japanese out.

And when the British returned to Burma with the re-occupation of Rangoon (now Yangon) in May 1945, they had to reckon with a powerful nationalist outfit in the AFPFL which had an army as one of its component units. That could have signalled trouble, but the British organized their act skilfully to avoid getting involved into a conflict situation with the nationalists.

Plans for restoring the pre-war status of limited self-government, holding of elections, drafting of a constitution by the Burmese and grant of Dominion status within three years were announced in May 1945 itself. Since these did not satisfy the AFPFL, which wanted immediate independence, the British Governor constituted an Executive Council with AFPFL in the dominant position in August 1946. And in December 1946, the British Prime Minister announced that Burma would be granted Commonwealth status or independence, as it chose, "by the quickest and most convenient way possible." The rest was easy. A conference was held in London between the British government and Burmese nationalists led by the AFPFL leader Aung San. In terms of the agreement reached in this conference in January 1947 for convocation of an elective constituent Assembly, elections were held in April in which the AFPFL secured an overwhelming majority. The new constitution of independence Burma was adopted in September 1947 which came into force from January 1948 and Burma became independent.

In Malaya, the situation was more complex because of two factors. First, pre-war British Malaya had a rather heterogeneous structure. It comprised the crown colony (the straits settlements), five unfederated Malaya states and four federated states, with varying degrees of direct and indirect British rule. It took many years after the end of Japanese occupation for a homogeneous Malay state to emerge to take over from the British.

The second factor which delayed the grant of full independence to Malaya was the divergent racial composition of the population of Malayan peninsula. The pre-war population of the peninsula consisted of 42.4 per cent Malays, 41.3 per cent Chinese and 14.8 per cent Indians. This population diversity prevented the development of a strong nationalistic sentiment in the region before the war. The British were in fact looked upon by the Malays as well as the Chinese and Indians as "protectors" of one from the other not only in name but also in reality. British rule had meant the establishment of rule of law and its impartial administration. This coupled with development of public services, communication facilities, education, health, sanitation, etc., had resulted in greater acceptance of British rule in Malay peninsula than in other colonial countries.

The common resistance to Japanese occupation during the war did weaken the internal barriers to development of Malay nationalism. It came to its own in the post-war period but it took almost a decade to grow to its full potential. Throughout the intervening period, the process of reconciling diverse political interests and formations continued unabated with the British acting their umpiring role with consummate skill. They never gave the impression of trying to hang on to the imperial idea, as the Dutch and the French did in respect of their former colonies.

The British re-entered Malaya in September 1945 after Japan's defeat. And in October 1945 itself, plans for the establishment of a Malay Union comprising the nine "protected" states and the former crown colony, except Singapore, with a degree of self-government were announced. When General Templer was sent as British High Commissioner to Malaya in 1952 to effectively deal with communist guerrillas active in jungle areas, he was instructed to go ahead with "the work of building up a Malayan nation and to give the peoples of Malaya an increasing responsibility for the management of their own affairs."[1]

Through years of tortuous negotiations involving the British and diverse parties, interests and territorial identities, a definitive stride towards self-government was taken in July 1955 when Federal elections to the Legislative Council were held. In the run up to the elections, the three principal political forces—the United Malay National Organization, Malayan-Chinese Association and Malayan-Indian Congress formed an Alliance to press for complete independence at the end of four years term of the new Legislative Council. The Alliance won a resounding victory by capturing 51 out of 52 elective seats in the 98 members Council. The U.M. N.O. Chief—Tengku Abdul Rahman—became the first Chief Minister of Malay Federation. This significant political advance was followed by a conference in London in January 1956 at which it was agreed to proclaim full independence for Malaya by August 1957 if possible. Accordingly, at the stroke of mid-night on August 31, 1957, Merdeka (independence) was proclaimed and Malaya became a fully independent member of the Commonwealth. And before the final consummation, the process of negotiations, settlements and constitutional arrangements leading towards independence was kept up without any break.

India: "The Jewel in the Crown"

To the British rulers, India was a different proposition altogether. For nearly two hundred years, it had been metaphorically "the jewel in the crown" of the world's most pervasive emperor under whose empire the sun never set. Eulogising the services of Robert Clive, who out-manoeuvred his French counterpart Dupleix in conquering South India for the British empire, Mecanlay wrote: "Such an extent of cultivated territory, such an amount of revenue, such a multitude of subjects, was never added to the dominion of Rome by the most successful pro-consul...."[2] By virtue of its size, resources and population, undivided India was more than metaphorically 'the jewel in the crown' of the British emperor.

Historically, the name 'India' or 'Indies' had been associated with fabulous wealth in the shape of spices, silk, gold, silver and precious stones, which the medieval Europeans coveted so much and which attracted a succession of European adventurers during the 15th century. It was the lure of the riches of the 'Indies' which goaded the Portuguese captain, Vasco da Gama, to round the southern-most tip of Africa, christened as the 'Cape of Good Hope' by the Portuguese King. Sailing north from the cape along the eastern coast, he entered the Indian ocean in 1497 and finally landed at Calicut in South India in May 1497. His adventurous journey to India reaped fabulous rewards as he sailed back to Portugal in 1499 with a Cargo worth sixty times the cost of his expedition. That was India to the empire-builders of western Europe, from among whom the British ultimately succeeded in having this prize land under their imperial sway.

It was the burning ambition of Christopher Columbus to

discover a new route to India (and China) by sailing westwards across the Atlantic, in keeping with the common conviction of geographers of his time that the earth was a sphere and that Asia lay to the west of Europe. It was in pursuit of this ambition that he sailed from a Spanish port in August 1492 westwards which ultimately led to the discovery of the New World (Americas). But, his enchantment with 'Indies' was so great that as he explored the Carribbean shores of present day America and encountered the primitive Carib people, he thought they were 'Indians' and designated them as such. Since then, the name 'Indian' has stuck to the original inhabitants of the American continents. They are still known as 'Red Indians', red because of the colour of their skin. Even in South East Asia, the present day Indonesia was known as 'East Indies' and Vietnam, Cambodia and Laos as 'Indo-China'. India thus had long remained a symbol of all the riches of the east in the eyes of the exploring and adventuring peoples of the west.

Having succeeded in weaving this fabulous country into their imperial net, the British were certainly not expected to let in slip out so easily. And they did show it in the face of growing nationalist demand for independence before the war. Unlike many of the colonial countries which got independence in the post-war independence boom, India had been deeply stirred by a strong nationalist freedom movement for at least 40 years. Starting with the Swadeshi movement in the wake of partition of Bengal in 1905, India had already gone through bitter struggles against British rule with ever widening mass base. The mass civil disobedience movement against the colonial regime launched by the Indian National Congress under Gandhiji's leadership in early 1921 had evoked tremendous response. According to one estimate, around 90,000 students across the country had left schools and colleges to participate in the freedom movement. Although the movement was withdrawn by Gandhiji on 12 February, 1922 when a violent mob lynched 22 policemen to death in village Chauri Chaura in eastern U.P., the overall struggle for independence continued. Gandhiji wrote in *Young India* on 23 February, 1922: "It is high time that the British people were made to realise that the fight that was commenced in 1920 is a fight to the finish......"[3]

And the 'fight to the finish' was still on when the Second World War began in September 1939 and ended in mid-1945. In the intervening years, the Indian National Congress under the presidentship of Jawaharlal Nehru adopted the memorable resolution declaring full-independence as its goal at its Lahore session in December 1929. This was followed by another round of mass civil disobedience movement in early 30's, negotiations, partial settlements, limited provincial autonomy, resignation of provincial governments on the outbreak of war and individual 'Satyagraha' (non-violence protest) against British war efforts launched by Gandhiji in late 1940. The crowded decade ended without any appreciable change in the conflict situation between the nationalists and the British. On the other hand, the outbreak of war only served to harden the stance and postures of both sides against each other. While the nationalist forces saw in the war their final chance of extorting independence as a price for cooperation in British war efforts, the British were not prepared to take any risks involved in grant of any significant degree of self-government in course of the war.

As the war situation worsened for Britain and her allies in 1941, there was considerable pressure on British government, headed by Churchill, by the U.S. and also Labour Party leaders to enlist cooperation from Indian nationalists in Allied war efforts. A new initiative was taken towards this end when in March 1942, a British Mission headed by Strafford Cripps, a left-wing Labour Minister reputed to be sympathetic to Indian aspirations, came to India to negotiate. The Cripps proposals promised India Dominion status and a constitution-making body after the war, with provision for Provinces to decide their own future status. (This was obviously to accommodate the Pakistan demand.) But the nationalist demand for immediate transfer of effective power, particularly in regard defence of the country during the war, was rejected. The British were firm about exercising complete control over defence related matters which, in war time, meant almost everything. The Congress was also opposed to some other ingredients of Cripps proposals, like promise of Dominion Status rather than full independence and option for provinces to have separate constitutional arrangements, but the talks failed mainly on the issue of immediate

all segments of the Indian people either. By the time it was launched, the Pakistan idea had caught the imagination of Muslim masses in the country. Under the spell of the Muslim League, which did not support the movement, the Muslim masses largely kept aloof from it. Territorially also, the movement was not as all pervasive as might appear from the distance of time now. It had little impact in the Southern parts of the country. Chakravarti Rajagopalachari (known as Rajaji), the towering nationalist leader from the south, had disassociated himself from the movement and was not even arrested at the time.

To add to the confusion, there was a subdued feedling of guilt among the orthodox Congress rank and file about the extensive scale of violence indulged in by young protesters and rural masses in course of the movement. Actually the entire course of the movement after the arrest of top leaders on 9 August, 1942 was violent, which was against the avowed Gandhian concept of non-violence. It was a challenge to Gandhiji's principles and perhaps to his conscience too. Though he blamed the British rulers for provoking the people into violence, he could not absolve himself completely for all the violence that went with the movement. He went through the ordeal of what he called a 'self-purification' fast for 21 days in prison beginning 10th February 1943 to atone for the violence of the rulers and the people.

With the failure of the 'Quit India' movement to move the British into any fresh initiative towards grant of independence, an ominous quiet descended on the scene. Nor was any initiative in the offing from the side of the nationalist forces, which were in a state of suspended animation. Jawaharlal Nehru was busy writing his famous book *The Discovery of India* inside the prison. Nobody seemed to know what was happening on the freedom front. The mass of students who had so excitedly jumped into the fray after the arrest of leaders on 9 August and shown extraordinary activism went back to their schools and colleges by the beginning of 1943. It was business as usual in the campuses, cities, towns and rural areas.

Outside the country, in South East Asia, something more spectacular was taking shape in 1942-43 in pursuit of the nationalist goal of independence. An Indian officer of the British Indian Army stationed in Malaya named Mohan Singh sought the help of the

Japanese to raise an Indian National Army to liberate India. It was a time when growing aspiration for independence in colonial countries of South East Asia has induced the nationalist forces to look upon the Japanese as liberators. As the Japanese went about ousting the old imperial powers in country after country, there was a growing feeling among the nationalists that liberation of their countries could be brought about with the help of Japanese armed forces. This idea had actually led the mainstream nationalist forces in the East Indies (Indonesia) and in Burma to welcome the Japanese conquerors initially, only to be disillusioned quickly. In the circumstances, it was quite in keeping with the contemporaneous sentiments prevailing in the region for patriotic Indians to think of Japan's assistance in India's liberation.

The Japanese welcomed Mohan Singh's idea and handed over thousands of Indian prisoners of war to him for raising the Indian National Army. The first division of the INA was formed in September 1942 with over 16000 men. As the Japanese were toying with the idea of an Indian invasion at this time, they encouraged the INA for sometime, but by December 1942, serious differences arose between the Japanese and INA officers. Evidently, the Japanese wanted the INA to play a purely subservient role in furtherance of their design to occupy India. They promptly arrested Mohan Singh and the INA dream received a setback.

The more effective phase of INA began with its reorganization by Netaji Subhas Chandra Bose after he set the Provisional Government of Free India at Singapore in October 1943. Apart from the Indian prisoners of war, civilian recruits from among Indians resident in Japanese occupied areas were also enrolled and INA headquarters were set up in Singapore and Rangoon. In 1944 summer, an INA battalion under the command of Captain Shah Nawaz accompanied the Japanese army in their Imphal campaign inside the Indian border. It was around this time that Netaji Subhas Chandra Bose made his famous broadcast on Azad Hind Radio addressed to Gandhiji: "India's last war of independence has begun... Father of our Nation. In this holy war of India's liberation, we ask for your blessings and good wishes." But by then, it was too late for the INA to succeed in their goal of liberating India by armed support from Japan. The Axis Powers were losing across the board and Japanese retreat in Asia began around mid 1944 until it ended in Japan's surrender a year later. With that, the INA dream of liberating India from outside ended in a shambles.

With all its transient glory, the INA story was virtually a non-event for Indians inside India till after the end of the war. With war-time censor on news, and in absence of present-day information facilities, nothing really was known about its patriotic actions beyond the borders of India. For the common people of India, ever more desirous of freedom, the 'Quit India' movement had come to represent the end of the road. In the few memorable weeks of patriotic fervour and extraordinary activism, hopes of imminent freedom had been raised to a feverish pitch. With the collapse of the movement and absence of any fresh signal or ray of hope from any quarter, a pall of gloom prevailed over the country. There was nothing but despondency and frustration in the air and the people were struck with a cripping sense of paralysis. So much so that even Gandhiji's 21 days fast in jail in February 1943 failed to arouse the people and rekindle hopes of freedom in the near future. There was considerable anxiety, concern and anguish in the minds of the people but hardly much hope. Some die-hard supporters of the Raj in the services and among the gentry said, "I told you so. The British are here to rule for ever." The common man agreed with a sigh.

In a way, the sense of despair was also linked with the changing course of the war. With the launching of the 'Quit India' movement against the British at their weakest moment, the Indian nationalists had virtually burnt their bridges with the Allied Powers. In the circumstances, change in the fortunes of the war in favour of the Allies from around early 1943 only appeared to strengthen the position of the British in relation to the Indian nationalists fighting for independence. This was evident in the unyielding attitude of the British during Gandhiji's 21 days fast. The hard-boiled imperialist Prime Minister of Britain, Winston Churchill, told his cabinet on this occasion that "this hour of triumph everywhere in the world was not the time to crawl before a miserable old man who had always been our enemy."[5] That said it all in no uncertain terms. If Churchill could say that in the middle of the war, while

Britain was still engaged in a "blood and tears" struggle against its enemies, what could the Indian nationalists expect from the British after their victory in the war?

Freedom in the Air

It was one of those miracles of history which happen once in several life-times. The long dark night of slavery enveloping the sub-continent which had seemed never-ending suddenly started breaking into a new dawn of freedom. And, paradoxically, the dawn this time round was heralded by the sun rising not in the east but in the west. For the freedom aspiring people of India, the period from 1942 end to mid 1945 had been one of utter gloom and despair, with freedom nowhere in sight. And suddenly, as if by an act of Providence, the gloom started melting into light and cheers. After three years of suffocating silence since the failure of the 'Quit India' movement, things started moving unmistakably towards a grand finale. It all started in mid 1945 and, ironically, just at the moment Britain and her allies came out triumphant in the deadliest war of history.

In May 1945, the Allied Powers finally emerged victorious in Europe and end of World War II was in sight. Precisely in their moment of triumph in a ravaging war, which they survived by the skin of their teeth, the British, initiated a process which would end in the liquidation of their Empire "that exceeded the most extravagant designs of Rome, Alexander the great, Chenghiz Khan, the Caliphs or Napoleon". For the Indian sub-continent—the coveted "Indies" of European explorers of earlier centuries— was the most precious constituent, the core of the Empire which they set upon the course of liberating. As soon after their European victory as June 1945, the British rulers announced the release of top Indian leaders from prison for negotiations. It was a great announcement which sent the right signals across the country. The end of the tunnel suddenly appeared in sight.

The tortuous course of negotiations between and among the colonial Government, Congress and Muslim League, the disputes and deadlocks are matters of recent history which need not be gone into at any length here, but merely touched upon. The first of the series of negotiations which were to follow was held at Simla in June-July 1945. By now, the two-nation theory had gripped the Muslim mind firmly and Jinnah was in a position to dictate terms. The Simla negotiations failed to resolve the deadlock between the Congress and Muslim League and the talks broke down on 14 July, 1945. But the failure of Simla dialogue was a relatively insignificant affair as far as the people's psyche was concerned. The significant fact was that the ice was broken and the process continued uninterrupted thereafter.

It got a tremendous boost when back in Britain the Labour Party came to power with resounding victory in general elections of July 1945. Clement Attlee, the Labour Prime Minister, was as much known for being sympathetic to India's independence as Churchill was for his love of the Empire. The Viceroy, Lord Wavell, was in England in August and returned to India after consultations with the new government. In September, he announced the Labour government's determination to go ahead with the task of bringing India to self-government speedily. The British cabinet took a decision on 22nd January 1946 to send a high powered Cabinet Mission to India to negotiate and hammer out a settlement for grant of independence. On 19 February, 1946, dispatch of the Cabinet Mission headed by Lord Pethic-Lawrence, a reputed old radical, was announced. And in March 1946, the Cabinet Mission landed in India with the avowed object of working out a constitutional arrangement for transfer of power to Indians.

It was one of the most pleasantly surprising changes in the attitude and conduct of the flagship imperial country of the world at that point of time. At the end of the Second World War, it may be remembered, most of Asia except China, Japan and Thailand, most of Africa and large parts of Latin America were still under colonial empires. Chester Bowles, two times U S ambassador to India and a known pro-India man, was to write later:" The British people have often achieved greatness, but they were never greater than in the dignity and decisiveness with which they relinquished their control in South Asia."[6]

As top national leaders started coming out of prison, a massive upsurge of patriotic sentiments swept across the land. Tamultuous welcome by huge crowds marked their release from jail. Jawaharlal Nehru came out of Almora jail with his manuscript of *The Discovery of India* to the cheers of large crowds that had thronged the jail gates. "Among his first statements," records his biographer M. Chalapati Rao, "was a word of cheers for those who carried on the freedom fight from underground and another word of cheer for the INA prisoners."[7] The young student activists of the raging and tearing "Quit India" struggle, sulking under the controversy regarding violence and non-violence, felt vindicated and went into ruptures. Over half a million people lined the streets of Bombay to welcome the leaders who came to attend the meeting of Congress Working Committee. The people of India seemed to be making up for their silence and inaction during the proceeding three years.

The patriotic upsurge touched a new peak when stories of the heroic deeds of Azad Hind Fauj (INA) for India's independence started spreading in the country. Deep nationalist sentiments were aroused throughout the country against the British over the trial of INA personnel in the winter of 1945-46. As the trial of INA personnel captured by the British during the war, began in Delhi's Red Fort, a new wave of support and sympathy for them swept across the country. The Congress decided to defend them and stalwarts like Jawaharlal Nehru, Bhulabhai Desai, Tej Bahadur Sapru, K.N. Katju and Asif Ali appeared in lawyer's robes in the defence. There were violent popular protests against the trials in Calcutta and Bombay in February 1946.

In that hour of glory, the young in big cities and small towns, showed a rare unity in standing up in vociferous support of the INA irrespective of their political and religious affinities. When an INA officer—Rashid Ali—was sentenced to seven years imprisonment by the colonial regime, students in Calcutta rose in loud protests on 11 February, 1946. The procession of protesting students this time was led by students wing of the Muslim League and joined by Congress and Communist student organizations. And when the INA heroes—Sehgal, Dhillon and Shan Nawaz went round the country in early summer, they received tumultuous welcome by milling crowds everywhere. The ecstacy of being around to welcome the coming of freedom was only to be experienced to believe and the youth considered themselves exceptionally lucky to have a taste of it.

Bliss it was to be living in India at the start of the year 1946. It was infinitely more so to be young and dreaming. After three choking years of paralysis, confusion, controversy and despair, the freedom scene brightened up miraculously. Independence was coming, independence after 200 years of alien rule. No one living in the sub-continent in those halcyon days had any doubt on that. And the fragrance of impending freedom intoxicated the young into a new euphoria. They scaled dizzy heights into the realms of fancy about the future of their dear land. The air of freedom created unlimited mental space to imagine utopias and fancy about unlimited possibilities. It was the stuff of which dreams are made.

References

1. *A History of the Far East in Modern Times*, Harold M. Vinache.
2. *Historical Essays*, Lord Mecanlay.
3. *India's Struggle for Independence*, Bipin Chandra and others.
4. *Ibid.*
5. *Ibid.*
6. *The New Dimensions of Peace*, Chester Bowles, 1955.
7. *Jawaharlal Nehru*, M. Chalapati Rao.

was infinitely more space for yearning and dreaming. After three [illegible] years of [illegible] confusion, controversy, and despair, the freedom seemed [illegible] unconsciously. Independence was coming, independence after 200 years of alien rule [illegible] in the sub-continent in those halcyon days had any doubt on that. And the fragrance of impending freedom intoxicated the young into a new euphoria. They soared dizzy heights into the realms of fancy about the future of their dear land. The air of freedom created a mental space to imagine utopias and dream about unlimited possibilities. It was the stuff of which dreams are made.

References

1. *A History of the Far East in Modern Times*, Harold M. Vinacke
2. *Historical essays*, Lord Macaulay
3. [illegible] from Churchill and others
4. [illegible]
5. Ibid.
6. *The New Dimensions of Peace*, Chester Bowles, 195[illegible]
7. *Jawaharlal Nehru*, M. Chalapathi Rau

2

The Shape of Things to Come

The Cabinet Mission Fiasco

The dream started souring sooner than one could imagine. The British Cabinet Mission that had arrived in March 1946 to negotiate a settlement for handing over power went into business in all earnestness. It held talks with the principal political parties and constitutional experts like T.B. Sapru and M.R. Jayakar lasting over seven weeks, without obtaining an agreed settlement. The main hurdle was the issue of partition of India which the Muslim League firmly demanded and the Congress vehemently opposed. The British, on the other hand, meant business and the Cabinet Mission had its brief prescribed. They were dead set to hand over power and quit as speedily as possible. In the circumstances, on 16 May, 1946, the Cabinet Mission on its won proposed a constitutional arrangement for an independent sub-continent which tried to accommodate both the Congress and Muslim League points of view as far as possible. The Cabinet Mission Plan, as it came to be known, also envisaged immediate setting up of an interim government comprising major political parties to run the country until a new constitution was framed and enforced. Having done this, the Cabinet Mission departed for England on 29 June, 1946, leaving the ball in the court of India's political parties to respond.

The core of Cabinet Mission proposals provided for an undivided Union of India with a very weak centre dealing only with defence, foreign affairs and communications, leaving all residuary powers in the jurisdiction of the provinces. To accommodate the Pakistan demand of the Muslim League, the plan provided for grouping of the Muslim majority provinces in eastern and western India, and for these groups to have constitutions of their own. Initially, the Muslim League accepted the proposals with several reservations. The Congress expressed its opposition to the scheme of grouping of provinces but decided to join the proposed constituent Assembly with the object of framing the constitution of a 'free United and democratic India.' Addressing the All India Congress Committee at Bombay in June 1946, Nehru clearly declared: "We are not bound by a single thing except that we have decided for the moment to go into the constituent Assembly."[1]

This virtually amounted to rejection of the proposal for grouping of Muslim majority provinces in the eastern and western wings which was supposed to accommodate the Pakistan demand in substance, if not in name. And Jinnah was the last person to take it lying down. He demanded clarifications from the British government on the Congress stand. The British tried to allay his fears on this score, but he was not satisfied. And on 27 July, 1946, the Muslim League Council finally rejected the Cabinet Mission Plan in toto and reiterated its demand for a separate, independent Pakistan. The League also gave a call to Muslims to observe 16 August, 1946 as 'Direct Action Day' to press for its demand. The stage was set for souring of the dream of independence swinging the sub-continent at the beginning of the year well before the year was out.

"The Great Calcutta Killing"

By now, the demand for Pakistan had taken deep roots in the minds and hearts of Muslim masses. Since it was as clear as day-light that the British were determined to withdraw from India sooner than later, this was their opportunity to realize their dream and they were prepared to go to any length to achieve it. It was now or never for them. "As early as 10th April, 1946" writes Durga Das, the veteran journalist of yester years, "he (Jinnah) summoned in Delhi a convention of some 400 members of the provincial legislatures elected on the League ticket. The rallying cry at this convention was the demand for an independent Pakistan. The Muslims, Shahid Suhrawardy declared, were straining at the leash, and Noon said even the exploits of Halaku, the Mongol conqueror, would be put in the shade by a *bloodbath* should their right to a separate state he denied."[2]

(Halaku or Hulagu was the brother of Mangu Khan, one of the successors of the great Mongol conqueror Chengiz Khan who had shaken the Eurasian world like a volcanic eruption during the first quarter of the 13th century. As Governor of Persia in the year 1258, Halaku sent a warning message to the Caliph at Baghdad over some relatively minor affair. The Caliph sent a rather offensive reply and Halaku's messengers were insulted by a mob in Baghdad. That was an invitation to the "Scourge of God," as Arab historians were used to describing Chengiz Khan. Halaku attacked and captured Baghdad after a seige of 40 days. "That was the end of the city of the *Arabian Nights*, and all the treasures that had accumulated there during 500 years of empire. The Caliph and his sons and near relatives were put to death. There was a general massacre for weeks, till *the river Tigris was dyed red with blood for miles*. It is said that a million and a half people perished."[3])

Came 16 August, 1946, the date of the first and the only major organized agitational call given by the Muslim League in pursuance of its demand for Pakistan. The Muslim League government of Bengal headed by Hasan Shahid Suhrawardy declared a public holiday to enable public servants to join in the agitational programme. Bengal was a solid bastion of the Muslim League and there was nothing unusual about the party government taking lead in organizing the agitation for Pakistan. It is not generally known that Muslim League was actually born in Bengal long before the birth of the idea of Pakistan. It was in the year 1906 that Nawab Salimulla of Dhaka originally founded the Muslim League. In the same year a Muslim delegation waited upon the Viceroy, Lord Minto, and demanded separate electorate for Muslims, which was promptly conceded. That being so, it was natural for Muslim League's 'Direct Action' to have its biggest impact on Calcutta, the capital of Bengal.

And what an impact it was? The suave, sophisticated Hasan Shahid Suhrawardy, the political head of Bengal government under the provincial Autonomy scheme of 1935-37, would never have imagined that Feroze Khan Noon's rhetoric at the League convention on 10th April would come so literally true and that also in the capital city of a government headed by himself. Nor for that matter Jinnah himself would have imagined the macabre dance of death his 'Direct Action' call was going to unleash on Calcutta. The holocaust that took place in Calcutta on 16 August,

1946 in the wake of the call for 'Direct Action' did not exactly paint the river Hooghly red, but was unmatched in savagery and scale. Never before in the shady history of inter-community riots in the sub-continent had so many human lives been lost in such a short time of a day or so in so brutal a manner.

Larry Collins and Dominique Lapierre describe : "At dawn on 16 August, howling in quasi-religious fervour, Muslim mobs had come bursting from their slums, waving clubs, iron bars, shovels, any instrument capable of smashing a human skull. They came in answer to a call issued by the Muslim League, proclaiming 16 August 'Direct Action Day ......' They savagely beat to a sodden pulp any Hindu in their path and stuffed their remains in the city's open gutters. The terrified police simply disappeared..... Later the Hindu mobs came storming out of their neighbourhoods looking for defenceless Moslems to slaughter. Never, in all its violent history, had Calcutta known 24 hours as savage, as packed with human viciousness. Like water-soaked logs, scores of bloated corpses bobbed down the Hooghly river towards the sea. Others, savagely mutilated, littered the city's streets. Everywhere, the weak and the helpless suffered most. At one crossroad, a line of Moslem coolies lay beaten to death where a Hindu mob had found them, between the poles of their rickshaws. By the time the slaughter was over, Calcutta belonged to the vultures. In filthy grey packs they scudded across the sky, tumbling down to gorge themselves on the bodies of the city's 6000 dead."[4]

Statesman, the sober English daily then wholly under English ownership and control, dubbed the horrendous carnage of 16 August as "The Great Calcutta Killing." In its leading article, the paper wrote on 20 August 1946: "The origin of the appalling Carnage and loss in the capital of a great province, we believe the worst communal rioting in India's history, was a political demonstration by the Muslim League...... The bloody shambles to which the country's biggest city has been reduced is an abounding disgrace, which owing to the Bengal Ministry's pre-eminence as a League Ministry, has inevitably tarnished seriously the All-India reputation of the League itself."

In the political arena, where the Indian National Congress and Muslim League were engaged in a bitter game of one-upmanship, with the British in a mighty hurry to withdraw, the grave human tragedy of Calcutta went largely unnoticed. No one seemed to be over much concerned about the horrendous human tragedy that Calcutta had gone through, as negotiations dragged on for the formation of an Interim Government of Indians in terms of the Cabinet Mission's short-term plan. The Viceroy's proposal for a 14-member Executive Council with 6 Congress nominees, 5 Muslim League nominees and three representatives of other minorities to be nominated by the Viceroy had been rejected by the Muslim League. The Viceroy then asked the Congress to form the Interim Government. The Congress readily accepted the offer and the Interim Government, with Jawaharlal Nehru as vice-president of the Executive Council, took the reins of administration on 2 September, 1946. The only impact of Calcutta Killings was to convince the Viceroy, Lord Wavell, that Muslim League's participation in the Interim Government was necessary to save the situation. To this end, Lord Wavell negotiated with Jinnah for over six weeks as a result of which the Muslim League's five representatives joined the Interim Government on 26 October, 1946. The labyrinthian goings-on at the political front could, at worst, be dubbed as kind of a Nedo fiddling while Rome was burning.

Reprisals and Counter-Reprisals: Noakhali and Bihar

The ghosts of Calcutta's 6000 dead did not lie buried in the depths of Hooghly. They raised their heads first in East Bengal, notably Noakhali, and then in other parts of the country, notably Bihar. Although the killings in Calcutta were started by Muslim League fanatics aided by anti-social elements, the Hindu backlash was even bigger resulting in heavier Muslim casualties. As news and rumours of Calcutta's Muslims having been slaughtered by rampaging Hindu mobs reached the predominantly Muslim areas of East Bengal, fanatical passions ignited another major conflagration. In the district of Noakhali Muslim masses in rural areas were aroused to a frenzy of revenge against their Hindu Co-villagers, in pitiable minority, with whom they had lived in peace for centuries. Normally docile, habitually peaceful rural folks of East Bengal turned into hysteric mobs crying for brutal revenge, not for anything done by their co-villagers but for the wrongs done to Muslims by the Hindus of Calcutta.

All on a sudden in October-November 1946, the obscure little known district of Noakhali hidden in a remote corner of the country, emerged from its obscurity to loom large on India's map. Gripped by unprecedented fanatical frenzy, rampaging Muslim mobs went after the minority Hindu villagers, killing, raping, pillaging and burning in village after village. Hundreds were killed, their women raped and kidnapped and many times that number fled their villages to safer areas far away. On 26 October, 1946, Acharya Kripalani, the Congress President, made the following statement at a Press Conference in Calcutta after an extensive tour of Noakhali and other affected areas of East Bengal: "The attack on the Hindu population in the districts of Noakhali and Tipperah was previously arranged and prepared for and was the result of League propaganda— it was absolutely communal and one-sided..... and there have been many cases of murders, forcible marriages, and religious conversions en masse."

Stories of Noakhali massacres and ravages hoged the headlines of newspapers day after day. As the news spread across the country, tempers rose and acute communal tension started building up in other parts of India. The Congress and Muslim League members of the Interim Government were busy out-manoeuvring each other in the Executive Council. The Viceroy had virtually abdicated and the once mighty colonial Government of India seemed to have gone into a coma.

Tension mounted as Hindu anger rose in the cow belt, particularly U.P. and Bihar. Madan Mohan Malviya, the great nationalist turned a Hindu leader who was ailing for sometime, died in deep anguish in U.P. But the Hindu backlash erupted with a vengeance in Bihar. The province of Bihar had the dubious distinction of witnessing the first major anti-Muslim riot of the century in the year 1917. It had broken out in the land of Babu Kuer Singh of 1857 fame over the issue of cow slaughter on the occasion of the Muslim festival of Id-ul-Zoha or Bakrid 1917. Bakrid Riot, as it came to be called, had resulted in large-scale massacre of Muslims in rural areas of Shahabad district of Bihar. The colonial administration had taken stiff measures to suppress the rioting and extensively deployed Mounted Police to curb violence in the affected areas. It was in the wake of the Bakrid riots that a regular Unit of Mounted Military Police was organized and based at Arrah, the headquarters of Shahabad district where it is still located. Relatively minor clashes between the two communities over such contentious issues as music before mosque, cow-sacrifice etc. have been endemic in Bihar, but violence on the scale of Shahabad Bakrid riots had not taken place after 1917 until October-November 1946.

As news of Noakhali atrocities on Hindus started pouring, a public meeting was held at Patna, the capital of Bihar, in which fairy speeches were made by an odd assortment of people, including some local Congressmen, condemning the happenings in East Bengal. Ironically, the meeting was held in the same Maidan where Gandhiji had held prayer meetings and preached his gospel of non-violence about seven months earlier during his prolonged sojourn at Patna in early summer of 1946. (From that, the place acquired the name 'Gandhi Maidan' which it still retains today). And more ironically, some among the speakers quoted Gandhiji's oft-repeated observation that non-violence did not mean cowardice or meek surrender to violence, out of context to devastating effect on the audience. Many among the crowd that listened to the speeches went back to their villages around Patna determined to avenge Noakhali under the grossly mistaken notion that it could after all be justified in Gandhian terms also.

And that proved to be the ignominious signal for the Hindu assault on Muslims in the rural backyard of Patna on a scale which Bihar had not known before. The carnage of Bakrid riots 1917 was a localized affair confined to the district of Shahabad alone, but this time round the macabre death drama was enacted in the districts of Chapra, Patna, Gaya and distant Monghyr and Bhagalpore districts also. It would be wrong to describe the bloody happenings of October-November 1946 as rioting between the two communities. It was an one-sided affair in which the worst elements among the majority community went after the blood of the minority community in large parts of central and eastern Bihar. 'Mian Mar' (Muslim bashing) is the name by which it is still known and it was so in every sense.

As assault, killing and loot of Muslim properties spread in the capital's hinterland, a large number of Muslim refugees poured into Patna which had a semblance of law and order. They took shelter with friends and relatives in Muslim localities besides large number being accommodated in the Anjuman Islamia Hall in the centre of the town. This created panic among the Hindu residents of the areas swarming with bitter and angry Muslims escaping the rural death-trap, whose numbers swelled by the day. As tension mounted, panic started gripping the University students residing in hostels and lodges situated in mixed localities. Until on a late October night war cries started in a prestigious University hostel occupied by Hindu students and a private lodge occupied by Muslim students a little distance away. For about half an hour, hysteric cries of "Har Har Mahadeo" and "Allaho Akbar" were exchanged between panic-stricken students of the hostel and the lodge, each side fearing an imminent attack by the other. No attack actually took place, but the event highlighted an ominous transformation in the youth situation. The same students who were renting the air with shouts of "Azad Hind Fauj Zindabad" on captain Shah Nawaz and other INA heroes' visit to the city six months earlier were now hurling the battle cries of "Har Har Mahadeo" and "Allaho Akbar" at each other.[5]

Two students residing in the hostel left to catch a train for their home town of Arrah, over 30 miles away, the next afternoon. Reaching Patna railway station around 5 p.m., they waited for one hour, two hours, three hours, indefinitely, but the train did not arrive. As the seemingly endless wait continued through the night, whispers were heard that the train had been attacked by killer mobs hunting for Muslim passengers. People talked in hushed tones as a chill went round the bones of the waiting passengers, both Hindus and Muslims. They started leaving the railway station in panic until only a few stragglers, including the two hapless students, were left at the platform during the rest of the night. They could not return back to their hostel after the nerve-wracking war cries of the previous night. The late autumn night at the open and desolate railway platform felt unusually chilly with the chill inside them on the news of the train killings.

No one knew how many were grabbed and killed that night,

but the train arrived half empty only the next day with dazed passengers in a state of shock. Frenzied mobs, it turned out, had stopped the train at wayside stations, searched for passengers who could be identified as Muslims and dragged and killed those who were so identified. No train arrived that day, till as long as the two students were at the station, from the other line running between Gaya and Patna. More such gory incidents, it transpired later, had occurred on this line which passed through some of the worst affected areas of the province.

Fazal Ahmad,[6] who was one among a delegation of five Ahmadiya Muslims who came from Quadian on a rescue mission to Bihar, recalls his visit to the borders of Monghyr and Bhagalpore districts in the wake of the massacres. The areas around Tarapur and Sultanganj police stations had been through killings on a large scale. He could see corpses lying scattered in paddy fields emitting foul smell. He was shown the house of one Sultan in which about 300 Muslim women had taken shelter. The house was raided by mariandiing mobs and all the 300 women done to death.

Syed Abdul Aziz, a barrister hailing from Bihar and one time Law Member of the Government of Nizam of Hyderabad, writes: "The offences of murder, arson and dacoity were committed in broad day light for hours and days by nearly all able-bodied Hindus of every village in certain localities...... A large number of dead bodies were thrown into the river, streams, tanks and wells. In one village no fewer than seven big wells were found chokeful of corpses."

In the overwhelming darkness of religious fanaticism that had enveloped Bihar for nearly a week, there were glimmers of fellow feeling and humanness in isolated corners. Fazal Ahmad recounts how a poor old Hindu woman risked her own and her adult son's life in saving the lives of his extended family members holed up in their ancestral house at village Uren in Monghyr district during that dark week. She had been obliged to the family in various ways but more than that her innate humanness had survived the blaze of communal hatred that was raging in the hearts of her co-religionists. She came forward and offered the services of her son to send message to the concerned authorities for saving the lives of the besieged Muslim family. Her son travelled all the way to the provincial headquarters at Patna with a message from the family head—seeking immediate protection from blood-thirsty crowds collecting in the surrounding areas. For fear of being detected or intercepted on the way, he carried the brief written message concealed in a *chunauti* (a tiny container) tied to his waist. The message was delivered to Prof. Akhtar Ahmad 'Urenvi", Fazal Ahamad's elder brother and a college teacher at Patna, who activated the provincial government to send an army contingent to rescue the beleaguered Muslims of his village. Fazal Ahmad's family and rest of the Muslims of village Uren were saved, thanks to the humanistic act of an old decrepit woman and her decrepit son.

The most sinister aspect of violence and retaliatory violence in Noakhali and Bihar was utterly inhuman cowardice of the aggressors. It was not as if they fought battles with their opponents who could more or less match their strength in numbers or otherwise. In all cases, they attacked and ravished the week and the hapless whom they far outnumbered and who could by no means defend themselves. "Nowhere were the aggression and retaliation evidence of bravery. There was no chance for a minority to redeem itself by acts of courage in defence; it was everywhere the majority that was brave enough to pounce on the outnumbered people of the minority community."[7]

The Muslim League government in Bengal was more concerned with advancing the cause of Pakistan than saving the lives of people whose destiny was in its hands. In Bihar, Congress was in power, whose leaders had no clue as to how to go about the business of maintaining peace and order. Having spent the best part of their lives agitating against the British rule, they had no idea of the art of governance which they were called upon to practice by a quick turn of events. A precarious Interim Government had assumed office at the centre whose members were in a similar predicament. In the circumstances, all that the members of the Interim Government and national leaders could do in the wake of Bihar killings was to visit the province and lash out at the unknown, abstract killers.

Jawaharlal Nehru and Rajendra Prasad visited Bihar and addressed a public meeting in Patna Maidan on 3rd November,

1946 denouncing the perpetrators of such heinous crimes in no uncertain terms. Nehru thundered: "By no standards of civilised conduct can acts of lawlessness and killing of neighbours be justified."[8] Rajendra Prasad exhorted: "Humanity demands that this mad orgy of loot, arson and murder must be stopped immediately even at the cost of great sacrifice, if necessary."[9] Jai Prakash Narayan said in a press statement: "I cannot say yet that I am in full possession of the facts, but it is clear from what I have been able to gather that terrible and gruesome things have happened in Bihar, to the eternal shame of the province and of the majority community here. The Hindus of Bihar have been guilty of heinous crimes and have committed deeds of abject cowardice and barbarity."[10]

All this amounted to so much sound and fury but nothing more. Jay Prakash Narayan went on to certify: "The situation happily seems to have been brought under control now, largely because of the whirl-wind tours of Pandit Nehru and the military and other security measures taken by the provincial government.... But its task might be made difficult, even impossible, if the Muslim League does not return to the path of sanity and forsake the politics of hatred and falsehood and of deliberate and planned incitement to violence. The events in Bengal and Bihar have proved the utter folly and futility of such politics, and have completely vindicated the stand and politics of the nationalist Muslims...... It is high time therefore that the Muslim masses looked around for better and truer leadership."[11]

So the colossal human tragedy of Hindus in East Bengal and Muslims in Bihar was trivialised into the never-ending polemies of Muslim League versus Nationalist Muslims or League versus Congress. Nothing else mattered, no matter how many innocent, unconcerned, defenceless Hindus and Muslims were massacred wherever they were in hopeless minority. No one cared if the killers were identified and brought to book by the law-enforcing agencies concerned. The professional agitators and protesters who held the reins of administration in the two provinces did not even seem to know or bother if murder, arson, loot and rape were heinous crimes under the law of the land and called for sustained action to bring the offenders to justice. Nothing of the kind happened. Not even serious and visible efforts were made in that direction. When one man kills another, the law is set in motion to catch him, put him on trial and get him punished by a court of law. And yet when thousands were killed by thousands in that black autumn of 1946, the 'benign' home - grown provincial governments of Bengal and Bihar dealt with the mass crimes like minor skirmishes in a football match. The pattern was set for the future, pointing to the shape of things to come.

Only one person in the whole of the sub-continent took the tragedy deep into his heart and reacted in the manner only he could react. It was the Mahatma. On 6 November, 1946, Gandhiji issued a long statement addressed "To Bihar": "Bihar of my dreams seems to have falsified them ..... Is it nationalism to seek barbarously to crush the fourteen per cent of the Muslims in Bihar?" He also announced to undertake a fast of penance for the inhuman crimes of the majority community in Bihar. He was not in charge of the governance of the country unlike the other Congress leaders who waxed eloquent on the enormity of the crimes and did nothing to restore the majesty of law. He worked on a higher, moral plane and had unshakable faith in the miracle that change of heart could bring about in the conduct of humans. In the ultimate analysis, he did not succeed in bringing about a change of heart among the Hindus and Muslims of the sub-continent to keep them united. But in the short-term context of the tragic happenings in Noakhali and Bihar, he did succeed to a considerable extent. In the early winter of 1946-47, he perched himself in a shattered hut in Srirampur village of Noakhali district to wipe the tears of ravaged Hindus and restore sanity among frenzied Muslims. And it was no less than a miracle that the harrowing events of October 1946 were not repeated in that region even during the worst days of partition riots in Punjab and elsewhere.

The British rulers had lost all interest in the governance of the country. Having decided to withdraw, they were just not interested in running the system they had evolved in course of their long rule. The Viceroy, Lord Wavell, was an able soldier but not so able an administrator and poorer still in grasp of India's political reality. He remained inextricably bogged down in resolving the unceasing quarrels between the Congress and Muslim League members of the Interim government from day one. The famous steel frame had developed gaping cracks down the line. The English civilians in the sub-continent were marking their time, waiting to depart, rather than administering the country. When, for instance, Bihar was in smoke, the English Governor of the province was holidaying in Bombay, for which he was roundly criticised by the daily *Statesman*. In such a situation of callous indifference all round, the ordinary men and women of India were left at the mercy of wolves of consuming hatred and brutality released by contemporary politics of the country.

References

1. *Constitutional Government in India,* M.V. Pylee.
2. *India From Curzon to Nehru and After*, Durga Das, 1971.
3. *Glimpses of World History*, Jawaharlal Nehru.
4. *Freedom at Midnight*, Larry Collins and Dominique Lapierre.
5. The writer himself was one of the two.
6. Fazal Ahmad who was then a lecturer in English in Ahmadiya College at Quadian, later joined the I.P.S. and rose to be the Police Chief of Bihar in early 1980's.
7. *Builders of Modern India: Jawaharlal Nehru*, M. Chalapati.
8. *Freedom Movement in Bihar*, Dr. K.K. Dutta, Vol. 3.
9. *Ibid.*
10. *Jay Prakash Narayan: Nation Building in India*, Edited by Brahmananda.
11. *Ibid.*

3

Dream Turned Nightmare

'Quit India' in Reverse

When the British started releasing the Congress leaders from prison immediately after Allied Victory in Europe in mid 1945, top political leaders realized that the struggle for independence had entered the final stage of negotiations and settlement. Durga Das captures the prevailing mood of the moment. "In India, the feeling that the curtain was now up on the penultimate scene of the political drama released a flurry of activity and counter-activity. The main actors in the domestic power struggle were the Congress and the League. Both sensed the proximity of freedom."[1] But none thought independence was so near, that it was coming as soon as it did. Nehru calculated it could take anything between three to five years for the British to finally withdraw. The Indian leaders were prepared for a prolonged period of negotiations, haggling, bargaining and also perhaps some muscle-flexing in between before the final dawn of freedom. After all 200 years of imperial rule could not be expected to end abruptly one fine morning.

To some inveterate freedom-fighters, British intentions would ever remain suspect. It was so even after Labour Party came to power in England and on 19 September, 1945 both the British Prime Minister Attlee and Viceroy Wavell announced their determination to hand over power to Indians 'Speedily.' They still thought of a fierce, long drawn out agitational programme against British rule and talked about it loud in public meetings and rallies. Jay Prakash Narayan was the most prominent mouth-piece of this school of thought. When the All India Congress Committee decided at its meeting at Bombay in July 1946 to participate in the Constituent Assembly under the Cabinet Mission Plan, he said "The Constituent Assembly is the creation of the British and it can never bring us the freedom we have been fighting for years." At the AICC meeting itself, he suggested that the Congress should prepare the country for another struggle for independence.

It was early summer of 1946 and a large crowd had collected in the Maidan at Arrah (Bihar) to see and hear Jay Prakash Narayan (J.P.). He was then a darling of the crowds, hero of 1942 movement who had so valiantly escaped from the colonial prison at Hazaribagh in the wake of the 'Quit India' movement to carry on the fight against the British from underground. Stories of his being tortured by the colonial police and prison officials in Lahore Jail on being re-arrested were doing the rounds in the country, lending an aura of romance to his personality in those days. Huge crowds gathered to have his *darshan* (seeing) wherever he went on being released from jail, particularly in Bihar. Roaring shouts of 'J.P. Zindabad' greeted him as he mounted the rostrum to address the meeting. He came straight to the point. A fresh mass agitation was essential to wrest freedom from the reluctant British imperialists. The Congress leaders were getting into the trap of negotiations which couldn't usher in independence. One of his prescriptions was that the top hundred Congress leaders should undertake a fast unto death demanding British withdrawal. By the time a couple of them died in the process, the country would achieve independence. It was a stunning prescription, but the audience was more interested in having his *darshan* and exhibiting their adulation for him rather than pondering over his sombre prescription.

To some, like this writer who as a young student was a part of the audience, the suggestion appeared rather odd and confusing at the moment, even though they had the highest regard for J.P. Thinking in retrospect, the idea of a mass agitation against British rule at that stage appears so much out of place and irrelevant. It proved to be so in less than a year from the time J.P. made the suggestion and repeated publicly in meeting after meeting. It was like the proverbial tilting at the windmill. The Congress and Muslim League leaders, who really counted in the run up to independence, of course knew better and played their cards accordingly. But even they — the principal actors in the drama—were taken unawares by the speed with which the British hurtled towards final withdrawal from the sub-continent.

Events moved fast on the constitutional front. The Muslim League contingent joining the Interim Government on 26 October,

1946 did not help bringing about a settlement. The issue of Pakistan versus United India remained as unsettled as ever. In fact, the Muslim League members in the Interim Government were all set to use their position in the Government to work for the creation of a sovereign state of Pakistan. The Congress on the other hand was banking on its numerical majority in the constituent Assembly to draft a constitution for a United Indian Republic. The Constituent Assembly met for the first time on 9 December, 1946. The Muslim League boycotted it. As the stalemate continued, the situation was compounded by Hindu-Muslim riots in different parts of the country.

To break the deadlock, the British Government invited the Congress, Muslim League and Sikh leaders to a conference in London. The conference failed to bring about an agreement between the Congress and Muslim League. Each side expected the British to pursuade the other to accept its point of view, failing which to impose a settlement favouring its own avowed goal. The British were not prepared to oblige either side. Nehru, Jinnah, Liaquat Ali and Sardar Baldeo Singh returned from London without being anywhere near a solution. The deadlock continued. Bitterness between Hindu-Sikh combine and Muslims increased.

On 20 January, 1947, the Constituent Assembly met without Muslim League participation and passed the objective Resolution for the establishment of a sovereign Indian Republic. At the end of January, the Muslim League repudiated the objective Resolution and called upon the British Government to scrap the Cabinet Mission Plan and dismiss the Constituent Assembly. In February, the Congress countered the Muslim League demand by demanding the removal of Muslim League members from the Interim Government. That signalled the final parting of the ways between the Congress and the League, that is, between the two dominant segments of Indian population which counted in the reckoning for independence.

What more could an imperial country ask for to hold on to its empire? The sub-continent could not be more pitiably dependant upon the British to adjudicate and, for all practical purposes, impose their own solution in regard to the future set up. If the British wanted to hang on to the empire, in some form or the other, as they did in the past or as some other imperial countries were trying to do elsewhere, this was their opportunity. But they had other ideas, as was amply evident from what followed immediately after the Congress-League final break-up. It was as if they were dead set on their course regardless of whatever happened to the Congress-League tangle, leaving no scope even for a second thought. The British resolve to get out of India was made clear and all speculations regarding their intensions set at rest on 20 February, 1947. On that momentous date, the British Prime Minister Attlee made a statement announcing British's "definite intention to take the necessary steps to effect the transfer of power into responsible Indian hands by a date not later than June 1948." If no agreement was reached by that time between the concerned political parties in India, the British Government would have to consider to whom it should transfer the powers of the Central Government. It would have to consider whether power should be handed over "as a whole to some form of Central Government for British India, or in some areas to the existing Provincial Governments, or in such other way as may seem most reasonable and in the best interests of the Indian people."

What more could the people of the Indian sub-continent struggling for independence ask for? What more proof of British intention to quit was needed? It was one of the rare paradoxes of history when the rulers were setting a deadline to set free the ruled. In August 1942, the Indian National Congress under Gandhiji's leadership had asked the British to 'quit India'. Less than five years later, the British set a deadline to quit India, even if the Indian political parties failed to agree among themselves on the future set up. It was "Quit India" in reverse par excellence; nothing less but with a difference. When we called them to quit, or the Congress did for that matter, they were fully set to take us on. What followed is history. They put all Congress leaders behind bars and suppressed the impromptu uprising within weeks with surgical efficiency, even though they were badly beleaguered in the war. What is more, they knew what they were doing or going to do and were fully prepared. But when they gave the ultimatum to quit, we were hopelessly unprepared, and paid the price of our unpreparedness in blood and tears of millions of our people.

Mountbatten's Nightmare

Simultaneously with the announcement of final withdrawal from India latest by June 1948, the British Prime Minister also announced the change of guard in Delhi's Viceroy's house. Lord Wavell was to be replaced by Lord Mountbatten who was entrusted with the task of effecting the transfer of power to Indian hands. The transfer was supposed to be done in a manner that would best ensure the future happiness and prosperity of India. The stage was set for the momentous events to follow, which not only brought freedom to the sub-continent but also much else.

Mountbatten had first visited India as a young ADC to the Prince of Wales (who as Edward VIII abdicated the British throne in 1936 on marrying an American divorcee). On that occasion, be recorded in his diary dated 17 November, 1921 that India, "is the country one had always heard about, dreamt about and read about." And while leaving the country, he had thought, "India is the most marvellous country and the Viceroy has the most marvellous job in the world."[2] But this time round when he landed in India on 22 March, 1947, his dreamland had turned into a veritable tinder box. With the Muslim League preaching Direct Action for achievement of Pakistan, and Congress tenaciously resisting it, Hindu-Muslim cleavage had reached an all time big. His predecessors had lorded over the country with grandeur, pomp and authority. Ironically, when he came with the proclaimed objective of liberating the land, he had the most unenviable task that any Viceroy of India ever had on hand. The young Mountbatten's dream was to be the Viceroy Mountbatten's nightmare.

He had his brief prescribed. Power was to be handed over before the deadline to whatever combination of provinces was possible under the circumstances, avoiding, as far as possible, the Balkanization of the sub-continent. And he went about his job in right earnest from the day he arrived in Delhi. By now partition of India had come to be virtually accepted by everybody as inevitable and Mountbatten's problem lay not so much in evolving a workable plan of partition. That was a relatively easy job. It was the human cost involved that proved to be his Achilles heel.

The conflict situation between Hindu-Sikh combine and

Muslims had by now reached alarming proportions in the Punjab, Sindh and North-West Frontier Province. Organized violence involving these communities was causing enormous destruction of life and property everyday. Mountbatten realized the magnitude of the horror that Punjab was going through when he visited a devastated Punjab village—Kahuta—in late April 1947. Larry Collins and Dominque Lapiarre describe the horrific scene: "For centuries, Kahuta's dirt alleys had been shared in peace by 2000 Hindus and Sikhs and 1500 Moslems... Kahuta's citizens as they had for generations, were sleeping side by side in mutual confidence and tranquillity. By dawn, Kahuta had for all practical purposes ceased to exist and its Sikhs and Hindus were all dead or had fled in terror into the night..... A Moslem horde had descended on the village like wolf pack, setting fire to the houses in its Sikh and Hindu quarters with buckets of gasoline. In minutes, the area was engulfed in fire and entire families, screaming pitifully for help, were consumed by the flames. Those who escaped were caught, tied together, soaked with gasoline and burned alive like torches.... A few Hindu women, hauled from their beds to be raped and converted to Islam, survived; others had broken away from their captors and hurled themselves back into the fire to perish with their families."[3]

Kahuta's destruction was not an isolated event. It happened to more and more villages and towns in the Punjab, Sind and North-West Frontier Province but more in Punjab, as days rolled by. Starting with the Muslim majority areas of west Punjab, killing, looting, burning and raping spread like a wild fire to the Hindu-Sikh belt of East Punjab where Muslims became the victims. Violence and retaliatory violence of the most brutal kind in the whole of north-west India became the order of the day. Thousands were slaughtered, burned, raped and abducted in innumerable villages and small towns in these provinces.

The conflagration spread to the cities— Lahore and Amritsar in particular— where the May temperature of 48°C soared many times with man made flames. Arson became the most widely used instrument of assault. "Lahore A veritable Inferno", "Amritsar Burning" screamed newspaper headlines. The entire land of the five rivers, the granary of India with the best irrigation system in pre-independence days, was up in smoke. Thousands fled their homes and were fleeing everyday to safer areas dominated by their own community. The time-honoured administrative machine of British India, which had remarkably maintained peace and order for over a century, was struck with paralysis.

People all over the country were numbed, resigned to utter helplessness. The Interim Government of India, comprising Indians themselves— both Congress and Muslim League—became utterly non-functional. Both Hindus and Muslims were dying dog's death in large numbers and their acknowledged leaders let them die like that without as much as raising a little finger. They were no more than guinea pigs to be sacrificed for the sake of political experiments going on in the vast laboratory that India had come to be.

But it was the response of the final arbiter— the Viceroy of India— who had come with full powers to handle the British withdrawal, which was most intriguing. The dynamic young Viceroy (Mountbatten was only 47 years old in 1947), a cousin of the British King and the former Supreme Allied commander in South East Asia who had valiantly taken on the formidable Japanese during the war, simply caved in when faced with marauding fanatics in India. There were no meaningful administrative efforts to put out the flame of violence or contain it, even though it was confined only to a corner of the country. Professional politicians, who are themselves responsible for the kind of mob violence that was rocking Punjab at that time, get away with talking only in terms of people's demands, people's anger and such other non-senses. But every administrator handling such violence knows that when it comes to the crunch, it is out and out a matter of law and order. And the corrolary fact that it can be controlled, contained and stamped out by effective handling. There could not be an iota of doubt that pre-partition riots in Punjab, Sind and North-West Frontier Province could have been controlled and stopped in a matter of weeks by effective policing. Nehru, Patel and Liaquat Ali, who were adorning the Interim Government seats, would not have known. Mountbatten would have known or ought to have known.

But he showed no will to act. He set his priorities wrong. In stead of paying attention to large scale killings and violence, he put in all his skills and energy in evolving an agreeable arrangement for handing over power to bleeding Indians. It was as if he was in a mighty hurry to pack up and go back from the scorching heat of Delhi and Lahore to the soothing, temperate summer of England. The result was the Mountbatten plan of June 3, 1947, which provided not only for the partition of India but also the partition of Punjab and Bengal. Mountbatten secured the acceptance of his plan by Congress and Muslim League leaders at a conference on 2nd June and the leaders announced their agreement in public on 3 June, 1947.

The fateful Mountbatten plan, which defined the political geography of independent Indian sub-continent (fated to be further re-shaped at the end of 1971) had the following main components:

(a) Partition of the country into an independent Indian Union comprising the Hindu majority provinces and an independent Pakistan consisting of the Muslim majority provinces in the west and east.

(b) Further partition of the Punjab and Bengal into Muslim majority and Hindu majority areas, the former going to Pakistan and the latter to the Indian Union.

(c) The Muslim majority Sylhet district of Assam was to have the option of joining East Pakistan through a referendum.

(d) Since the Muslim majority North West Frontier Province was having a Congress government led by Dr. Khan Saheb at the time, it was given the option to decide through a referendum whether to join Pakistan or India. (The result was a foregone conclusion and as a face-saving device, Khan Abdul Gaffar Khan's Red Shrits or "Khudai Khidmatgars" boycotted the referendum demanding the third option of an independent 'pakhtoonistan', which was not available. The Frontier Gandhi, as he was reverentially called in India, felt betrayed by the Congress leadership and spent the rest of his life mostly in exile).

(e) The princely states in the sub-continent were denied the option of independence, which some of them claimed. They were to opt for either the Indian Union or Pakistan.

(f) Power was to be finally handed over to the successor Governments of India and Pakistan as early as 15 August, 1947. *This was the most vital part of the plan* from the stand point of our analysis here.

Apart from partitioning the country and creating Pakistan, which had become unavoidable, the Mountbatten Plan was favourable to the residual Indian Union in every other way. By providing for partition of the Muslim majority provinces of Punjab and Bengal, it allowed predominantly Hindu areas of these two provinces contiguous to the Indian Union to become parts of independent India at the cost of Pakistan. It was a definite departure from the principle of provinces as a whole going to Pakistan or Indian Union on the basis of the religious majority of the population. (It was of course workable because the Hindu majority parts of the two provinces, by a queer coincidence, were continguous to the Hindu majority Indian Union.) The Plan did not even look at the Muslim League demand for a corridor between its western and eastern wing, which was made from time to time by Jinnah but not persisted with. By denying the option of independence to princely states, most of which were Hindu majority, it further helped the Indian Union to add to its territory. It did create Pakistan but otherwise ensured that India remained as big as possible.

Jinnah said he got a 'trunkated Pakistan,' but he had no option but to accept it at that stage of his life. If Larry Collins and Dominique Lappierre are to be believed, Jinnah was living on borrowed life, nursing a terminal lung ailment severely limiting the years of his life still left to him. Having travelled so far almost single handed to come within touching distance of his cherished goal of an independent homeland for India's Muslims, he was not in a position to stay back and refuse whatever he was getting, even a 'trunkated Pakistan'. But it was not only a 'trunkated Pakistan' that came into being in mid August 1947. The sub-continent was trunkated in more senses than one. Independence created a trunkated Pakistan, a trunkated India and above all, a trunkated humanity, almost literally.

Heroes of Clay

The British answer to the developing human tragedy, reflected in Mountbatten's decision of immediate withdrawal was, to the say the least, most queer. By all accounts, the bloodbath in the Punjab and north-west was getting out of hand and called for immediate and effective intervention, which the British Indian administration alone could provide. And precisely at the moment the country needed administering most, the time tested administration decided to abdicate for political reasons. The facile argument advanced then and still touted by recent historians— both English and Indian— was that Hindu-Muslim hostility had reached a stage where any delay in British withdrawal could be disastrous. But disastrous for whom? For the unfortunate people of the sub-continent who went through the worst human disaster of their recent history anyway? If a patient's condition worsens and he becomes critical, it does not behove his treating doctor to run away from him leaving him at the mercy of his family members having no idea of how to treat him. The only plausible explanation is that the British decided to abdicate at the time they did only to avoid a disaster to their own prestige and image in India and the world.

In whose favour they were abdicating anyway? The political parties— the Congress and the League whose followers were killing each other, as Churchill was to say, "with the ferocity of cannibals?" How could politicians who had spent a life-time in protesting, demonstrating and agitating grow into sound administrators of law and order overnight? Even the will to act firmly of many of them, particularly at lower levels, could be suspect. Only the utterly gullible and ignorant would buy the reasoning that hasty British withdrawal was motivated by the pious intention of preventing more killings. It was no more, and no less, than jumping out of a leaky boat in stead of trying to repair the leak and rescue the people on board or running out of a house on fire rather than fighting the fire and making efforts to save the people trapped inside.

One fateful Monday morning on 6 August, 1945, the first atomic bomb was dropped on the quiet, sleepy Japanese town of Hiroshima. The blast directly killed around 60,000 Japanese men, women and children and injured over 100,000, destroying a sea port city of about 250,000 people in one go. It resulted in Japanese surrender a few days later and brought about the end of the Second World War. Arguments have continued since then about the rights and wrongs of the American decision to drop the atomic bomb on Hiroshima. The most serious argument justifying the decision was that if Hiroshima had not been bombed, the war would have continued on the Japanese main land for quite a few months more. That would have entailed more loss of life and more destruction of Japanese cities and towns, prolonging the agonies of Japanese people. It is difficult to imagine a more callous defence of the bombing of Hiroshima. The British decision to abdicate power in a huff leaving large populations at the mercy of killers, rapists and looters could not be considered any the less callous. In terms of loss of human lives it turned out to be five times more lethal and destructive than the bombing of Hiroshima.

Nor did the political leaders of the sub-continent acquit themselves any better in the epic human tragedy accompanying the partition. The 'Great Calcutta Killing' of August 1946 had served adequate notice on the political leadership about the shape of things to come. They failed to take it. They received bloody reminders from Noakhali and Bihar. They refused to wake up. And even as they were signing the 3rd June agreement in Delhi, the whole of north-west India was burning. They declined to open their eyes and see the macabre dance of death right in front of them or in their backyard. It is not only from hind sight that they invite such a harsh judgement. The impending holocaust, a direct result of the callous game they were playing on the political chessboard, was as clear as day light at that time itself to anyone who wanted to see. The British saw it and cleverly ran away just in time to evade the blame, which though would ever remain attached to their conduct at the fag end of their long rule over the country.

The 16 August Calcutta Killing was indeed a watershed in the tortuous course of events leading to the sub-continent's independence. It set the pattern of muscle-flexing by protagonists of Pakistan and their opponents in the months to come. The fight for independence was no longer against the British but against each other, which, in the circumstances prevailing at that time, meant Hindus and Muslims. The sporadic Hindu-Muslim riots that the country had known before were now sanctified by a new sacred cause. The Muslims fought in the name of a separate holy homeland while the Hindus for an independent *Akhand Bharat*

(United India). It was a fight not between two organized political groups or cadres pitted against each other, but involving unconcerned followers of the two religions in innumerable villages and towns of the country. And in every case, it was an one-sided affair in which the community in brute majority in an area butchered the community that was in hopeless minority in that particular area. It was the same in Noakhali, Bihar, Punjab and North-West Frontier Province. And while this macabre game of massacres went on in the name of political struggle for sacred causes, the political leaders were blissfully busy in their own game of one-upmanship.

The Calcutta Killing itself was the end-product of the first ever call for 'Direct Action' by Muslim League in support of the Pakistan demand. And the League's 'Direct Action' call was the direct result of the ambivalence of the Congress in regard to the Cabinet Mission's Plan of May 1946. It was remarkable that both the Congress and Muslim League had initially accepted the proposed constitutional arrangements, albeit, with certain reservations. The initial agreement over such a tangled issue as Unity of India versus partition was a highly positive factor of great significance. It was a highly promising signal for continuing patient negotiations to narrow down the remaining differences to within workable limits. Once the basics were agreed upon, it could certainly be not beyond the ingenuity and capacity of the negotiators to work out a solution accommodating both seemingly opposite points of view. The Cabinet Mission initially appeared to have achieved the impossible.

But it was the attitude of the Congress articulated forcefully by Nehru, who had become the Congress president, which drastically changed the entire course of events. He emphatically told the AICC in mid 1946 that once the Constituents Assembly was formed (evidently with a clear Congress majority), it could go its own way (regardless of whatever the Cabinet Mission Plan envisaged). His biographer, M. Chalapathi Rao, writes: "The Constituent Assembly had always meant to his historical sense a revolutionary step and he saw in the proposed Constituent Assembly an instrument of revolution. It was to be brought into being by the British Government, but when it met, would develop a volition of its own and go its own way. He had other Constituent Assemblies in mind and the way the States General of France, when summoned by the Bourbans, had gone ahead and paved the way for a revolution was specially in his mind."[4] If Nehru did actually think so, it could only be said to be amateurish India in 1946 was not France in 1789 nor were British the Bourbans. His categorical assertion that the Congress was not bound by a single thing "except entering the constituent Assembly and going ahead with constitution making" torpedoed the very structure of the Cabinet Mission Plan as a whole. For the Plan while providing for a United India with a weak centre also provided for a grouping of provinces into Hindu majority and Muslim majority entities. You could not accept one part and reject the other. If you are playing cricket, you have to observe the rules of the game and cannot lay down your own rules to suit your side.

It was too much to expect Jinnah to accept the position openly taken by Nehru, the Congress president, on the role of the Constituent Assembly. The very raison de' etre of the Pakistan demand was to save the Muslim minority from being overwhelmed by the vast Hindus majority in the determination of the future set-up. Right or wrong, the demand had overwhelmingly captured the imagination of the Muslim masses. Right or wrong, the Muslim League at least had a case. The Hindus and Muslims had co-existed in India rooted in their medieval moorings as parallel societies for centuries. The growth of modern nationalism to supercede socio-religious diversities was too slow and too feeble to have any perceivable impact.

Jinnah himself had once articulated the Hindu-Muslim dichotomy in an interview to Beverly Nichols, the controversial English Journalist who visited India in 1943-44, in the manner of a brilliant lawyer that he professionally was. His words: "There is nothing in life which links us together: our names, our clothes, our foods— they are all different... We challenge ourselves at every point of the compass. Take one example, the eternal question of the cow. We eat the cow, the Hindus worship it."[5] For a thorough bred western-oriented, non-religious person like Jinnah, who admitted of no distinction between beef and pork and was always immaculately attired in western dress, these were strange words to mouth. But his observations rang ominously true and he used it to telling effect. To cite just one example, the first major anti-Muslim riot to rock British India in 1917 was over the issue of cowslaughter during Bakrid. In a country where any number of human beings are killed to avenge the killing of a cow, Jinnah was after all not that wide of the mark.

In such an environment of acute socio-religious and political polarization, initial acceptance of the Cabinet Mission Plan by both the Congress and the League had held out a ray of hope. It was not only a question of India remaining united, but of the two major religious communities living in peace after the foreign balancer was gone. It was a great opportunity which both parties, particularly the Congress as the major partner vitally interested in keeping India United and its two major religious communities in harmony, could have seized with both hands. But Nehru's romantic visions about the proposed Constituent Assembly, equating it in his mind with the States General summoned by Louis XVI in 1789 which brought about the French Revolution, let the opportunity go. Once Jinnah realised that the Congress meant to use its majority in the Constituent Assembly to thwart the grouping of Muslim majority provinces, he withdrew his initial acceptance and rejected the Plan in its entirety. In his desperation, with the British Government wavering, he gave the call for 'Direct Action' which resulted in 'The Great Calcutta Killing'. That proved to be the turning-point in the entire course of events. The point of no return had reached. The clock started moving back from reconciliation to confrontation ending in the bloody partition of the country.

Blood-soaked Freedom

The agreement of 3 June, 1947, which was to bring about the independent States of India and Pakistan, allowed only 72 days time for the leaders to assume the mantle in their respective States. The period was too short to enable them to be fully prepared for the onerous task of governance which lay ahead. Not that they were much keen themselves to do any meaningful homework. Elated beyond measure at having achieved their life's dream of independence, they had immense confidence in themselves to prove equal to the task. All the tragic events of the past one year, all the killings and destructions, they pursuaded themselves to believe, could somehow be traced to the colonial administration. Once the devil of the British Raj was gone, leaving them free to govern their own people, all the wounds and scars of the past would disappear and all ugly happenings stop. They were leaders of their people in their own right, darlings of their masses who swayed and swung to their tunes. Now in their hour of triumph and glory, with the basket of cherished freedom to offer, they were sure their people would listen to them more. They thought they could stop all the evil acts their misguided hordes were indulging in lately by a wave of their hand or a word of their mouth. They could not be more wrong.

Jinnah was the first to give a stirring call to his people in the new-born State of Pakistan to forget the past and eschew all differences based on religion. In his memorable address to the constituent Assembly of Pakistan on 11 August, 1947, he said: "If you change your past and work together in a spirit that every one of you, no matter to what community he belongs, no matter what relations he had with you in the past, no matter what is his colour, caste or creed, is first, second and last a citizen of this state with equal rights, privileges and obligations, there will be no end to the progress you will make. I cannot emphasise it too much. We should begin to work in that spirit and in course of time all these angularities of the majority and minority communities— the Hindu community and the Muslim community— because even as regards Muslims you have Pathans, Punjabies, Shias, Sunnies and so on and among the Hindus you have Brahmins, Vaishnavas, Khatries, also Bengalis, Madrasis and so on—will vanish... You are free : you are free to go to your temples, you are free to go to your mosques, or to any other places of worship in this state of Pakistan... We are starting in the days when there is no discrimination, no distinction between one community and another, no discrimination between one caste or creed and another." And then referring to the Roman Catholics and Protestants being equal citizens of England, the Quade-Azam went on to say "Today you might say with justice that Roman Catholics and Protestants do not exist; what exists now is that every man is a citizen, an equal citizen, of Great Britain and they are all members of the nation. Now, I think we should keep that in front of us as our ideal and you will find that in course of time Hindus would cease to be Hindus and Muslims would cease to be Muslims, not in the religious sense, because that is the personal faith of each individual, but in the political sense as citizens of the State."

The tone of a totally modern liberal nationalist, steeped in British democratic traditions, was unmistakably noticeable in the speech. No liberal democrat, with howsoever impeccable secular credentials could have better defined the basic principles he would wish his new born nation state to adopt and follow. For once, Jinnah threw off the mask of a communal leader par excellence, which he kept wearing all through his single-handed crusade for Pakistan. Once his ultimate goal was achieved, he came to his own and showed up for what he was — a fully modern liberal nationalist with no religious hangovers at all. He thought his people would listen to and follow his words, now that he had brought to them what they craved for, in the same way as they had done in course of his crusade. For once, he was sorely mistaken.

It goes to Jinnah's credit that he thought of the danger his nascent state was exposed to as it started on its course and gave out his mind in clear and emphatic terms. He had tenaciously preached and struggled for a separate homeland for India's Muslims. When he got it, he took the first opportunity to proclaim loud and clear that the new state was for all who inhabited it irrespective their religion. He thought he needed to correct the aberration of religious exclusiveness Pakistan was vulnerable to, in the background of the complexions of the political movement which brought it about. But if he meant his pious exhortations to stop his marauding co-religionists from going after the blood of the sizeable Hindu-Sikh minority still left in his Pakistan, his words fell on deaf years.

Nehru, on the other hand, had no such compulsion to re-define the character of the newly independent nation state he was going to preside over. The Congress had always carried on the freedom struggle in the name of all the inhabitants of the country belonging to all religions. It was another matter that it failed to win the confidence of the Muslim masses in general and draw them into the national movement by and large. That failure incidentally, was the most tragic aspect of our freedom movement and its final outcome. Not necessarily because the sub-continent was split territorially, first in two and then in three parts, but because the mind and hearts of the people were also split. The partition of India caused a horrendous rupture of Indian humanity casting a dark shadow over the subcontinent which continues to envelop it even 50 years after independence. And instead of the shadow receding with the passage of time, it has gone on thickening all along until it has come to envelop the entire sub-continent in a deep dark night which seems never-ending.

The failure of the Congress to carry the Muslim masses with it was a collective failure resulting from a variety of historical, social and political factors, perhaps beyond the control of the Congress or its leaders. Nehru in any case had no reason to nurture any guilt complex on this score. He was as far away from any religious particularity, in fact from religion itself, as anyone could be. He prided in describing himself as a westerner by education, Muslim by culture and Hindu by birth. His unexceptionable and unsullied secular credentials obviated the need for referring to the Hindu-Muslim question in his first address to his people on the eve of independence.

With his compulsive obsession with the perspective of history, he felt free to soar high when he addressed the momentous session of the Constituent Assembly on the midnight of 14-15 August, 1947. He thundered: "Long years ago we made a tryst with destiny, and now the time comes when we will redeem our pledge, not wholly or in full measure, but very substantially. At the stroke of the mid-night hour, when the world sleeps, India will awake to life and freedom. A moment comes, which comes but rarely in history, when we step out from the old to the new, when an age ends, and when the soul of a nation, long suspended, finds utterance. It is fitting that at this solemn moment we take the pledge of dedication to the service of India and her people and to the still larger call of humanity."

Even as Jinnah was delivering his sermon and Nehru recalling his "tryst with destiny", large numbers of their countrymen were being slaughtered en masse, their homes and assets burned and destroyed, women and girls raped and kidnapped daily, hourly.

Hundreds of thousands were thrown out on roads and rugged pathways, exposed to sun and rain and marauding hordes, fleeing to safety on either side of the border in Punjab, leaving the corpses of their near and dear ones behind. It was freedom soaked in blood, not of those fighting for and wresting freedom from the British, but of thousands and thousands of innocent men, women and children caught in the vortex of brutal frenzy generated in course of the run up to transfer of power. They had to go through the dreadful carnage as a direct result of the callous and clumsy manner in which the British, Congress and the League ushered in freedom in the sub-continent. To these hapless victims of the orgy of death and destruction, Jinnah's pious homilies and Nehru's "tryst with destiny" rhetoric rang not only hollow but outrageously cruel.

Alan Campbell-Johnson, staff member of Mountbatten, gives a blow by blow account of what the people of Punjab were going through in the wake of independence, as recorded in his diary : "16 August, 1947."

"Even as we met, momentous news was coming in from both the partitioned provinces which provided at once a warning and an example.....In the Punjab the people are taking the situation into their own hands. What Jenkins has aptly termed the war of succession has broken out in full fury in the land of the five rivers... In view of the grave Punjab developments, Nehru and Liaquat have decided to go together at once to Ambala and thence to Amritsar...."

"27 August 1947

Mountbatten then turned to a general account of what was happening in Punjab. The Sikhs, he said had launched an attack, just as Giani Kartar Singh and Tara Singh before 3rd June had told him they would. Mountbatten had expostulated with them at the time, stressing that the British would have gone. It would be Indians fighting Indians. But they were adamant and had in fact observed that they were waiting for us to go. The situation was now out of their control. In an area less than two hundred by one hundred and fifty miles containing some seventeen thousand inhabited localities and only about the size of Wales, some ten million people were on the move."[6]

About Lady Mountbatten's visit to the heartland of communal frenzy, Campbell-Johnson records on 28 August, 1947: "Her report on the situation on both sides of the boundary is disquieting enough. The refugees are now in a state of mass hysteria. Neither side has any trust in the intentions, assurances or actions of the other Dominion."[6]

Within fifteen days of independence, Nehru and Liaquat Ali, the Prime Ministers of India and Pakistan decided to fly to Lyallpur and Lahore with a small press party to see the plight of refugees in west Punjab. Durga Das, a senior journalist who accompanied them, describes the scene: "we took off from Amritsar and landed at Lyallpur, where half a million Hindus and Sikhs begged for safe passage to India. It was the day of 'Rakhi' when a Hindu sister ties a thread around her brother's wrist, thus committing him to defend her honour. A dozen women came to the Circuit House, where we had made our headquarters, and tied the symbolic thread on Nehru. The act brought tears to their eyes, and Nehru was visibly moved. He responded to their plea that he fly over Jhang and Chiniot to lift up the thousands of refugees who had gathered there from the dispair in which they had been plunged. As our Dakota passed over these places, we saw huge crowds looking up at the aircraft and we could almost feel a vast sigh rise upward to meet it.

"This trip delayed our arrival at Lahore airfield by ninety minutes. There I met the Governor, Sir Francis Mudie, who had been Home Member under Wavell, and Giani Kartar Singh. 'What the devil are you doing here?' Mudie asked me in a voice betraying panic. 'To see what the Frankenstein monster you and we all have let loose has done to innocent people', I retorted. He snapped back, "you wanted independence. Now you have it".... Giani Kartar Singh was in tears and appealed to Nehru to save the hundreds of thousands of Hindus and Sikhs who had gathered in various towns in west Punjab, seeking protection in numbers.

"Most touching were the replies of the refugees whom we spoke to when we came across a long caravan on the way to India along the road through Sheikhupura, where the worst slaughter had occurred. An old peasant said: 'This country has seen many changes of rulers. They have come and gone. But this is the first time that with a change of rulers, the riyaya (subjects) is also being forced to change— and flee their homes.' An elderly woman, not aware she was addressing Nehru but judging him an important personage from his dress and demeanour, said: *'Partitions take place in all families. Property changes hands, but it is all arranged peacefully. Why this butchery, loot and abductions? Could you not do it the sensible way families divided*?"[7]

In one short, wry, crucible question, the elderly woman said it all. That was the crucial question to which all the wisemen of Britain, India and Pakistan, Mountbatten, Nehru and Jinnah, had no answer then. No one has any answer even now, half a century after independence. And no one will have any answer in future. It will ever remain a tragic question mark on the manner in which the transfer of power was brought about.

Alan Campbell-Johnson, Mountbatten's Aide, records about their aerial view of refugee movement on 21 September, 1947: "As we approached the Ravi we had our first aerial vision of the scale of this desperate exodus. We were looking down on one of the greatest movements of population in recorded history.... we flew, in fact, for over fifty miles against this stream of refugees without reaching its source... As we flew back into India we came down low over the northern most of the Muslim refugee convoys making its slow and painful way along this main Lyallpur-Lahore road.... This column, therefore, must have been at least forty-five miles long... Today we saw for ourselves something of the stupendous scale of the Punjab up-heaval. Even our brief bird's eyeview must have revealed nearly half a million refugees on the roads."[8]

"22 September 1947:

In the past few hours, reports have come in of no fewer than four serious attacks on refugee trains, two on Muslims in Jullundar and at the Beas bridge and two on non-Muslims in the Lahore area. During his visit Liaquat had referred to one train starting off with two thousand passengers of whom only seven hundred had arrived at the other end..."

Butcheries on refugee trains on both sides assumed horrific proportions through September-October 1947. The total brutalisation of humanity was tellingly reflected in a sordid placard displayed on a train that arrived with corpses and mutilated bodies into the Indian territory. It read *Pakistan ka Tohfa* (Gift from Pakistan). The devastating impact of such provocations on the mass of Muslim refugees fleeing to Pakistan, who had to bear the brunt of retaliatory violence, could be well imagined.

A former Army Vice-Chief, Lt. General S.K. Sinha (Retd.) who as a young major was posted to the Staff of General Russel in charge of Delhi and East Punjab command in those turbulent times, writes:" The civil administration in these parts had virtually ceased to exist and we had almost completely taken over responsibility for the maintenance of law and order... Apart from ensuring the security of life and property of the people, we also had to escort large numbers of refugees both by foot and on train. Mass migrations on a scale unprecedented in history were in progress and escorting these large refugee columns to the Pakistan border was indeed a very difficult problem. The trains carried eight to ten thousand refugees each (most of them packed in goods wagons) and the foot columns often extended up to 30 miles in length. There had been several unfortunate incidents and these poor refugees had been attacked time and again both in India and in Pakistan."[9]

The end-product of freedom at the time and in the manner it came was half a million to one million people dead and well over ten millions uprooted from their hearths and homes. According to the judicial finding of G.D. Khosla, around half a million people lost their lives in the partition holocaust. At a conference of about two hundred American and other specialists on terrorism held in March 1976, some statistical studies were presented regarding the toll taken by terrorist violence during the preceding years. One study presented at the conference disclosed that approximately 4600 lives were lost in scattered terrorist actions and around three quarters of a million in all forms of civil strife the world over during the decade of 1960's. In comparison, the loss of at least half a million lives in the Indian sub-continent in a short span of only about 4-5 months immediately before and after partition tells its own story. The dream of early 1946 had turned into the worst nightmare for millions in the sub-continent by the end of 1947.

References

1. *India From Curzon to Nehru and After,* Durga Das, 1971.
2. *Freedom At Midnight*, Larry Collins and Dominique Lapierre.
3. *Ibid.*
4. *Builders of Modern India: Jawaharlal Nehru*, M. Chalapathi Rao.
5. *Verdict on India*, Beverly Nichols, 1944. The book had evoked great controversy in those days and elicited rejoinders from others.
6. *Mission with Mountbatten*, Alan Campbell-Johnson, 1951.
7. *India From Curzon to Nehru and After*, Durga Das, 1971.
8. *Mission with Mountbatten*, Alan Campbell-Johnson, 1951.
9. *Operation Rescue,* Lt. General S.K. Sinha PVSM (Retd.)

4

Freedom to Kill

Paradox of History

It is a cruel paradox of the sub-continent's history that about a hundred times more human lives were lost during its liberation than in the entire course of its conquest by the British. And while the negligible loss of life of combatants involved in the British conquest of India was spread over around a half a century or so, the colossal sacrifice of innocent human lives accompanying its liberation took place in less than a year. What is more stunning, the imprecedented scale of blood bath on the eve and in the wake of liberation was not a result of any showdown or clash of arms with the British. On the other hand, half a million to a million people of the sub-continent died fighting among themselves. In fact, during the peak of the partition holocaust, when thousands of refugees packed in trains were being pounced upon and massacred on either side of the border, any Englishman could freely move about through the worst affected areas absolutely unmolested. One Col. F.H.B. Ingall, of 6th Lancers, a cavalry officer of the British Indian Army, travelled unescorted from Amritsar to Lahore and back many times during those days without any fear or harm. (Later in his life, Col. Ingall migrated to America and wrote a book on his life and times in the sub-continent.)

To set the records straight, a flitting peep into the sub-continent's history, particularly regarding its subjugation by the British, is perhaps called for. The decisive armed conquest of India by the British may be traced back to the Battle of Plassey fought between the forces of Nawab Sirajuddaula of Bengal and Robert Clive in June 1757. The British victory of Plassey, which proved to be a watershed event in the chain of developments that made them the masters of India, took the toll of only 500 Indian soldiers who were killed in that fateful battle. Of course, Robert Clive manoeuvred the British victory at Plassey by causing defection of

Mir Jaffar, Sirajuddaula's commander, and others, almost without much of a fight. But even the subsequent more closely fought Battle of Buxar between the vast combined forces of Mir Kasim, the Nawab of Bengal, and the Nawab of Oudh, in October 1764 resulted in casualty of only about 2000 Indian officers and soldiers. And victory at Buxar confirmed the position of the British as the unchallengeable power in Northern India as a whole, paving the way for their ultimate victory over Marathas and Tipu Sultan in the west and south on way to establishing the Indian Empire.

Neither the four Anglo-Mysore wars—1767-69, 1780-84, 1790-92 and 1799—nor the three Anglo-Marathas wars—1775-82, 1803-1806 and 1817-18—which consolidated the British position as the Paramount power in the sub-continent, involved any large scale casualties of combatants and destruction of civilian lives. None of these so-called wars was anywhere in the nature of the ferocious and devastating wars launched by foreign invaders from the north-west like Nadir Shah and Ahmad Shah Abdali during the 18th century, or by the alliance of Muslim kingdoms of South India against Vijayanagar earlier in the 16th century. Nadir Shah's conquest of Delhi in March 1739 was accompanied with massacre of about 30,000 people in Delhi alone. And in the battle of Talikota on the banks of river Krishna in January 1565, in which King Rama Raya of Vijayanagar was decisively defeated by the Deccan Sultans, about 100,000 soldiers and citizens of Vijayanagar were slain. Historians record: "Never perhaps in the history of the world has such havoc been wrought and wrought suddenly, on so splendid a city, teeming with a wealthy and industrious population in the full plenitude of prosperity one day, and on the next seized pillaged and reduced to ruins, amid scenes of savage massacre and horrors beggaring description."

Earlier still, in the historic battle of Panipat of 1526 fought between Sultan Ibrahim and Babar, about 40,000 to 50,000 soldiers had died fighting in the battlefield. Babar himself recorded in his memoirs that on reaching Agra after his victory, he gathered from the accounts of "natives of Hindustan" that forty or fifty thousand soldiers had perished in the battlefield of Panipat. It was Babar's victory in this momentous battle which heralded the Establishment of Mughal Empire in India. In sharp contrast, the wars fought by the British to build their empire in India would appear to be kind of a sport which the British and the local Nawabs and satraps indulged in at the time. In any case, the Anglo-Mysore and Anglo-Marathas wars in the Deccan, or the battles at Plassey and Buxar for that matter, were no more than skirmishes between the rising British power and decaying indigenous feudal kingdoms. They were more in the nature of battles of wits, intrigues and manipulations than real clash of arms between two-well-organized armed forces or fighting machines. The British won the day on the strength of their diplomatic skill, intelligent handling of feuding Nawabs and Maharajas and superior military strategy. Above all, they won because they had arrived in the modern age while the local powers in India were still living in medieval times.

Dwelling upon numbers of human beings killed at the time of independence, or at any other time in India's chequered history, may appear to be a maudlin way of looking at things. But ignoring it altogether while gloating at independence, as people in the sub-continent are used to doing, would be nothing short of monumental callousness. To the political practitioners and people generally in the sub-continent, particularly the post-independence generation, those hundreds of thousands who were butchered at the altor of freedom were not Indians or Pakistanis to be remembered while remembering the coming of freedom. No they were not human beings, not worth remembering anyway. They just did not exist. Never did.

One may blank off those unknown, abstract victims of independence—half a million or one million—from one's memory, but can it be done in respect of some of the topmost national leaders of countries of the sub-continent which gained independence in 1947? Apart from the huge numbers of forgotten people who could not live to see the dawn of freedom, every top leader of every country of South Asia was annihilated almost on the morrow of independence by his own people. It would appear that the most important freedom that the people of South Asia got from the British was the freedom to kill. They started making full use of this morbid freedom from the moment they achieved it and have continued to do so down to the present times. That is the story of South Asia's 'progress' from freedom to violent order, the subject matter of this book.

Bullets in the Crowns

India was long hailed as the "Jewel in the Crown" of British emperors who reigned over the magnificent Indian empire for nearly two hundred years. But the crowns that their successors, in the countries into which the Indian Empire was split, wore after independence were riddled with bullets, literally. The topmost leader or the head of government of every country of South Asia which gained independence after British withdrawal fell victim to assassin's bullet sooner or later. What was "jewel" to the British crown turned into bullets to the crowns of those who succeeded the British in their respective countries. It was not an aberration, a one-time happening, a mad act or mishap. A mad act or mishap could happen in one country, at the most in two. But it happened in every country of South Asia which became independent. There definitely was a pattern in it, which has come to be a permanent features of political life in all these countries. The assassination of top national leaders with the advent of independence was symbolic. It set the tone for what was to follow on a much larger scale as years rolled by.

Aung San of Burma

The first lethal shot war fired in Rangoon (now Yangon) the capital of Burma, which was a province of India under the British until 1937. Aung San was the topmost nationalist leader of Burma at the time of its independence. He was foremost among the "Thirty Heroes" who after helping the Japanese to oust the British initially soon started working to liberate Burma from the Japanese. Aung San organised his Burmese Defence Army to drive the Japanese out of Burma. By August 1944, the other resistance groups in Burma working to liberate the country from the Japanese formed the powerful Anti-Fascist Peoples Freedom League (AFPFL) led by Aung San. When the British returned to Burma in May 1945, AFPFL led by Aung San was the most authentic nationalist outfit to negotiate with the British and herald freedom. Accordingly in August 1946, an Executive Council of eleven members, six from the AFPFL led by Aung San and five from other parties, was constituted by the British Governor of Burma to function as an interim Government pending the grant of full independence. Aung

San had broadly the same position in Burma as Jawaharlal Nehru in the Interim government set up in India in September-October 1946.

Aung San headed the Burmese delegation at a conference in London in December 1946 in which details about the transfer of power to the Burmese were finalized. It was categorically announced that Burma would be granted Commonwealth status or independence, as it desired, by the quickest possible means. In January 1947, it was agreed upon to constitute an Elective Constituent Assembly for drawing up the constitution of an independent Burma. In April 1947, elections to the Constituent Assembly were held in terms of the settlement reached in January. Predictably the AFPFL led by Aung San won an overwhelming majority of seats confirming its position as the principal nationalist political organization to take over from the British. The process of constitution-making for the independent republic of Burma started in right earnest.

But even before the task could be completed, nemesis struck from which Burma never recovered in course of the last 50 years. On 19 July, 1947, Aung San and six other members of the Executive Council (Interim Government) were assassinated while engaged in a cabinet meeting. Burma was formally declared independent on 4 January 1948, but the principal architects of its independence were removed from the scene by assassin's bullets about five months before assuming the mantle. Agents of opposition groups led by U. Saw were blamed for the killing. The process of annihilation of top South Asian leaders by their own people, freed from the bondage of the British, had begun.

Thakin NU, a pious Buddhist, succeeded Aung San and carried the AFPFL and the Government along the agreed course. The unfinished task of constitution-making was completed and the new constitution adopted on 24 September, 1947. Burma was granted independence by the Treaty with Britain dated 17 October, 1947, which came into force on 4 January, 1948. But Burma was not to be the same again. The assassination deprived the newly independent nation of the services of its ablest and most experienced political leaders at a time it needed them most. It showed in no uncertain terms in the political fortune of independent Burma leading to its lapse into military dictatorship, from which it is still struggling to extricate itself.

Incidentally, Ms Aung San Suu Kyi, the most visible symbol of pro-democracy movement in Burma and a Nobel laureate, is none other than the daughter of the assassinated leader Aung San. When the military regime called a general election in Burma on 17 May, 1990, the 'National League For Democracy' led by the charismatic Aung San Suu Kyi achieved a sweeping victory. The people of Burma appeared to have atoned for the sin of the July 1947 assassination by giving an overwhelming victory to the daughter of the principal victim. But the military regime failed to oblige by honouring the electoral verdict, and Burma continues to be as far away from democracy as ever.

The tragedy of Burma came eloquently to world attention in September 1988 when widespread student agitations broke out demanding the end of dictatorship. Starting from Rangoon University, students from all other major campuses in Burma came on the street in a firy campaign for major democratic reforms. But on 18 September, 1988, General Saw Maung captured power in a coup-like manner and embarked on brutal repression. In a frightful display of state terror, thousands of prodemocracy students were massacred by trigger-happy soldiers and several thousands fled the country into neighbouring Thailand and India. The ghosts of Aung San and his six colleagues are still haunting the corridor of power in Burma.

Mahatma Gandhi: Assassination Most Sinister

He was the lone crusader for human values during the bloody days of partition independence. Even as India and Pakistan were preparing to usher in the new-found freedom in style and ceremony, regardless of the blood-spilling in Punjab and elsewhere, Gandhiji was away on his sacred mission of saving Bengal from communal madness. Well before the appointed date of Nehru's "tryst with destiny", the Mahatma withdrew himself from the inaugural scene of freedom he had fought all his life to bring about. He spent the day— 15th August, 1947—which is celebrated every year with great fanfare by weilders of power—fasting in a small unostentatious house in a Muslim locality of Calcutta. He birthed himself there to prevent by his healing presence a much feared repetition of what had happened just a year before.

While Nehru and Liaquat Ali, Prime Ministers—designate of India and Pakistan, were bubbling with confidence in their capacity to stop the communal frenzy sweeping either side of the border in the west. Mountbatten was not so confident. He was seriously concerned about Calcutta and the east going up in smoke. The great Calcutta killing of a year ago, which actually started the series of communal carnage in the sub-continent, hang heavy on his mind. It was too recent to be brushed aside or shrugged off easily. Any communal flare up in Calcutta at that stage had the ominous potential of engulfing East Bengal, Assam, Bihar, U.P., in fact the whole of the north and north-eastern India, into conflagration on a scale he would shudder to imagine. Mountbatten had anyhow managed to put together a combined force of the two Dominions called the Punjab Boundary Force under an English commander—Pete Rees—who had earlier commanded a Division on the Burma front under him, to control the situation in that region. (The force utterly failed to maintain even a semblance of peace and had to be subsequently dishanded.) Gandhiji's decision to station himself in Calcutta was his only hope of peace being maintained in the whole of the east, even though he kept his fingers crossed.

H.S. Suhrawardi, the last Chief Minister of undivided Bengal, was a more worried man. His amateurish handling of the first 'Direct Action' call given by the Muslim League had resulted in the massive Calcutta carnage, with heavy Muslim casualties, only a year earlier. The heavy load of Calcutta's dead on his conscience was compounded by the fear of a repetition of the event in the wake of the happenings in Punjab. He had learnt his lesson and was not prepared to risk another holocaust in his province. He went out of his way to cultivate Gandhiji and pursuade him to stay in Calcutta as a caution against the hot wind of communal frenzy sweeping across the west. Gandhiji stayed on in Calcutta during that critical period out of his own convictions, but also obliged Suhrawardi by doing so. In the bargain, he made Suhrawardi restrain the Muslims of East Bengal from going the Noakhali way, and, what was more exacting personally to him, asked Suhrawardi to stay with him in the humble home he was himself living in Calcutta.

For saking his well known luxurious life style, Suhrawardi did stay with Gandhiji in the latter's humble way during his sojourn at Calcutta in pursuit of peace and amity. And he was amply rewarded for that. Calcutta's Muslims were saved, East Bengal Hindus were saved and the entire region remained calm. Mountbatten was rewarded too for putting his trust in Gandhiji's soothing presence in that area. The solitary saviour did in the East what his 55000 strong Punjab Boundary Force could not do in the north-west. It was the Mahatma's miracle that the whole of undivided Bengal was spared the blood bath that Punjab was going through in those mad times.

Anger of Hindus on the fanatic fringe started building up against the Mahatma from that time. "What was he doing" many whispered, "protecting the Muslims of Calcutta when Hindus were being massacred in Punjab"? Some fanatic Hindu youths threw stones at the house where Gandhiji was staying in Calcutta. It was a time when Hindus and Muslims no longer counted as human beings. They were reduced to mere numbers—the numbers of those killed on either side. It happens only in times of big wars between nations when, for instance, people talk in terms of so many Germans or Russians killed in a bomb attack or battle. In war time, perfectly sane, normal citizens of a country start gloating at the number of people of the enemy country dying in course of an action or fighting.

During the First World War when England and Germany were arraigned against each other, one Prof. Glibert Murray of England wrote in Hibbert Journal in October 1914: "When I see that 20000 Germans have been killed in such—and—such engagement and next day that it was only 2000, I am sorry."[1] Prof. Hibbert was no Jingoist or ultra nationalist in his views and attitudes. He was in fact an opponent of war as such and inclined towards neutralism or pacifism in the peace debate going on in Britain before the outbreak of the First World War. But once the war started and Britain and Germany were locked in life and death struggle, even he felt happy if the number of German casualties in any engagement was large rather than small. Most people in India and Pakistan at that time had the same feeling about Muslim and Hindu casualties respectively as Prof. Murray had about German casualties in 1914.

That was Gandhiji's real undoing and ultimate rejection of all that he stood for. And that by the very people among whom he preached his gospel all his life. But he was not the one to give up even if all his people deserted him or no one listened to him. He was essentially a loner in the midst of the crowds that thronged around him and he didn't mind being so without them. He had failed in preventing what he called the "vivisection of India," but he would persist with his mission to prevent the "vivisection" of hearts of the people who stood divided into two nations. His commitment to the cause cast him in the role of the greatest protector of Muslims in what remained of India in the wake of partition. Even leaders of the new state of Pakistan, who were now unable of protect their flock in India whom they had aroused to fanatic pitch before partition, started grudingly acknowledging Gandhiji as the sole protector of Muslims in India.

And the Mahatma did perform his role with the same devotion and dedication which he had given to the cause of independence earlier. When a relatively minor communal trouble flared up in Calcutta in September 1947, he undertook another of his celebrated fasts, which had the desired result of restoring peace. When devastated and furious Hindu-Sikh refugees started rampaging the Muslims of Delhi in bloody revenge, he rushed to Delhi to restore sainty. He felt ashamed that Dr. Ansari's daughter and son-in-law had to take shelter in a hotel and Dr. Zakir Hussain could not move about freely in Delhi, and said so to everyone who cared to listen. His healing words at daily prayer meetings had the desired effect in limiting the damage and bringing about progressive improvement in the situation.

He was focused at that time on protection of Muslims in India because they needed it. After having vociferously and aggressively campaigned for Pakistan which could not accommodate or protect those left in India, they had soured their relations with the Hindus to a breaking point. The influx of Hindu-Sikh refugees with blood-curling tales of atrocities committed on them in Pakistan added to their predicament. Gandhiji perceived the serious threat situation they were in and responded to it in the way only he could. But it was not as if he was oblivious of the monumental sufferings of Hindus and Sikhs left in Pakistan at the time of partition. As the situation in Delhi improved, he was thinking of visiting Pakistan to bring solace to Hindus and Sikhs. Durga Das reveals that "he told me one day that he had decided to visit Pakistan accompanied by General Shah Nawaz Khan of the INA. They had planned to leave in mid-February. He wanted the Hindus and Sikhs and Muslims restored to their homes."[2]

Meanwhile, a crisis situation developed in Indo-Pak relations early in January 1948 over distribution of assets. An accord had been reached between the two countries according to which among other things, India was to pay a cash balance amounting to Rs. 57 crores to Pakistan and Pakistan was to withdraw the raiders from Kashmir. But Pakistan subsequently changed its mind on Kashmir and India refused to turn over the agreed balance of Rs. 57 crores to Pakistan. It was believed that Nehru and Mountbatten were in favour of honouring the agreement in respect of payment to Pakistan, but Patel was adamant. Liaquat Ali Khan dubbed India's refusal to pay as an attempt to "strangulate" Pakistan financially. (This found its echo subsequently in Jinnah's last recorded Independence Day message as Governor General of Pakistan, as follows: "Disappointed in their efforts by other means to strangulate the new State at its very birth, our enemies yet hoped that economic manoeuvres would achieve the object they had at heart... they prophesied that Pakistan would be left bankrupt, and what the fire and sword of the enemy could not achieve would be brought about by the ruined finances of the State."[3]

Gandhiji felt it was India's moral obligation to pay the amount to Pakistan. It was immaterial that Nehru also perhaps had the same view. To Gandhiji, it was more than a question of moral obligation alone. It was also necessary, he felt, to help the new state of Pakistan out of its initial financial difficulties. His reaction was quick and unequivocal. Pakistan must be paid the amount. And to lend his support to the cause, he went on an indefinite fast at his Delhi camp. Patel finally yielded, the Government of India yielded, and payment of Rs. 57 crores to Pakistan was announced. Gandhiji broke his fast.

The cup of anger of those burning with the fire of revenge against Pakistan was full. Among them was one Madan Lal Pahwa who had lost his dear ones and everything else in Sind (Pakistan) and was now a refugee in Delhi. Among them were Nathu Ram Godse and Gopal Godse who represented the extremist fringe of Hindu backlash against Muslim communalism. They ganged up to commit the most heinous crime against humanity. On 30 January, 1948 Nathu Ram Godse shot at Gandhiji thrice from point blank range at his afternoon prayer meeting at Delhi, killing him instantly. It was the assassination of the century.

His final acts—fasting for ensuring payment to Pakistan—and extra solicitousness and activism for protection of Muslims in India after partition, were aimed at healing the wounds of partition. All through the five and a half month he was allowed to live after independence partition, he kept striving to restore peace and goodwill between India and Pakistan, a cherished dream of the common people of the two states which is still as far away as ever. It was as if he was seeking an answer to the simple question put before Nehru by the elderly refugee woman in Lahore circuit house at the peak of partition carnage: "Partitions take place in all families... but it is all arranged peacefully, could you not do it the sensible way families divided?" All his endeavours during the five and a half months that he lived after independence were in the direction of making amends for the insensible or atrocious way India and Pakistan divided in 1947.

If Gandhiji had his way, India and Pakistan would have divided, if they had to, as brothers, as families do, and not as adversaries. In recent times, many countries in the world have split or separated but they are not pointing the dagger at each other's throat as India and Pakistan are doing today. After end of communism in Europe, the central Asian Republics of Kyrgyzstan Turkmenistan, Turkestan, Tajikistan, Uzbekistan, and Kazakhstan separated from Russia, but they formed a commonwealth of independent states to coordinate and cooperate with each other in diverse spheres. The erstwhile state of Czechoslovakia split into two separate states—the Czech and Slovak Republics. Earlier still, Singapore separated from Malaysia, both one-time British colonies, quite peacefully. They all separated when separation became unavoidable for one reason or another, but did so as friends, not enemies. That was Gandhiji's dream, after India divided, and he worked for it till the last day of his life.

One of the most appropriate comments on his assassination comes from Frank Moraes, the Englishman who lived and worked as a newspaperman in India for over forty years through the later British rule, the Gandhian era and early post-independence years. He writes: "I like to think of him in the last weeks of his life when, oppressed by the horror of the partition killings and separated by vital differences from some of his closest colleagues— a lonely, tired, enfeebled, and mentally anguished man—he yet insisted indomitably that justice should be done to all without fear or favour, to Hindus, Muslims, Sikhs, Christians, and all who sought the protection of India.... He died as perhaps he would have liked to—in the cause of Hindu-Muslim Unity and understanding, felled by the gun of a fellow Hindu. That was Gandhi's finest hour".[4] But that was South Asia's darkest hour, the shadows of which have turned it into a sub-continent of darkness.

Liaquat Ali Khan of Pakistan

Even as he accepted Mountbatten's 3 June partition/ Independence Plan, the Quaid-i-Azam lamented what he got was a "moth-eaten" Pakistan. The sombre observation, made apparently in the context of taking West Bengal and East Punjab out of Pakistan, was actually true in more senses than one. Territoriality apart, it was even more true of the ethnic, linguistic, cultural and class composition of what the polity of Pakistan was going to be. Perhaps Jinnah knew it and was conscious of it; perhaps he was not. But his observation concealed more than what it revealed at the time. For the only thing that linked the East Bengalis, West Punjabis, Sindhis, Pukhtoons and Baluchis who comprised the new state of Pakistan, with each other was religion. A revealed religion with the finality of the Prophet's message, Islam is no doubt a great cementing force. But it is a religious order, a religion, perhaps the fastest growing religion in the world,— and not a political organization. In case of the newly created state of Pakistan, Islam could not be expected to be a substitute for a mature and sound political organization to carry forward the task of nation-building and state building. That was Jinnah's predicament at the time of the birth of Pakistan.

In his first and last independence day message of 14 August, 1948, the Quaid-i-Azam told his countrymen: "The foundations of your state have been laid, and it is now for you to build, and build as quickly and as well as you can." The task needed a strong political instrument with grass root organization and support, like the Congress party in India, as well as competence and skill in the mechanics of governance. The Muslim League, which had spearheaded the agitation for creation of Pakistan, was simply not in a fit state to carry out the task. The core of Muslim League leadership in both the western and eastern wings comprised the land-owning elites as well as upper middle class professionals like lawyers and businessmen. For garnering support of the masses, they depended on the Islamic appeal exercised through Pirs and Mullahs. But in this regard also, they were given to kind of a political double think and double speak, which incapacitated them to an extent. While they sold the concept of an Islamic state to the masses, the League elites toyed with the idea of establishing a modern liberal state, which created a dichotomy of sorts in their of thought and action sapping their efficacy. With its lop-sided, hollow organizational structure and political scyzophrenia of its leadership, the League was just not the appropriate instrument for nation-building in the new state.

Its credentials for state building through sound governance were still more dubious. The Muslim League was definitely not a well-knit governmental unit by the very character of its leadership, particularly in the western wing. Jinnah knew it and had little trust in the will or capacity of political leaders he had at his disposal to run the machinery of government with any degree of skill. So much so that three of the four provincial governors under him in west Punjab, Frontier and East Bengal were British. And they were not mere ornamental heads of provincial governments either. The Quaid relied on them to keep the feuding and blundering politicians under sheath. They sent regular reports to Jinnah on the functioning of the provincial cabinets and the prevailing factionalism. The common theme of their reports was that the politicians were not allowing the administrative machinery to function with its pre-independence efficiency. (How true it was and it is even today not only in respect of Pakistan but also India.)

There is evidence to suggest that during the closing days of his life, the Quaid-i-Azam was fed up with the intrigues and feuds of Muslim League politicians of Punjab, the heart land of Pakistan, and had given them up as beyond redemption. Sir Francis Mudie, the English Governor of Punjab, had in fact written to Dr. Khalid B. Sayeed, an academic living abroad, about Jinnah's utter disgust with them in those days. As Governor General, Jinnah "had become so disgusted with the performance of the Muslim League ministry in Punjab that he told the Governor that he would wash his hands of them and that his policy was to let the ministry 'stew in its own juice' of intrigues and feuds."[5]

The greatest weakness of the Muslim League was its total dependence on the Quaid-i-Azam not only during the period of the movement for creation of Pakistan but also after it came into being. There was complete lack of able second and third line leadership in the League to carry forward the task of building up on the foundations laid by Jinnah. And the tragedy of Pakistan was that it lost its creator and founder just after a year of its birth. Jinnah was already a terminally sick man when Pakistan came into being and had little time of his life left to give it a solid footing. His independence day address of 14 August, 1947 proved to be his valedictory message to the people of Pakistan. The great helmsman passed away quietly on 11 September 1948, leaving the ship of Pakistan in rough seas.

The only leader who had the ability, vision and a semblance of authority, after Jinnah, to steer clear the ship of Pakistan through rough weather was Liaqualt Ali Khan. Jinnah was too towering and over-powering a leader to groom any successor as such. But Liaquat Ali had come up to be in a position to succeed him on his own by virtue of his leadership qualities and standing in the Muslim League in course of the movement for Pakistan. Like Jinnah, he was steeped in the traditions of modern, western education, liberal, unbigoted, tolerant and had visions too. During his visit to Delhi as Pak P.M. on 19 Sept., 1947 at the height of partition killings, Nehru remarked that the talk of war (between the two new states) was "completely wild and absurd." Liaquat reacted: "I agree that talk of war is absurd.... Pakistan wants peace for all nations but specially with India. We are after all two parts of the subcontinent. *We could never dream of waging war against India*".[6] (Ironically, India and Pakistan have gone through three wars since their inception as independent states, and one of his successors— Z.A. Bhutto—talked of waging a "thousand years war" against India. But Liaquat at least had the vision, at the time of partition, of permanent peace with India).

After Jinnah's passing away, Liaquat Ali chose to remain the Prime Minister of Pakistan, allowing a lesser political leader—Khwaja Nazimuddin—to become the Governor General. That was quite in keeping with the traditions of parliamentary democracy which Liaquat evidently wanted to develop in Pakistan. The first task that needed his urgent attention was to get on with the work of constitution-making which had got bogged down into serious controversies by the very nature of Pakistan's composition. After meeting for the first time on 10 August, 1947, the Constituent Assembly was stuck up in controversies relating to the place of Islam, national language, representation of the eastern and western wings, rights of minorities etc. in the new set up. Even the basic principles on which the constitution was to rest could not be formulated during Jinnah' life time.

In the circumstances, adoption of the objectives Resolution by the Constituent Assembly in March 1949, defining the basic objectives of the constitution, was a great achievement for which Liaquat could take legitimate credit. He was within his rights to describe it as "the most important occasion in the life of the country next in importance only to the achievement of independence." What was more significant, the objectives enumerated in the Resolution admirably combined due reverence to Islam with essential attributes of a modern republican constitution. The Resolution represented a remarkable reconciliation of the demand for an Islamic state with the liberal democratic predilections of the founders of Pakistan. For once, the nagging ambivalence or dichotomy in the thoughts and pronouncements of political leaders in those formative years was resolved to everybody's satisfaction. That was certainly an achievement. Pakistan still had a leader who could bring it about.

The Resolution contained reference to religion and Islam in the following terms:

"Whereas sovereignty over the entire Universe belongs to Allah Almighty alone, and the authority which he has delegated to the state of Pakistan through its people for being exercised within the limits prescribed by Him is a sacred trust. Where as the Founder of Pakistan Quaid-i-Azam Muhammad Ali Jinnah, declared that Pakistan would be a democratic state based on Islamic principles of social justice......

Where is the principles of democracy, freedom, equality and tolerance and social justice as enunciated by Islam should be fully observed:

Where in the Muslims of Pakistan should be enabled individually and collectively to order their lives in accordance with the teachings and requirements of Islam as set out in the Holy Quran and Sunnah."

The reference to Allah (God) Almighty and Islam was made in broad and generic terms which could be quite consistent with a liberal democratic dispensation. To leave no scope for doubt on this account, the Resolution went on to emphasise the rights and interests of minorities as follows:

"Wherein adequate provisions should be made for the minorities freely to profess and practice their religion and develop their culture....

Wherein should be guaranteed fundamental rights including rights such as equality of status and of opportunity, equality before law, freedom of thought, expression, belief, faith, worship and association, and social, economic, and political justice, subject to law and public morality:

Wherein adequate provision shall be made to safeguard the legitimate interests of minorities, and backward and depressed classes."

What more could anyone ask for by way of safe-guarding the rights of religious minorities in pursuit of their religion and culture? What greater guarantee could a basic document like the objectives Resolution provide for preservation and protection of minorities' interests? In spite of repeated references to Islam in the broadest possible context in this first policy document, it is clear that the founding fathers of Pakistan did not intend it to be a theocratic state. And it is an eloquent testimony to the leadership qualities of Liaquat Ali Khan that he was able to get it adopted by the Constituent Assembly.

But the intrigues of his country's semi-feudal politicians particularly in the western wing, started catching up with Liaquat. It started with a whispering campaign against Begum Liaquat who was a well educated modern lady freely taking part in public activities. Ironically, the ire against Begum Liaquat was openly voiced by a political out-fit—Majlis-i-Ahrar which before partition was opposed to the very idea of Pakistan. In a speech delivered on 27 August, 1948 in village Bhullar (Punjab), the Ahrar leader Sahibzada Faiz-Ul-Hassan described Begum Liaquat Ali Khan and other women who did not observe 'pardah' as prostitutes. The Ahrars were at that time leading a violent campaign against the Ahmadis in Pakistan demanding their declaration as non-Muslims.

Ahrars apart, who targeted him by proxy through his Begum, Liaquat was getting more and more isolated from the Muslim League politicians themselves. Not because they had anything against him personally, but because he was the only leader who could keep them under control, which they would rather do without Mohammad Ayub Khan, one time President of Pakistan, describes the scene: "Towards the end, Liaquat was being challenged from several quarters; politics became regionalised, with the result that the Prime Minister was forced to depend more and more on the refugee group. The tension in the Punjab was growing because of the squabbles between the Nawab of Mamdot and Mian Mumtaz Daulatana".[7] In the midst of such murky goings-on, getting more and more lonely, Liaquat Ali Khan, the Quide-i-Millat as he had come to be known, was assassinated while addressing a public meeting at Rawalpindi on 16 October, 1951.

The assassination was routinely investigated. No lights could be thrown on those behind the dastardly act. No one knows till this day. In the words of Mohammad Ayub Khan again, "There were all kinds of wild rumours and some Cabinet Ministers and highly placed individuals were accused of having plotted the murder.... I know the Begum Liaquat Ali Khan still thinks the

Government did not try hard enough to investigate the assassination and bring the culprits to book." And he goes on to add, "It was my belief at the time that Liaquat Ali Khan could have blossomed into an active and positive leader of the nation. I hoped he would put his foot down and crush all the intrigues. Unfortunately he did not live long enough to give a clear lead and direction to the country."[8] Another top leader of South Asia killed by his own people after achieving freedom from British rule, but that was not the end.

S.W.R.D. Bandaranaike of Sri Lanka

Sri Lanka was the only colonial country in South Asia which graduated to full independence peacefully and smoothly through several stages of constitutional reforms effected by the British over a period of more than a century. There were no fireworks or pyrotechniques on either side in the process of transition from the colonial status to full independence under the Commonwealth. The transformation was achieved entirely through peaceful negotiations between the British and the western educated elitist leadership of the country, stage by stage. It was almost like the gradual, natural growth of Canada and Australia from British colonies to independent Dominions of the Commonwealth.

It was in 1802 that Sri Lanka (then Ceylon) became a British crown colony and was placed under a Governor assisted by an Advisory Council. The first step towards self-government was taken in 1833 when the Advisory Council was replaced by a Legislative Council in which financial and economic issues could be debated. The Legislative Council was first expanded in 1910 and then again in 1920 giving majority to non-official members. Meanwhile some political associations (not parties) demanding further constitutional reforms appeared on the scene, like the Ceylon Reform League (1917) and Ceylon National Congress (1919). They were not satisfied with the limited powers enjoyed by the Legislative Council and agitated for more.

To accommodate the demand, another dose of constitutional reform was given in 1924. Under it, a majority of members of the Legislative Council were to be elected and all powers of the council could be exercised by elected members. That marked a significant advance, but was still not considered enough by the growing nationalist opinion, because the executive powers were still exclusively in the hands of the Governor and his officials. In the circumstances, the elected majority of the Legislative Council functioned more as an opposition to the executive than a partner in the governance of the country.

The first real advance towards greater share of people's representatives in the governance of the country was made by the introduction of the Donoughmore constitution in 1931. It was based on the recommendations of the Donoughmore commission which went into the working of the constitutional reform of 1924 and found it wanting. The new constitution provided for the establishment of a state council consisting of 58 members, 50 elected on the basis of territorial representation and 8 nominated by the Governor, which function as a Unicameral Legislature. The state council was divided into seven Executive Committees each headed by an elected member of the council with the status of Minister. In absence of broad-based political parties, apart from elitist and sectional associations like the Ceylon Reform League, Ceylon National Congress, Ceylon Indian Congress, Muslim Political Association etc., cabinet system as such could not be introduced at that stage. But the constitution of Executive Committees was a step towards the evolution of the cabinet system subsequently.

The most notable advance towards representative democracy inaugurated by the Donoughmore-constitution was the introduction of Universal suffrage in 1931. Under the earlier reform, voting right was restricted by property, income and educational qualifications, which made it a privilege of a very small percentage of the population. With the introduction of unrestricted adult franchise, door was opened for the eventual establishment of a fully-fledged responsible government in the island colony. Interestingly, none of the mainstream nationalist groups like the Ceylon National Congress had made any demand for adult franchise before it was introduced, except a radical fringe. The leaders of the Tamil community were in fact opposed to the idea of extension of franchise at that stage. Sir P. Ramnathan, the undisputed Tamil leader, went to the extent of saying that universal adult franchise would mean "the transfer of the political power to a dangerous mob who may be easily misled by schemers and speculators bent on selfish ends." (To many in India today, Ramnathan's forebodings would appear to have come literally true in some states of the country.)

The dyarchical features of the Reforms of 1931 presented working difficulties and demands for further reforms towards a more responsible government persisted. In 1938, the Governor of Ceylon examined the constitutional question afresh and formulated a "Reforms Despatch" suggesting substitution of the Executive Committee by a more responsible cabinet system. But with the outbreak of the Second World War in 1939, the proposals were kept in abeyance and any further reform temporarily stalled.

The process was revived again in 1943 when the British Government declared "the grant of full responsible government in all matters of internal civil administration" as the objective of the reform process and invited the Ministers to draft a suitable constitutional scheme. The Ministers led by D.S. Senanayake went ahead with preparation of a Draft but could not reach complete unanimity on all points. The Imperial Government finally appointed a commission (the Soulbury Commission) for suggesting a draft constitution. The commission visited Sri Lanka in December 1944 and submitted its report in October 1945. The report envisaged a fully responsible government for Sri Lanka, with the cabinet system and a bicameral legislature, with certain limitations on the powers of the Parliament to restrict or prohibit free exercise of any religion, aimed at safeguarding the rights of religious minorities.

The Soulbury Report, was the basis of the Ceylon Independence Act of 1947 which, though, removed the proposed restrictions on the legislative powers of the Parliament in respect of minorities. The Ceylon Independence order-in-council of 1947 simultaneously abolished the reserve powers of the governor. After its coming into force on 4 February, 1948, Ceylon achieved independence from the British empire, D.S. Senanayake became the First Prime Minister of independent Sri Lanka. But immediately, Defence and External Affairs Agreements were signed which tied Sri Lanka to Britain in matters of defence and foreign policy. The important ingredients of these agreements were grant of military bases to

Britain on Sri Lankan soil and adoption of a pro-western foreign policy by Sri Lanka. The agreements amounted to leaving Sri Lanka less than fully independent in matters of defence and foreign policy, which aroused considerable political controversy in the country in subsequent years.

The above account would show that self-government was achieved by Sri Lanka through a gradual process of peaceful settlements spread over a century, step by step. What is more, the initiative at every step was taken by the British themselves rather than any strong nationalist political movement for independence agitating for it vociferously. The reason was the absence of any broad-based nationalist political party or parties in Sri Lanka to conduct a sustained movement for independence before 1947. The organizations which pressed for constitutional reforms from time to time like the Ceylon Reform League and Ceylon National Congress were in the nature of political groupings of English educated elites with their activities confined to Colombo and some other urban centres. They remained in the state the Indian National Congress was in the days of Dadabhai Naoroji, M.G. Ranade, Surendra Nath Bannerji, Gopal Krishna Gokhle etc., almost till 1947. And their activities mainly consisted of submitting memoranda and petitioning the British Government for reforms and doses of self-government.

There were some other sectional organizations which represented different communities inhabiting the island country, as in case of Malaya before independence. These were the All-Ceylon Tamil Conference, the Ceylon Indian Congress, Muslim Political Association, the Moors Political Committee and the All-Ceylon Malay Association. They stood for safeguarding the interests of their respective communities. In any case, all political groupings and associations which counted limited their activities to strictly constitutional and peaceful methods. All were middle class parties representing the upper crust of society without any involvement of the larger masses. And achievement of self-government within the British Empire by peaceful negotiations was the avowed objective of all their activities.

In the circumstances, when freedom came almost as a gift of the Imperial Power in 1947, the diverse political groupings thought of combining together to form a broad based political party for running the cabinet system of government. And the United National Party (UNP) was born in 1947 incorporating such groups as the Ceylon National Congress, Sinhala Maha Sabha, Ceylon Muslim League and Moors Association, the latter three groups having come up in the State Council during the operation of the Donoughmore constitution (1931-47). It was a paradoxical case of national independence from foreign rule giving birth to a national political party rather than the other way about.

From its origin, the UNP was a coalition of upper classes including the business interests in Colombo, land-owners and planters held together by personalities rather than any worthwhile organizational structure. The UNP leader D.S. Senanayake, who was the first Prime Minister of independent Sri Lanka, was no "loudly passionate hero-leader "either. In the words of one writer, "the 1947 transfer of sovereignty consisted of the replacement of conservative, moderate, aloof British civil servants by conservative, moderate, aloof British-educated Ceylonese notable."[9] According to another, the Ceylonese leaders who took over from the British "resembled the former colonial rulers in everything but the colour of their skin."[10] In the event, advent of independence in Ceylon saw the emergence of a national political party in the UNP but not for a mass political leader or a national hero.

Of all the groups included in the UNP, the Sinhala Maha Sabha had the potential of linking it to the larger Sinhalese (Buddhist) masses who constituted more than 70 per cent of the total population. If this large chunk of the population came into the mainstream of active politics, the even tenor of political change could be rocked into an upheaval. It was left to a new, somewhat charismatic leader, S.W.R.D. Bandarnaike, to exploit this potential to the full in the years following independence. A minister in D.S. Senanayake Cabinet in charge of Health and Local Government, he resigned in 1951 and formed his own Sri Lanka Freedom Party. "Himself Oxford-educated, vaguely Marxist and essentially secularist in Civil matters, Bandarnaike undermined the authority of the English-speaking (and bi-ethnic Colombo) patriciate by appealing openly, and one suspects somewhat cynically, to the primordial sentiments of the Sinhalese, promising 'Sinhala only' linguistic policy, a place of pride for Buddhism and the Buddhist clergy, and a radical reversal of the supposed policy of 'pampering' the Tamils."[11]

Within five years of its formation, the Sri Lanka Freedom Party came to the centre stage of the country's politics. And in the elections of 1956, its leader S.W.R.D. Bandarnaike was swept into the office of Prime Minister on the crest of a Sinhalese cultural, religious and linguistic revivalism. It did not matter to him or anybody else that in the process about a hundred lives were lost in wild Tamil-Sinhalese riots in 1956. A certain amount of tension between the thrifty, industrious and aggressive Tamil minority and the somewhat relaxed Sinahala majority was inherent in the situation, but the two committees had lived peacefully side by side for centuries. The centuries-old peaceful equation between the two communities was broken by somewhat ideologically inspired mass hatred against each other, with disastrous consequences for the future of the country. There were more serious Tamil-Sinhalese riots in 1958 resulting in loss of around 2000 lives. Clifford Geertz sums up: "The first definite move towards a resolute, popularly based, social reform government led, therefore, not to heightened national unity, but to the reverse-increased linguistic, racial, regional and religious parochialism."[12]

That was one side of Soloman Bandarnaike's emergence as the first charismatic mass leader of his country. The other, more rosy side was the shift of political power from the westernized middle and upper classes to the common urban and rural masses. Many hailed it as kind of a social revolution. In the sphere of foreign policy, he was identified with withdrawal of British military bases in Sri Lanka, opening up of diplomatic relations with socialist countries and adoption of non-aligned posture in international relations. He emerged as a vigorous exponent of the Bandung spirit and Nehru's policy of non-alignment, which created a very favourable image in India. In any case, Soloman Bandarnaike became the most widely known leader of independent, resurgent Sri Lanka outside the country. His vocal opposition to the British and French military action against Egypt on the Suez Canal issue put him among the foremost leaders of non-aligned movement and Afro-Asian solidarity.

He emerged as the first mass leader of independent Sri Lanka on the wave of rising Sinhala (Buddhist) nationalism, which intensified the conflict situation between the Sinhala majority and Tamil minority. After the brutal Tamil-Sinhalese riots of 1958, Bandarnaike tried to mend fences with the Tamils by introducing the Tamil Language Act No. 28 of 1958. It provided for the use of Tamil language in education, public service examinations and administration in the Northern and Eastern Provinces. As a popular and populist leader of the Sinhalese Buddhist masses, he went about reforming and regularising the affairs of Buddhist religious institutions. And precisely at his moment of glory, in September, 1959, S.W.R.D. Bandarnaike was shot dead not by a Tamil but by a Sinhalese Buddhist monk, who had been given an opportunity to place his grievances regarding administration of religious institutions. One more distinguished name was added in the list of giant leaders of South Asia who fell to the bullets of the people they led after freedom from British rule.

Sheikh Mujibur Rahman of Bangladesh

The first partition of the sub-continent in 1947 gave birth to Pakistan; its second partition in 1971 gave birth to Bangladesh. The first time in 1947, India was partitioned into two; the second time in 1971, it was Pakistan's turn to be partitioned into two. Both the partitions were preceded by a tenacious campaign for separation of varying intensity and complexion by the people of the seceding units, though the campaign was of shorter duration the second time round than the first. And both partitions were accompanied with unprecedented scale of blood bath taking a toll of between half a million to a million human lives.

But the similarities end there. The first partition was the result of agreement, however grudging and reluctant on the part of India, between the separating parties brought about by the departing imperial ruling power. The second one was effected after a bloody struggle between the parent country (Pakistan) and the seceding unit (Bangladesh) with active Indian military intervention on behalf of the latter. The massacres accompanying the first partition were the result of killings and counter-killings in course of internecine violence indulged in by the people of the two parts. The carnage preceding the second partition was almost entirely one-sided, perpetrated by the armed might of the parent state to suppress the upsurge for secession technically dubbed as edition. Above all, while the first partition represented the separation of a minority from the majority, the second one was a queer case of the majority separating from the minority. Yes it was literally so. For the erstwhile East Pakistan accounted for 66 per cent of the population of United Pakistan, with West Pakistan having only 44 per cent of the total. And it was East Pakistan which seceded from West Pakistan, and converted itself into Bangladesh, and not the other way about.

Right from the inception of the independent state of Pakistan, the issue of equation between the Western and Eastern wings remained involved in serious controversies. Successive Prime Ministers and Presidents struggled to find a magic formula which could equate the 66 per cent population of East Pakistan with 44 per cent of West Pakistan. It was one of the thorny issues, along with many other controversial questions like the place of Islam, national language etc. which delayed the adoption of a full-fledged constitution for Pakistan by about 9 years. It was only on 23 March, 1956 that the first formal constitution of the Islamic Republic of Pakistan came into force. Till then, the Government of India Act 1935 and the Indian Independence Act 1947, with necessary modifications, remained the working constitution of Pakistan.

Every step in the constitution-making process was dogged by the East-West question. Even as Prime Minister Liaquat Ali Khan presented the interim report of the Basic Principles Committee on 21 November 1950, East Pakistani members of the Constituent Assembly strongly criticized it for seeking to whittle down their majority in the contemplated constitutional set up. The full report of the Basic Principles Committee presented in the Constituent Assembly by the next Prime Minister, Khwaja Nazimuddin on 22 December, 1952 proposed equal representation of both the Western and Eastern wings in Pakistan's Parliament which raised considerable controversy. The East Pakistani members strongly resented the 'parity proposal', apprehending their artificial conversion from majority to minority under the proposed arrangement. Yet, the first constitution of Pakistan which came into force on 23 March 1956 adopted the parity principle in providing for a Unicameral federal legislature (National Assembly) with equal number of members from each wing. The National Assembly was to have 300 members, 150 each from West Pakistan and East Pakistan.

Pakistan's first constitution prepared after tortuous labours of a succession of Prime Ministers and Presidents over a period of nine years lasted only about two and a half years. It was unceremoniously abrogated by President Iskander Mirza who, backed by the Army Chief General Ayub Khan, assumed all powers in a peaceful coup on 7 October, 1958. Iskander Mirza of course proved to be a mere front man of General Ayub Khan who promptly dispensed with him and himself became the president of Pakistan on 27 October, 1958 inaugurating the first military regime of Pakistan. Ayub Khan sought to legitimise his rule by introducing the scheme of what he called 'basic democracy' in the country. Under it, 80,000 'basic democrats' were to be elected from the whole of Pakistan who were to constitute the electoral college for election of the President as well as members of the national Parliament. But even in this scheme, the principle of parity between West and East Pakistan was kept intact. The total number of 'basic democrats' to be elected was equally divided between the two wings. (The total number was subsequently raised to 120,000).

The second constitution of Pakistan, handed down to the people by President Ayub Khan, came into effect on 1st March, 1962. Although all real powers vested in the President, the constitution did provide for a Unicameral legislature at the centre for whatever it was worth. As a sop to the East Pakistanis, Dacca was made the principal seat of the Central Legislature termed as National Assembly. But in the composition of the National Assembly also, the principle of parity between East and West Pakistan was stuck to. All seats in the National Assembly were to be shared by the two wings in equal numbers. The parity principle became so sacrosanct that even the number of members of Provincial Assembly was to be the same for each of the two wings. (Under the one-Unit plan enforced by Ayub Khan, the whole of West Pakistan was converted into a single Province.) Both West and East Pakistan had provincial Assemblies consisting initially of 155 members each, which was subsequently raised to 218 members each.

It was left to the much maligned, much berated Yahya Khan, successor to Ayub Khan as the last President of United Pakistan, to give constitutional shape to East Pakistan's numerical majority. A professional army chief who was fond of his drinks and other good things of life with little clue about the Knitty-gritty of politics, General Aga Mohammad Yahya Khan was catapulted to Pak Presidency on the wave of an anti-Ayub upsurge. Ayub Khan's fortune was on the decline since the failure of his gamble in the Indo-Pak war of 1965 and popular resentment against him kept mounting. It was compounded by growing political suffocation under his regimented regime as years rolled by, until it erupted into a strong popular movement for his ouster by the end of 1968. And exactly after ten years and five months of Bonapartist rule, characterised by political stability and economic growth, Ayub Khan was forced to resign and hand over power, in absence of any other established political institution, to the Army Chief— General Yahya Khan on 25 March, 1969. In the circumstances, Yahya Khan's ascent to power was more by default than by design.

The popular movement which brought him to power was not only against Ayub Khan personally but also against the regimented or dictatorial character of his regime. After over a decade of choking political stability enforced by a Bonapartist regime, political forces in Pakistan in both the western and eastern wings were craving for full play. In the west, political leaders of all the original provinces of Punjab, Sind, Baluchistan and NWFP were set against Ayub's One-Unit Plan and wanted to revert back to their separate status. The East Pakistanis, of course, had their own traditional grouse against domination by the west. Yahya Khan, as the new President, had to reckon with the popular demand for restoration of proper parliamentary democracy and he was quite conscious of it.

True to his mandate, he set about demolishing the structure of soft dictatorship, miscalled "Basic Democracy," built by Ayub Khan through the second constitution of 1962, and restoring democracy in doses. He defined his task in no uncertain terms in his first major broadcast to the nation on the night of 31st March, 1969: "I wish to make it absolutely clear that I have no mission other than the creation of conditions conducive to the establishment of a constitutional government. It is my firm belief that a sound, clean and honest administration is the prerequisite for sane and constructive political life and for the smooth transfer of power to the representatives of the people elected freely and impartially on the basis of adult franchise. It will be the task of the elected representatives to give the country a workable constitution and find a solution to all other political, economic and social problems that have been agitating the minds of the people."

True to his words, he promulgated the Legal Framework order of 1970 which provided for a National Assembly having 313 seats. And, the wonder of wonders, allotted 169 seats in it to East Pakistan and 144 seats only to the western wing distributed among all the four provinces of Punjab, Sind, Baluchistan and NWFP in proportion to the respective populations of each of the five provinces. (The One-Unit Plan of President Ayub was abrogated and West Pakistan was split into the original four provinces.) It was for the first time since the establishment of Pakistan that the principle of parity between the eastern and western wings in the country's constitutional set-up was abandoned. Even the interim report of the basic principles committee presented to Pakistan Constituent Assembly by the first Prime Minister— Liaquat Ali Khan—On 21 November, 1950 had talked of parity between the western and eastern wings in regard to representation in the national legislature. It was for the first time that East Pakistan was allowed representation in the National Assembly in proportion to its population, which established its due position as the major component of the state of Pakistan.

It goes to Yahya Khan's credit that he not only promulgated the constitutional order giving due recognition to East Pakistan's numerical majority on paper but also implemented to on the ground. He successfully organized general elections in the whole of Pakistan in December 1970 in accordance with the provision of his scheme granting majority representation to East Pakistan in the National Assembly. Incidentally, that was the first ever country-wide general elections (including the provincial Assemblies) held in Pakistan since it came into being. That was Yahya Khan's finest hour, but by a queer twist of destiny, it proved to be his doom and that of the Republic of United Pakistan. In the national elections, Sheikh Mujibur Rahman's Awami League secured 167 out of 169 seats allotted to East Pakistan, giving it absolute majority in the National Assembly of United Pakistan. Zulfiquar Ali Bhutto's Pakistan People's Party (PPP) emerged as the largest party in the four provinces of West Pakistan, but was no match to Sheikh Mujib's Awami League overall. That was the beginning of trouble for the ruling Establishment of Pakistan comprising the Army, civil services, politicians and business houses.

By winning 167 out of 169 East Pakistan seats in the elections, Sheikh Mujib performed a feat never achieved by any political leader of the sub-continent before. Even Nehru at the peak of his popularity in India had not reached the level of success for his Congress party in the general elections of 1952 which Sheikh Mujib achieved for his Awami League in Bangladesh in December 1970. He emerged as the supreme, undisputed and undisputable leader of East Pakistan embodying all the urges and aspirations of Bengali speaking majority of Pakistan. Above all, he emerged as the leader of the political party which commanded an absolute majority in the newly elected national legislature of Pakistan.

And yet he was neither invited to form the government at the centre nor to play the role his representative status entitled him to do in shaping the destiny of the country. Having come thus far in his soldierly stride to restore democracy, President Yahya Khan ran into rough weather with the pillars of power in Pakistan. He convened the session of the newly elected National Assembly on 3 March, 1971 to draft a new constitution, but had to abruptly adjourn it in the face of Z.A. Bhutto's threat of boycott. That was the end of Yahya Khan's affair with constitutionalism and representative democracy. The die had been cast. The Bengali Muslim nationalism in the east had to be suppressed by force of arms to preserve the solidarity of monolithic Muslim nationalism symbolised by Pakistan.

The decision of such explosive potential cannot really be understood unless viewed in perspective. The decision of a military crackdown on East Pakistan might appear abrupt on the surface, but in essence it was not that abrupt after all. It was actually rooted in, and culmination of, a long-standing thought process discernible in the central leadership of Pakistan right from its inception. Dr. Khalid B. Sayeed, an India-born political scientist settled abroad who once taught in Dacca University in early fifties, writes: "The central leadership adopted the view that a significant number of influential Bengali Muslim leaders were probably not completely loyal Pakistanis. It was suspected that such leaders not only believed in retaining the Bengali language and culture but admired Tagore and were not opposed to the steady and surreptitious influx of Hindu ideas and other cultural influences from across the border ...... This conception, laced with the orthodox or Jamaat-i-Islami view that even Muslims in these parts of the sub-continent were not really pure and strict Muslims, led many to regard Bengali Muslims as an inferior breed who needed to be purified even more rigorously... In fact, the collision course on which the Pakistani leaders embarked was disastrous and disruptive from the beginning.... In social gatherings, one could hear West Pakistani and other Muslims from Urdu-speaking provinces of India referring with scorn to the Bengali's devotion to his language and to his inability to pronounce correctly Muslim names. Even after Bengali was adopted as one of the two state languages, Governor Monem Khan attempted during the Ayub era to ban the broadcast of Tagore's songs or poems over Dacca radio and to prevent the import of Bengali books from Calcutta."[13]

The inexorable logic of such a mind-set, identifying Muslim nationalism in the sub-continent with Urdu language and cultural milieu of North Indian and West Pakistani Muslims, hurtled Yahya Khan's government towards a disastrous confrontation with the unprecedented upsurge of Bengali Muslim nationalism. For some time after the aborted National Assembly session of 3 March, 1971, facade of a dialogue with Sheikh Mujib was kept up while making all preparations for a military cracked down. General Tikka Khan, with the dubious distinction of having tamed the rebellions Baluchistanies earlier, was already in position as the Governor of East Pakistan. The brink was reached on 23 March, 1971, when Pakistan's Republic Day was declared as "Resistance Day" in East Pakistan. Hundreds of Bangladesh flags went up atop homes, shops, schools and public buildings all over Dacca and Pakistan national flag was burnt publicly. What followed is described by David Loshak :" On March 25, without another word to Mujib, the President and Bhutto returned to Karachi... That night the holocaust began."[14] As soon as President Yahya Khan safely landed at Karachi, Green signal was given for the pre-planned military crack-down.

A British Journalist, Simon Dring of the *Daily Telegraph*, London gives an eyewitness account: "The first targets as the tanks rolled into Dacca were the students. Caught completely by surprise, some 200 students were killed in Iqbal Hall, headquarters of the militantly anti-government students union, as shells slammed into the building and their rooms were sprayed with machine-gun fire. Two days later, bodies were still smouldering in their burning rooms, others were scattered outside and more floated in a nearby lake..."[15] Simon Dring and Michel Laurent, a French photo journalist, who were present in Dacca during those fateful days, estimated that Pak army killed 7000 people in Dacca in those two days and nights, besides around 15,000 more in other areas like Comilla, Jessore, Chittagong etc.

The point of no-return had been reached. The Pak army's brutal onslaught on East Pakistanis that eventful night gave birth to Bangladesh. It must be said in fairness to Sheikh Mujib that almost till the last hour, he was agitating only for full autonomy encapsuled in his famous "Six Points", and not for secession as such. He claimed that since Bengalis were in a majority in Pakistan, secession had no meaning for them. The military onslaught finally closed that option. On 17 April, 1971, six leaders of the Awami League declared the formation of the first "Independent Sovereign Democratic Republic of Bangladesh" in a mango grove 300 yards from the Indian border near a village renamed as Mujib Nagar. Sheikh Mujib was declared the President, Sayed Nazrul Islam acting President, Tajuddin Ahmed Prime Minister and Col. A.G. Osmani Commanding Officer of the Mukti Bahini.

The rest of the story until the formal emergence of Bangladesh as an independent republic in December 1971 is recent history and need not be gone into here. It is the story of brutal repression resorted to by Pak army for nearly nine months in course of which close to a million lives were lost, majority of them Muslims, in the towns and rice fields of the erstwhile East Pakistan. Nearly 10 million people, both Hindus and Muslims, which came to about 15 per cent of the total population, escaped into India. Finally, with the outbreak of Indo-Pak war on 3 December, 1971, the Indian army actively intervened on the side of the beleaguered Bengali rebels in the on-going civil war. The issue was settled in favour of the Bengalis by the surrender of Pakistan Army at Dacca on 16 December, 1971. Bangladesh was born.

Sheikh Mujib had been imprisoned by Pakistan Government on charges of sedition during the period of the civil war. He returned from Pakistani prison on 10 January, 1972 to tumultuous welcome by the bleeding people. The euphoria of the Bengali people on his return to Dacca that temperate winter day, in spite of all the wounds of the civil war, was to be seen to believe. After decades of uneasy co-existence with the aggressive, domineering West Pakistanis and frustrating tussle with the ruling elites for a place under the sun in Pakistan, the Bengali Muslims had come to their own. The end of the tunnel had been reached and they were masters of their own destiny. And the one leader who had led them out of the tunnel was Sheikh Mujibur Rahman. He was given the effectionate name of "Banga-bandhu" (Brother of Bengal) and hailed as the Father of the Nation.

In terms of the Declaration of Independence issued from the non-decrepit little village renamed Mujib Nagar in April 1971, Sheikh Mujib was the President of the Sovereign Republic of Bangladesh when he made his triumphant entry into Dacca on 10 January, 1972. On the very next day, he issued the first Provisional constitutional order abolishing the Presidential system and providing for a parliamentary form of government. Accordingly Justice Abu Sayeed Chowdhury, an ex-Vice-Chancellor of Dacca University, was sworn in as President and Sheikh Mujib as Prime Minister at the head of a 14-member cabinet.

One of the main tasks of his government was to frame a proper constitution for the newly liberated republic. He addressed to the task in earnest and the Constituent Assembly completely dominated by his Awami League, did in ten months what Pakistan Constituent Assembly had taken nine years to do. It framed and adopted a constitution providing for parliamentary democracy on 4 November, 1972, which came into force on 16 December, 1972. The first parliamentary national election under the new constitution was held in March 1973 in which Sheikh Mujib's Awami League secured an overwhelming majority. But that was almost the end of his success story.

Faced with multifarious problems of governance of a country ravaged by a devastating civil war, with shattered institutions of civil administration compounded by growing political indiscipline, Sheikh Mujib found his system of multi-party parliamentary democracy severely wanting. On 25 January, 1975, an Act was passed scrapping up the multi-party parliamentary system and replacing it by a single-party presidential system. The ruling party was re-christened as the Bangladesh Krishak Shramik Awami League (BAKSAL) which proceeded to run the country with Sheikh Mujib as the President.

But his single party rule ended in less than eight months, and what is more, that was the end of Sheikh Mujib himself. On the night of 15 August, 1975, armoured vehicles rolled once again into the streets of Dacca, not of the Pakistan Army but of his own Army of Bangladesh, and moved on to his residence. Seized with a murderous frenzy, a group of middle level army officers shot dead Sheikh Mujibur Rahman and ten of his family members present in the house in one bloody sweep. Tajuddin Ahmad, the Prime Minister of Bangladesh government in exile proclaimed in April 1971, and his other close associates were also killed in cold blood in the wake of Mujib's assassination. The saga of the charismatic Sheikh Mujib, the popularly acclaimed 'Banga bandhu' of three and a half years ago, the Father of the Nation, came to an abrupt end, in the same way as that of all charismatic mass leaders of South Asia after independence.

Sheikh Mujib's assassination completed the circle of physical liquidation of every top South Asian mass leader after the end of the British Raj. It was not merely a question of what Sheikh Mujib, or for that matter the other assassinated leaders of their countries, did or did not do to please or displease their people. No leader, however great, towering or charismatic, can please or satisfy all people he is called upon to lead. Not even God Himself, if there be a God and He were to assume the leadership of a country, could please all His countrymen. Even a saintly leader like Mahatma Gandhi seemed a villain to the likes of Nathu Ram Godse and Madan Lal Pahwa for his solicitude for the Muslims of India and

Pakistan. The kind of fate that these illustrious leaders met at the hands of the very people they helped to liberate was rooted in the sick socio-political culture of their people. The chain of assassinations symbolised the free play of the cult of violence and politics of blood-shed which has come to be the trade mark of South Asian political regimes after freedom from British rule.

References

1. *The Abolition of War*, Keith Robbins.
2. *India From Curzon to Nehru and After*, Durga Das, 1971.
3. Quoted in an article on Jinnah by Dr. Sachchidananda Sinha in *The Hindustan Review* of September 1949.
4. *India Today*, Frank Moraes, 1960.
5. *Politics In Pakistan: The Nature and Direction of Change*, Khalid B. Sayeed, 1980.
6. *Mission with Mountbatten*, Alan Campbell-Johnson, 1951.
7. *Friends not Masters*, Mohammad Ayub Khan (then President of Pakistan), 1967.
8. *Ibid.*
9. *Old Societies & New States*, Clifford Geertz, 1971.
10. *Pacific Affairs*, D.K. Ragnekar, 1960.
11. *Old Societies & New States*, edited by Clifford Geertz, 1971.
12. *Ibid.*
13. *Politics in Pakistan: The Nature and Direction of Change*, Dr. Khalid B. Sayeed, 1980.
14. *Pakistan Crisis*, David Loshak, 1971.
15. *Ibid.*

5

The Violent Society

An Area of Violence

It has come to be the sub-continent of violence, blood and tears par excellence. At the beginning of the momentous 20th century, about to fade into the pages of history, the Indian sub-continent was the coveted paradise of the world's imperial regime in more senses than one. The British were the envy of the other imperial powers for being the masters of this vast, ancient land of peace and variegated culture. In a relatively short time span of 50 years since the empire folded up, it has turned into a land of unceasing turbulence, terror and blood spilling. George VI, the last British King to preside over the empire had one great regret—that he never visited the marvellous land. He said as much to his cousin, Lord Mountbatten, on the eve of the latter's departure to the sub-continent for negotiating and handing over power.

In the words of Larry Collins and Dominique Lapierre, "Indeed George VI would die without ever setting foot on that fabulous land. There would never be a tiger hunt for him, no parade of elephants jangling past in silver and gold ....."[1] If the ghost of George VI were to visit the Indian sub-continent today, it would not be amused by the jangle of elephants "in silver and gold" but shocked by the shots of Kalashnikovs and loud thuds of RDX. It would not be able to enjoy a " tiger hunt" in the wilds of Bengal or central India or big game hunting in Rajputana. Instead, it would cry over the head hunting of humans going on unabated in Kashmir, Karachi, Jaffna, North Eastern India, and even Bombay, Lahore and Delhi not infrequently. What was once the most peaceful colonial country in the world has turned into a land of ceaseless violence and bloodshed in course of just 50 years.

The highest common factor (HCF) that characterises the countries of South Asia— India, Pakistan, Sri Lanka and Bangladesh —is their proneness to violence. People of these countries are ever ready to take to the stick, dagger or gun against each other, their own countrymen, at the drop of a hat, or turban or topee. They may not be anywhere in the reckoning in affairs of the world, in proportion to their numbers, but they have certainly come to count among the world's most violent peoples. It is as if they have reverted, after freedom from imperial regime, to the Hobbesian State of Nature which is characterised by a war of each against all and all against each. They seem to be making up for the passivity or peaceful predilections of their grandparents and great grandparents during around two centuries of the British Raj.

Violence in the sub-continent ranges from destruction of public property, looting, burning of private property, mob assaults on individuals and groups, and assassinations to large scale massacres. Uprooting railway tracks, setting fire to railway stations, post offices and other government establishments, damaging and burning transport buses etc. are common forms of public protest in India. Wanton destruction of public utilities, which are so scarce and ill-managed in an underdeveloped country like India, is somehow sanctified by the hallowed memory of August 1942. The large scale destruction of railway tracks, telegraphs lines and other public property in course of the August 1942 violence may or may not have contributed to freedom from British rule, but it has certainly prescribed the format and set the pattern which all protesters and agitators religiously follow in India. (No one would like to remember that Mahatma Gandhi had to go on a 21 days fast to atone for the spate of violence in the wake of his 'Quit India' call to the British.)

Considerable heat verging on a certain amount of violence is inherent in big protest demonstrations of any kind all over the world. Some of the most politicised, intense, exciting and massive protest demonstrations took place in countries of western Europe at the peak of youth upsurge of late sixties against the savagery of Vietnam war. Two of such demonstrations organized by left wing student groups against the Vietnam war—one in Paris and the other in London—may be mentioned here in view of their massive size and intensity. On the evening of 10 May, 1968, about 30,000 French students collected in the centre of Paris and blocked traffic for two miles. As their attempt to march towards the French broadcasting station was thwarted by the police, they proceeded to occupy the Latin quarter and construct barricades to obstruct the police from approaching them. The siege of Latin Quarter by thousands of militant students led by Cohn-Bendit continued beyond mid-night when the police intervened at about 2 a.m. The police used teargas grenaders to choke and disperse the students but the crowds fought back and continued the occupation. The confrontation continued till the early morning hours without the students yielding ground. By around 6.30 a.m., the police units were withdrawn and the main demands of the students were conceded by the French government the very next day. In course of the entire 12 hours siege by frenzied mobs of students, no harm whatsoever was caused to the citizens of the Latin Quarter or any damage done to public property. Not even a glass pane of a house in the neighbourhood was broken or any citizen injured even though the students battled it out with the police throughout the night.

The other, even more massive demonstration was held in London by the Vietnam Solidarity Campaign (VSC) on 27 October, 1968. Tariq Ali, the famous Pakistan-born Marxist intellectual based in England who was one of the leading organizers of the demonstration, writes: "When I arrived at the embankment where we were assembling, the sight was joyous. This was much more than a demonstration of solidarity with the struggle of the Vietnamese. It was an assembly of those who regarded the capitalist order in Europe as doomed. The significance of the turn-out (over 100,000) was not lost on the state. This was the largest explicitly revolutionary demonstration in Britain since the twenties. A survey showed that an overwhelming majority of those who marched that day were hostile to capitalism..... That was the mood that day ..... And as tens and tens of thousands of predominantly young people came together that day they expressed an optimism about the future. The world had to be changed and France and Vietnam proved that it is possible to move forward...... For our part the demonstration had gone according to plan. 'The Times' had alleged that we were planning to overthrow the state. They were to mock us the next day for having been so peaceful."[2]

A sharp contrast to the gigantic student demonstrations in Paris and London in 1968 is provided by what happened in Bihar in March 1974. The students formed a Bihar State Students Struggle Committee in February 1974 to press for fulfilment of some generic demands like improvement in educational facilities, removal of unemployment, eradication of corruption etc. They gave a call for a big demonstration in front of the Bihar State Assembly at Patna on 18 March, 1974. On the appointed day, a large number of demonstrators assembled at the Assembly gates, many coming on commandered state transport buses, and tried to force entry. When the police resisted, they took to furious stoning. The police resorted to lathi-charge, tear-gas shells and ultimately firing causing injuries to many. As the demonstrators dispersed, they went on a rampage in the city causing widespread arson, violence and destruction of public and private property. The premises of the oldest daily newspaper of Bihar, *The Search-light* were ransacked and totally burnt, the press, newsprint and all. The Patna Railway Station was set fire to and damaged. A petrol pump was also set a flame and completely burnt. For almost a week, student mobs attacked, ransacked and damaged innumerable post offices, railway stations, state transport buses and other government establishments in wide areas across the state of Bihar. It was only after Jay Prakash Narayan came out of his self-imposed semi-retirement and took over the cause giving it the aura of "Total Revolution" of his dream, that the spate of meaningless violence was stopped and some order restored in the movement.

No one really cares or takes notice of such destructions, least of all the politicians or government of the day, even though the people in general are seriously hampered in their day today life. Destruction of public property and state utilities is the accepted mode of public protest in India and nobody looks askance at that. It invites no public disapprobation, as if the properties or utilities damaged or destroyed belonged to an alien ruler or an alien country. The shadows of August 1942 violence and destructions still hang over and determine the course of all public agitations and protests in India. It is the kind of violence involving loss of human life which is what people consider as violence worth taking note of. In this respect, the tone was set by the orgy of violence and blood-bath immediately proceeding and following the partition/ independence of India. Since then we, the people of the sub-continent, have not looked back. We have reached a stage when we hear violence, see violence, smell violence and breathe violence every day, every hour. Violence is in the air, organized, not so organized, un-remitting, relentless violence, that is.

Sometime there is a cause. It may be communal (religion based), linguistic, regional, ethnic or tribal or whatever. Any particularist or primordial sentiment would do to arouse people to worst kind of brutality against fellow humans. Sometime there is no recognisable cause. In that case, a cause is invented or conjured up, if necessary by digging into history, "Some old unhappy far off things and battles long ago." And violence, most babaric and elemental, resorted to by one group against another. That leads to counter violence, retaliatory violence, serial violence, violence against Muslims in India leading to violence against Hindus in Pakistan, in Bangladesh. In India itself, it is not only Hindus versus Muslims or Hindus and Sikhs versus Muslims, as it was at the time of partition, but Hindus versus Sikhs and vice versa, Hindus versus Hindus, and one caste against another. Similarly in Pakistan, it is not only Muslims versus Hindus or Sikhs, but Muslims versus Christians, Muslims versus Muslims, Shias versus Sunnis and so on. The name of the game is violence, which has a logic of its own, and the game goes on in the whole of the sub-continent, cause or no cause.

Hindu-Muslim Violence: India, Pakistan-Bangladesh—Pre-Independence Scene

Of all forms of group violence, which this book is primarily concerned with, violence against each other by major religious communities, mainly Hindus and Muslims, has been the most distinguishing trademark of India, Pakistan and Bangladesh (erstwhile East Pakistan) since independence. All the three countries continue to be rocked by orgies of communal violence of varying intensity with ominous regularity. Not that there was complete peace and harmony between Hindus and Muslims before. Conflicts of ideas, religious beliefs and practices are inherent in any society comprising two or more major religious communities. To that extent, a certain degree of communal irritation and even sporadic violence have been endemic in the sub-continental situation. There used to be isolated cases of Hindu-Muslim riotings or skirmishes, mainly confined to one pocket or another, in undivided India before independence also. Cow-slaughter, an anthema to Hindus— and music before mosque-equally opposed by Muslims—were constant irritants, as they still are, which caused relatively minor clashes between the two communities here and there occasionally.

At times, there were more serious riotings also over one issue or another, as in Bengal and Punjab during Moharram in 1923. In May, June and July 1923, communal riots occurred in Amritsar, Sindh and some cities of U.P. also. In September 1924, there was serious rioting in Kohat (now in Pakistan) in which over a hundred lives were lost. Earlier still in 1917, there was a very serious communal flare up in and around village Piro in Shahabad district of Bihar over cow-slaughter during Bakrid in which around four to five thousand people, mostly Muslims, lost their lives. And there was the famous Moplah rebellion in 1921 down south in Travancore state (now Kerala) which though was primarily directed against the British authority turned against Hindu landlords and upper classes with violent religious fanaticism.

Barring these occasional flare-ups, which were exceptions rather than the rule, Hindus and Muslims lived by and large in peace and harmony across the sub-continent without fear or distrust of each other. For religion as such does not breed violence. Dildar Khan observes: "The popular belief is that communal violence is the product of differences in religious practices and symbols followed by different religious groups. This is a false belief. Communal violence is not the product of religious differences, practices symbols, but it used these to further certain interests."[3]

Durga Das recalls with deep nostalgia the state of Hindu-Muslim relationship in a Punjab village during his childhood in early 20th century. "In these troubled days, my thoughts often flash back to a vivid picture of Hindu-Muslim harmony of long years ago. Arrayed on two sides are long-bearded Muslim divines engaged in hot disputation over the precise interpretation of an injunction in the Holy Koran. The arbiter seated at the head of the assemblage is a Hindu.[4] The arguments go backward and forward, and at the end, my father pronounces the verdict. Nodding their heads in amiable agreement, the devines depart, each with a reverential salaam. Incidents like this underscore the mutual respect and understanding that nourished a climate of tolerance and harmony in rural India over the decades."[5] A more eloquent testimony to religion in itself not breeding conflict and violence would be difficult to imagine. That would show religion or divergent religious beliefs do not necessarily produce conflict situations or communal violence. The reasons are to be looked for in other areas which will be explored later.

The First Post-Independence Decade

The persistence, tenacity and ferocity of communal violence in post-independence Indian sub-continent are commonly attributed to large scale communal killings at the time of partition/ independence. This fascile assumption is also belied by facts. History—recent history at that—does broadly colour the perceptions of people, but does not guide or motivate the hum drum life and conduct or behaviour in ordinary course as much as many of us imagine. The remarkable fact is that following the communal holocaust accompanying the partition, relative peace prevailed on the Hindu-Muslim communal front for more than a decade. The story of large scale orgy of communal violence began in India at the end of the fifties or beginning of the sixties, well over a decade after partition, with chain reaction in Pakistan. How come? What explains the astonishing passivity of our communal fanatics, in spite of the bloody background of partition riots, during the first 12-13 years of independence? But first, the facts.

The chain of major communal riots involving large scale violence started with the flare-up at Sitamarhi in Bihar on the occasion of Ramnaumi festival in April 1959. The trouble spread to rural hinterland of Sitamarhi town causing extensive destruction of life and properties of Muslims at the hands of rampaging Hindu mobs. The ostensible provocation was display of beef or cow-slaughter but once the rioting started, with free play of arson and killing, it went on for well over a week on its own momentum without anybody asking or caring about the origin. Reacting to the event, Jay Prakash Narayan (J.P.) said in a press statement dated 27 April, 1959: "The curtain has not yet lifted from the tragic events at Sitamarhi. Particularly the origin of the sudden flare-up on Ramnaumi day in Sitamarhi town seems to be still shrouded in mystery. What is so far known of the story is a very sad commentary on the Hindu mass mind... In these days of degeneration and decay of Hinduism, the sacredness of the cow has however become a meaningless and therefore dangerous superstition which sometimes leads misguided Hindus to the wilful and wanton destruction of the most valuable and sacred form of life on this earth, namely human life."

The 60's—An Ominous Beginning

In early 60's, there were serious riots and counter-riots in India and Pakistan against their respective minorities. Violence against Muslims in Jabalpur was countered by violence against Hindus in Karachi. J.P., steadily emerging as the nation's conscience-keeper, reacted in a statement to the PTI: "Every sensible Indian must have been deeply grieved by the Jabalpur incidents. How thin our vineer of humanity and how week our feelings of national unity are, could find no better witness than the wicked deeds committed there. And, as if not to be left behind by Indians in inhumanity and wickedness, Pakistanis went berserk in Karachi. The authorities too of that city seemed to have entered the competition, for if their opposite numbers in Jabalpur were slack, those in Karachi went one better and let goondaism have free play right under their nose."

It was now the turn of the eastern part of the sub-continent to go through its share of communal nightmare. Hindu-baiting started in East Pakistan in the wake of theft of the holy relic from Hazratbal mosque in Kashmir. Muslims took out angry processions to protest the theft in Khulna and Jessore on 3 January, 1964 which generated violence against Hindus. Although the holy relic was recovered on 4 January, disturbances continued leading to flight of Hindus to West Bengal. This led to anti-Muslim riots in Calcutta for several days. While Calcutta was returning to normal, fresh wave of violence against Hindus erupted in Decca, Narayanganj and other areas of East Pakistan resulting in brutal atrocities against the minority communities—Hindus, Christians and Buddhists. The result was large scale influx of Hindus and tribal refugees into the eastern region of India.

Their tales of atrocities committed by Muslims and sight of refugee special trains ignited communal passions not only in Calcutta but also in neighbouring Rourkela and Jamshedpur industrial belts of Orissa and Bihar during March-April 1964. Soon the entire tribal belt of Chhotanagpur in Bihar was engulfed in a spate of killing, looting and burning of Muslims at the hands of Adivasis of the area. It was for the first time that tribal anger was aroused against Muslims of the region, who had a bitter taste of tribal wrath against them. Large scale violence and destruction over a wide area in the tribal belt of Bihar and Orissa continued for nearly a month before the authorities could succeed in restoring peace.

In a press statement in March 1964, J.P. said: "The recent and recurring outbursts of sudden and cruel violence against Muslim citizens of this country as retaliatory punishment for the acts of Muslim citizens of Pakistan are a matter of the gravest anxiety for every thinking Indian. If Indian Hindus kill Indian Muslims for no other reason than that Pakistani Muslims have killed Pakistani Hindus, it is (among other things) a complete vindication of the two-nation theory."

Visiting Jamshedpur immediately after the riots and spending four days ascertaining the facts J.P. wrote a letter to the Speaker of Lok Sabha on 9 April, 1964 giving vent to his anguish. Among other things, it said : "I visited all the affected areas in the city but did not have the stomach to visit more than two of the 17 Muslims refugee camps.... As for the nature of atrocities committed, I do not think any holds were barred. Every kind of revolting deed was done. Seen in the mass, the tragedy was terrible enough, but some individual instances were fathomless indeed in their cruelty and degradation."

If there were riots in industrial-tribal belt of eastern India on provocation from East Pakistan in 1964, there were serious riots in Ranchi and neighbouring areas in 1967 without any provocation from either wing of Pakistan. The riots in Ranchi-Hatia industrial area in August 1967 erupted out of violent protests by Hindus against Bihar Government's move for making Urdu the second official language of Bihar. The violence spread over several days took toll of 184 lives, 164 of them Muslims and 19 Hindus, besides looting, burning and destruction of large number of houses, shops and business premises.

The chain of communal riots continued unbroken with another serious outbreak in Nagpur in June 1968. But more virulent rioting and violence causing bigger loss of life and property erupted in Ahmedabad in September, 1969, which spilled over to several districts of Gujrat state like Baroda, Kaira, Junagadh, Amreli, etc. The immediate cause was an altercation between some Sadhus at Jagannath temple and Muslims assembled at a nearby Dargah of a Muslim saint on the occasion of Urs on 18 September, 1969. The event snowballed into a series of major clashes between the two communities in the city during the next few days in most of which the Muslims were at the receiving end. At the end of it all, the official estimate put the number of dead at 512, of whom 413 were Muslims and 24 Hindus. The estimated loss of property was valued at well over Rupees 40 million.

The sister state of Maharashtra soon followed suit with a series of communal riots in Bhiwandi, Jalgaon and Mahad towns in May 1970. Of these, the riots in Bhiwandi were the most virulent. Bhiwandi town of Thane district has a large concentration of Muslim population engaged in its flourishing power-loom industry. With Muslims constituting about 65 per cent of its total population, Bhiwandi had been prone to communal tension and incidents had been taking place off and on. In this background, rioting started on 7 May, 1970 when a large Shiva Jayanti procession was brick-batted on shouting some provocative slogans while passing through a Muslim locality. Between 7 and 12 May, 1970, 78 persons (59 Muslims and 17 Hindus), were officially admitted to have been killed and six Muslim women gang-raped, though the unofficial estimates put the figures much higher.

On 8 May, 1970, anti-Muslim violence rocked the city of Jalgaon with great ferocity. The trouble started over such a trifling event as an argument and altercation between a Muslim and some Hindus at a betel shop. And it struck the city with such virulence that 42 Muslims and one Hindu were killed in the matter of a few hours only on 8 May. The worst part of the tragedy was that 39 of the 42 Muslims who lost their lives that day, died of suffocation and burns as they were locked inside a building set on fire.

Disturbances also spread to Mahad town and many parts of Thane district in the wake of Bhiwandi riots and tapered off after a weak or so.

After the Maharashtra riots of May 1970, there was lull on the communal front on account of monumental political developments in the sub-continent during the major part of the troubled decade. The Indo-Pak war of 1971, birth of the independent Republic of Bangladesh, intense political agitation in India culminating in the infamous 'Emergency', coup d' etat in Bangladesh and political turmoil in Pakistan monopolised people's attention. They were much too pre-occupied with these phenomenal happenings to allow any free play to their proclivity towards communal fire-works. They have a tendency to revert back to the game of mutual injury and annihilation when times are more normal.

And times did seem to be returning to normal, at least in India, after the 'Emergency' regime was voted out of power in 1977. And the lull on the communal front was broken with the return of communal violence. The account was re-opened at the historic little town of Sambhal, once the capital of legendary Prithviraj Chauhan, in March 1978. Sambhal, sub-divisional town of Moradabad district in U.P. has, like Bhiwandi, a pre-dominantly Muslim population. On 29 March, 1978, a notorious Muslim communalist who also happened to the leader of rickshaw-pullers, gave a call for Bazar bund to press for their demands. His men had a tiff with a Hindus betel shopkeeper who refused to close his shop. With that the spark was lit and a rampaging mob of about a thousand Muslims went after the Hindus in a killing and looting spree. At the end of the day, 25 persons lost their lives, 23 of them being Hindus, apart from destruction of shops and establishments including a timber godown and a Khandsari factory owned by Hindus.

There was a relatively less destructive outbreak of communal violence in Aligarh city of U.P. on 5 October, 1978 which resulted in considerable damage to property and killings. Aligarh, incidentally, has been a chronic trouble-spot in respect of Hindu-Muslim conflicts because of its mixed population ratio—60 per cent Hindus to around 40 per cent Muslims. Perhaps the role of its celebrated University in furtherance of separate Muslim nationalism before partition still rankles in the minds of the two communities. There had been minor communal riots in Aligarh in 1962 and 1971 also. And there was another bout of attacks and counter-attacks between the two communities at Aligarh in June 1979. The issue this time was opening of a cinema theatre owned by a Hindu in a predominantly Muslim residential locality.

But the cake was taken by Bihar once again when large scale communal rioting started at Jamshedpur on 11 April, 1979. In any story of violence and lawlessness in independent India, Bihar pops up like a sore thumb over and over again. This time round it happened on the occasion once again of Ramnaumi celebrations in the steel city. Although April 5 was the actual Ramnaumi day, processions could not be taken out in the city till 11 April due to considerable disputations, including litigation in court, about the route. When the procession did actually come out, it stopped opposite a mosque and refused to proceed ahead until some Hindus arrested earlier in this connection were released. As large crowds gathered at the spot, a bomb exploded and some stones were thrown on the static procession from the side of the mosque. That was the signal for a flare up of communal frenzy which consumed around 200 lives by the time it was over. Arson, destruction and killing continued non-stop for over 24 hours in course of which there were pitched battles also between the two communities. Official reports put the death toll at around 120, more than half being Muslims. Unofficial estimates put the figure much higher.

In the words of one writer, "It was as if by some remote control mechanism the entire city burst into flames, thereby substantiating the theory that sections of the rapidly antagonistic Hindu majority and those of the Muslim minority ... had carefully planned their strategies of assault and defence."[6] The most barbaric episode of the story relates to the treatment meted out to an ambulance load of Muslim refugees being taken to a refugee camp. A mob of rioters intercepted the ambulance on the way and set in on fire. All its occupants including women and children were burnt to death.

The 80's—the Most Violent Decade

The brutalities of communal violence at Jamshedpur were more than matched by those at Moradabad in U.P. in August 1980.

While Jamshedpur riots of 1979 broke out in course of Ramnaumi celebrations by Hindus, the Moradabad riots of 1980 started on the day of Id prayers by Muslims. And while Hindus and Muslims fought pitched battles at Jamshedpur, Muslims and the police fought pitched battles in course of the riot at Moradabad. Finally, while the riots at Jamshedpur were the culmination of days of disputation, litigation and perhaps preparation on the part of Hindus and Muslims, the Moradabad explosion was entirely abrupt and that also on the issue of a pig.

There was a little background to it though Muslims and Harijans living near the Idgah in separate *bustees* (colonies) side by side had strained relations for sometime since kidnapping of Harijan girl by some Muslims in March 1980. The girl was subsequently recovered and the accused arrested. When the girl was being married to a boy of her community in July 1980, the Muslims obstructed the marriage procession on the issue of music before mosque and trouble erupted. There was heavy brick batting from both sides and many houses were looted before the situation could be brought under control.

In this background, when a pig from the nearby Harijan colony (Harijans usually keep pigs as domestic animals) strayed into the Idgah at the time of Id prayers on 13 August, 1980, there was flutter in the congregation. (It may be remembered that Muslims are as blind in their hatred of pigs as Hindus in their worship of cows). The Muslims asked a policeman on duty to chase the pig away but he refused. Heated exchanges between the congregationists and the police took a serious turn. To add fuel to the flame, some stones were pelted on the policemen posted there who retaliated with counter brick batting. That started rioting on a scale which the brass city of Moradabad had not known before. It was partly communal and partly anti-police. Police opened fire on the congregation inside the Idgah, about 50,000 strong, comprising unarmed Muslims including children and aged who had assembled to offer Id prayers. Many were crushed to death in the stampede that followed, besides those killed by police bullets.

The dispersing Muslim mobs indulged in mass looting and arson in course of which a number of Harijan slums were ravaged. A sepoy of the Provincial Armed Constabulary (PAC) was burnt to death and two others were hammered to death. The trouble spread to the surrounding rural areas also where it assumed pure communal complexion. The exact number of lives lost during those few days of anarchy and unchecked violence would never be known. Post-mortem was performed on at least 145 dead bodies which were recovered by authorities. A large number of bodies were not traced. Upwards of 200 persons were feared killed according to unofficial estimates.

Even after the major outbreak subsided, Moradabad remained disturbed for the next two months. Trouble erupted again in September on the Hindu festival day of Raksha Bandhan (Rakhi). And there were series of stabbings and killings at the end of October costing at least 14 lives.

The Moradabad conflagration of 1980 August proved to be a watershed event of sorts. It inaugurated a sinister series which scarred distant regions of India with bouts of communal violence year after year throughout the 80's. There were riots after riots in one part of the country or the other making the decade of 80's a decade of communal riots. There were wide-spread riots in Nalanda district of Bihar taking a toll of 80 lives between 30 April and 7 May, 1981.

Hindu-Muslim conflicts erupted 19 times in Baroda area of Gujarat state in course of the years 1982. Major riotings took place in October 1982 when the Hindu festival of Dussera and Muslim festival of Muharram coincided and again for the 19th time in December when the city police commissioner was transferred. Jaspal Singh, the police commissioner who had somehow won the confidence of local Hindus for effective handling of goonda elements among Muslims earlier, was shifted from Baroda on pressure from Muslim leaders. This sparked off riots in the city which left about 12 persons dead in course of three days. The year 1982 also witnessed major communal riots in Meerut city of U.P. in September. A dispute had arisen over a temple and a Mazar in adjacent buildings in March 1982 which escalated in large scale violence in September.

The year 1983 was even more disturbed. There were Hindu-Muslim riots of varying intensity and duration at Bijapur, Bellary and Malur in Karnataka, Malegaon in Maharashtra, Hyderabad in

Andhra Pradesh and Hazaribagh in Bihar. Of these, the riots in Hyderabad city, notorious for its sharp communal divide since pre-partition days, were most tenacious and persistent. Stray stabbings, killings, looting and destruction of property continued intermittently for around three weeks in September 1983.

The city of Hyderabad went through another round of communal violence in 1984. Trouble flared up first when a Hindu procession was stoned while passing through a Muslim locality on 22 July, 1984, and incidents including stabbings continued for over a week. For the second time, another big Hindu procession was brickbatted from Muslim house-tops in September 1984 which resulted in more serious disturbances and devastations. It was only after the army was called up, indefinite curfew imposed and large number of people arrested that order could be restored. But the most devastating occurrence of communal violence took place in Maharashtra state in May 1984. In the wake of a Bund call given by Shiv Sena in Bombay on 17 May, violence erupted simultaneously in Bombay city and the powerloom township of Bhiwandi some 50 kms away on 18 May, 1984. The unprecedented scale of violence shook the commercial capital of India and destroyed the flourishing powerloom township of Bhiwandi. Well over a hundred persons were killed, over 10,000 people rendered homeless and properties worth millions of rupees destroyed. It was the communal violence of the decade.

If Maharashtra exploded in 1984, the neighbouring Gujarat did it in the following year. In respect of multiple violence of every conceivable variety, the year 1985 belonged to Gujarat, Ahmedabad in particular. Early in the year, the State Government announced an increase of 18 per cent in jobs to be reserved for so-called other backward castes, which meant reduction in job opportunities for the rest of the castes. A bitter anti-reservation agitation started which became more and more violent, involving the beneficiary and adversely affected caste-clusters. And by April 1985, what started as inter-caste rioting turned into inter-religion rioting and violence on a scale which was astounding even by Ahmedabad standard. S.K. Ghosh aptly describes the scenario: "Ahmedabad was in throes of violence from April 1985. Everybody, it seemed, was fighting everybody. The upper castes were fighting the lower castes, the working classes had turned against the middle classes, Hindus were fighting with Muslims, the police were battling with the people and the press and government was fighting the opposition."[7] The city was literally reduced to the Hobbasion 'State of Nature." And the violence was not confined to Ahmedabad city alone. It spilled over to other cities of Gujarat also like Baroda of 1982 fame, Rajkot, Bhavnagar and Surat. The riots continued intermittently till the end of May, 1985 taking hundreds of lives, a large number of them Muslims.

But that was not the end of the story as far as Ahmedabad was concerned. By now Ahmedabad had became a metaphor for Hindu-Muslim blood-spilling. It erupted again in July 1986 in a big way. On 9 July, 1986, a Hindu Rathyatra procession was brickbattled while passing through a particular locality, and hell broke loose in the city. Hindus were stabbed and killed in Muslim dominated areas and Muslims were ravaged in Hindu majority areas. In this sudden spurt of violence, at least 48 lives were lost, according to official reports, though unofficial estimates indicated much higher casualty figures.

Even as Ahmedabad was recovering from one conflagration to be consumed by another, an ordinary, innocuous looking event took place, which would have gone unnoticed in any modern civilized society. On February 1, 1986, the doors of a crumbling vintage mosque at Ayodhya in which nobody had offered namaz for years, which was also claimed as birth place of Lord Rama by Hindus, were opened by authorities at the termination of some old prohibitory orders. And that inaugurated an ominous cycle of Hindu-Muslim bitterness and violence from which India, and in fact, the entire sub-continent, is yet to fully recover.

From 1986, onwards, the Ayodhya dispute came to the fore, consequent upon the unlocking of the doors of the disputed structure by the authorities. As the movement for construction of Ram temple at the disputed spot caught the imagination of Hindu masses, particularly in the Hindu heartland, communal tension continued to build up resulting in innumerable incidents, skirmishes and recurring conflicts in different parts of the country during the second half of the 80's. There were serious communal riots at Meerut, Sultanpur, Moradabad, Pilibhit, Shahjahanpur,

Jaunpur, Varanasi and Allahabad in U.P. over the Ayodhya (Ramjanmabhoomi-Babri Masjid) dispute leaving about 60-70 persons dead and numerous injured. The surcharged communal situation in the country led to riotings the disturbances in areas not known for trouble before. A piece of careless publication in a Bangalore newspaper outraged the religious sentiments of Muslims so much that they indulged in rioting and violence at Bangalore on 30 November, 1986. The trouble soon turned into communal violence and spread to surrounding areas on 1st December. Many lives were lost and considerable damage caused to public and private property before peace could be restored. The country seemed to be sitting on a power keg of communal violence.

The violent decade ended with another big communal conflagration in Bihar, this time in and around the silk town of Bhagalpur in the grim autumn of 1989. It ravaged the urban and rural areas of Bhagalpur district with savage ferocity resulting in massacres of hundreds of men, women and children, mainly Muslims. The Prime Minister of India, the late Rajiv Gandhi, visited Bhagalpur to ensure speedy restoration of peace. But the riots continued unabated, spreading deeper in rural areas, for days after the Prime Minister had come and gone devastating Muslim lives and properties on a wide scale.

The 90's—Ayodhya Explosion

The 90's opened ominously with the Ramjanmabhoomi-Babri Masjid dispute dominating the communal scene and heightening Hindu-Muslim tensions across the board. Political parties had a hey-day garnering mass support of one or the other of the two major religious communities by fanning, instead of making efforts to cool down, communal passions. While the avowedly Hindu political leaders were raising the Hindus' hope of building a magnificent Ram temple at the disputed site in Ayodhya to a feverish pitch, the miscalled "secularists" were raising Muslims' religious passions against it to hysteric proportions. The flash point was reached on 6 December, 1992, when a frenzied Hindu mob fell upon the vintage structure called Babri Masjid, known and valued more as a historic relic than a place of religious worship, and razed it to the ground. On account of sustained building up of religious passions over the issue by the so-called 'communalists' and 'secularists' over the years, the unfortunate demolition of the structure caused much more communal violence across the sub-continent than it would have done in ordinary course.

There were widespread riots in India, started this time by the Muslims violently protesting against the demolition. The Muslim protest became particularly violent in Bombay city where it had to be suppressed by heavy police firing resulting in heavy casualities among the rioting Muslims. There were allegations of the predominantly Hindu police force of Bombay city going after the Muslim rioters in abandon and using excessive force to quell them. (The matter is still before a commission of Enquiry set up by the incumbent Congress government and scrapped by the successor government but revived under orders of the Supreme Court.) Muslims were fanatically aroused and in many areas across the country where they were in a substantial majority, they indulged in varying degrees of violence against Hindus. Everywhere it was the same story of local majority ravaging the local minorities, which has been the hallmark of communal violence in the sub-continent since the time of independence.

Conforming to the basic unity of mass behaviour across the sub-continent, as brought out in earlier chapters to be corroborated in chapters ahead, violence against Hindu minorities spilled over across the borders of India also. Pakistan has hardly any Hindu population worth counting but there are many Hindu places of worship scattered over the country. These were promptly decreted or destroyed by Muslims in retaliation for Ayodhya demolition. Bangladesh, on the other hand, still has a sizeable number of Hindus left in the country who came in for sharp retaliation at the hands of the Muslim majority. In those few days after December 6 Ayodhya demolition, there was wide-spread Hindu hunting in Bangladesh in course of which numerous Hindu houses were attacked and ransacked, their inmates maimed and killed and innumerable temples and shrines destroyed.

The sheer inhumanity of persecuting innocent men and women for the fault of their co-religionists in another country shook Taslima Nasrin, the famous Bangladeshi feminist intellectual, to the core. She pored her heart out on the plight of the minority community in her own country in her celebrated novel entitled *Lajja* (shame), written in a record time of seven days of intense anguish. In her preface to the book, she says: "It is disgraceful that Hindus in my country were hunted by the Muslims after the destruction of the Babri Masjid. All of us who love Bangladesh should feel ashamed that such a terrible thing could happen in our beautiful country. The riots that took place in 1992 in Bangladesh are the responsibility of us all, and we are all to blame. Lajja is, a document of our collective defeat".[7]

Vernacularisation of Polity

The story of vicious and escalating communal violence in India, with spill-over in Pakistan and Bangladesh, after independence would remain incomplete without answering the question raised at the beginning of the sub-chapter. How to explain the relative communal peace in India during the first 12 years after independence, in spite of bitter memories of the partition holocaust? The answer lies in the complexion of India's political leadership and Indian polity generally during the first post-independence decade. The first generation rulers of independent India, freedom-fighters who assumed the mantle after British withdrawal, were all metropolitan (English) educated nationalists steeped in liberal traditions of modern nationalism. They were as far away from backwards-looking particularist and primordial ideas as 20th century is from 16th century. The top three— Mahatma Gandhi, Jawaharlal Nehru and Sardar Patel — were all barristers -at-law—from London and so was Dr. B.R. Ambedkar, the Chief architect of the Indian Constitution. All the rest of the political stalwarts setting the tone of political behaviour — C. Rajgopalachari, Moulana Azad, Dr. B.C. Roy, Sarojini Naidu, Gobind Ballav Pant, B.G. Kher etc. were highly educated persons, leaders in their own right, who led the lesser men and were not led by the latter.

Among the younger leaders emerging on the democratic opposition spectrum, Jay Prakash Narayan had his higher education in America and Dr. Ram Manohar Lohia in Germany. The guiding star of the CPI, representing the main leftist opposition in India, was Rajni Palme Dutta, an erudite Marxist intellectual based in

England having close links with international Communist movement. Even the second rank leaders of the Congress Party who took over the role of governance in the states of the Union were well educated persons following in the footsteps of the more illustrious nationalist leaders who were in command at the national level.

The doyen of them all was of course Jawaharlal Nehru who presided over the destiny of India since independence with an authority which could hardly be matched by any democratic leader anywhere in the world. And Nehru had had the most metropolitan of metropolitan education that any nationalist leader could have had. His earliest tutor at home was an Irishman, F.T. Brooks, who was a follower of Mrs. Annie Besant of Home Rule Movement fame. At the age of fifteen, he was sent to England for his schooling at Harrow, a school established in 1572 which had provided Britain with four Prime Ministers—Pitt, Palmerston, Baldwin and Winston Churchill. When approaching the age of eighteen, he joined the University at Cambridge in October 1907, from where he graduated at the age of twenty. Joining the Inner Temple at London after Cambridge, he passed his Bar examinations in the summer of 1912 and returned to India after over seven years' stay in England. All through his stay in England, he maintained deep interest in the growing nationalist movement back home in India and was inclined towards the extremist viewpoint represented by Tilak.

With such a cosmopolitan, outward and forward looking nationalist leader at the helm, backwards and inward looking particularist ideas could not prevail in India as long as he had complete sway over the people. And it was not Nehru alone but the whole lot of second and third rung political leaders who constituted the governing elite had received fairly high level of education, metropolitan in origin and modern in content. They were sufficiently imbued with the precepts and practices of modern nationhood which supercedes all other narrow loyalties——religious, ethnic, clanish, tribal etc. They were educated in a tradition of exogenous inspiration drawn from western societies epitomising modern nationalism. As long as they, the first generation political successors of the British, held sway and called the tune, India was held back from lapsing into all manners of pre-national parochial conflicts and violence, of which communal violence was only a part, even though a major one.

But the danger was always there, ever since India emerged as an independent nation state, which it had not been before. The danger lay in the gaping chasm, wide gap between a modern, exogenous, outward looking governing elite and largely uneducated or even illiterate mass rooted in a variety of indigenous traditions, beliefs and superstitions. One way of resolving the dualism and bridging or at least reducing the gap was to educate and modernise the masses with a hurricane speed to bring them up in the era of modern nationalism. This was a stupendous task of which perhaps Nehru alone was fully conscious and kept striving untiringly in the post-independence era. Commenting on the magnitude of the job in 1959-60 when Nehru was still on the scene, Frank Moraes observed: "Nehru can no more escape the past than can India. Five millenniums of history look down upon him. His task is to carry forward a people who range sociologically from the primitive to the most sophisticated... By any standards this constitutes a stupendous challenge. Add to these depressing factors a socio-religious pattern with strong divisive urges, and the gigantic proportions of the job which faces India's government and people can be better understood."

Nehru at least kept up the effort as long as he lived, but he himself started imperceptibility losing his grip on the affairs of the nation during later years. Ever since his dream of lasting Indo-Chinese friendship started souring in the wake of Chinese occupation of Tibet and escape of Dalailama to India in 1959, he was on a down slide. He was finally shattered after the Indian debacle in the short India-China war of October-November 1962, from which he never recovered. It was no accident that the major spurt in communal riots in India started in 1964—the fateful year of Nehru's death—and has since continued unabated, except for a brief interlude in the 70's brought about by exceptional political developments in the sub-continent.

Nehru's successors chose the easier option of bridging the gap. If the masses rooted to the narrow parochial loyalties of religion, caste and clan could not be brought up to the level of modern nationalism, the governing classes would themselves go down to the level of the masses. In fact, this slide down of the ruling elite had stated in the states and lower down at the national level even in Nehru's life time towards the end of the fifties. It assumed serious proportions after his departure from the scene. The institution of adult franchise made the temptation to court the masses by catering to their particularist loyalties of religion, caste, language, region etc. irresistible. The social and political elites who by virtue of their education and apprenticeship under the Mahatma and Nehru were supposed to lead the masses, started being led by them instead. They increasingly pampered and nourished narrow, pre-national loyalties and blind hatreds of the masses in order just to mobilise their electoral support and capture or retain power.

The growing vernacularisation of education after independence made it more and more inward-looking and insular. That brought about a sea-change in the character and style of the new, post-independence political elite who steadily replaced the old guard in post-Nehru era: Norms and standards of political conduct and behaviour got fast eroded. All niceties and finer nuances of democratic polity, even basic humanistic values were increasingly superseded by the obscenities and crudities of political power game. In the close-doorist socio-political milieu, bereft of exogenous inspiration, shunning all modernistic ideas of the civilized world outside, the vernacular political elites signalled the onset of sharp deterioration in the standards and quality of political life. And since politics had and has an overwhelming impact on society as a whole in all newly independent underdeveloped states, it meant sharp decline in the quality of social life too. The elites and the masses alike were given more and more to stewing in their own 'Swadeshi' juice of primordial differences, ancient hatreds and better forgotten historical wrongs. The result was a disastrous lapse into the whirlpool of violence and disorder, the like of which had not been experienced since the establishment of Pax Britannica.

Vernacularisation of polity and society was compounded by vernacularisation of the bureaucracy or the civil and administrative services. The vernacular edition of the celebrated 'steel frame' of the Raj days which was known for its objectivity, impartiality and work culture, was entirely unequal to the task of keeping peace and order. It sailed along merrily with the vernacular political elites in splitting and splintering the society rather than holding it in one piece. On a visit to the IAS training academy at Mussourie sometime after the Ayodhya demolition, Praful Bidwai, a well-known journalist, was shocked to learn that the IAS trainees had loudly hailed and celebrated the Babri Masjid demolition on the night of 6 December, 1992. In sheer disgust and anguish, Bidwai wrote two lead articles in *The Times of India* lamenting the decline in the standards of the elite civil service in India since independence and scratching to discover the reason. Thereby hangs a tale.

Nehru and Patel tried to establish the institution of IAS in the mould of the old ICS of British times in order to withstand the pulls and pressures of indigenous politics and keep the country together. The service was to be manned by the pick of India's educated youth and it started off as such. But like most other institutions of civil and political society in independent India, the IAS was also steadily tinkered with, diluted and rendered infructuous over a period of time. By a conscious decision of the political executive, the mode of recruitment of the service was so amended as to shun the top class material among the youth and bring in the second-raters. Through the report of the Kothari Commission, entrusted with the task of suggesting dilution in the mode of recruitment, the floodgates of the IAS were thrown open to all kinds of mercenary mediocres who could cram their way into the elite services. The ostensible objective was to ruralise the civil services, but in the process the very fabric of the services was over-stretched and torn apart. That explains the kind of jubilation in the IAS academy on the Ayodhya demolition which Praful Bidwai laments about. The decline in the quality and standard of the services has since been further accelerated with ever increasing quantum of reservations and quotas for this category or that.

The sharp acceleration in the incidence of communal violence in India after the balmy years of the 50's, particularly after Nehru's departure, is explained by the increasing vernacularisation of the polity and administration. The vernacular power elites, comprising both the politicians and civil servants, distorted and contorted the ideals of the society as a whole, making it more communal, more fanatical, more splintered and more violent.

Muslim-Muslim Violence in Pakistan

End of the Giants-Quaid-i-Azam and Quaid-i-Millat

The Hindu-Muslim problem in Pakistan had largely been solved at the time of partition itself, albeit the other way about. With massive migration of Hindus from what was then West Pakistan at the time of partition and immediately after that, there was hardly any Hindu population worth reckoning left in what is now the state of Pakistan. Those who could not migrate, or most of them, were circumcised, made to eat beef and converted to Islam. Pakistan literally became the 'land of the pure', which the name literally means, on its very birth. That should have augured very well for internal peace and harmony in the land. As it turned out, it did not. If there were no Hindus and Sikhs to bash about, there were diverse sects and some groups among the Muslims themselves to exorcise or fight with. The paradox of Pakistan is that even after emerging as a pure Muslim state from day one, it has been troubled with sectarian and group violence of one variety or another almost from its coming into being.

In fact, the sub-continental virus of inter-community violence caught up with Pakistan earlier than India, thanks to the long innings Nehru had as the supreme leader of the Indian state. Pakistan was not so fortunate. It lost its founder, Quaid-i-Azam Jinnah, just over a year after its birth. And Jinnah was no less-religion neutral (that is a much better term than 'secular' which has been so prostituted by its so-called protagonists in India as to mean exactly the opposite of what it does—complete non-religiosity in the affairs of state) in his outlook and personal life than Nehru. In the words of Larry Collins and Dominque Lapierre, "A more improbable leader of India's Moslem masses could hardly be imagined. The only thing Moslem about Mohammad Ali Jinnah was his parents' religion."[8]

As for his public policy, there can be no more eloquent testimony to his unquestionable religion— neutrality in matters of state than his landmark address to the Pakistan constituent Assembly on 11 August, 1947, already quoted in part earlier. The concluding part of this speech is a most authentic exposition of unadulterated, religion-free modern nationalism, from which the multifarious brands of mock 'secularists' in India can learn a lesson or two. It is worth re-quoting here: "You will find that in course of time Hindus will cease to be Hindus and Muslims will cease to be Muslims, not in the religious sense, *because that is the personal faith of each individual*, but in the political sense as citizens of the state." The most remarkable aspect of this gem of a piece is that it consigns or confines religion to where it belongs—the mind and heart of each individual. Which unfolds the modern concept of religion as a private enterprise of every individual and not a public enterprise of the state, as an individual affair and not a monolithic collectivity affecting matters temporal.

For reasons of recent history of the sub-continent, Mohammad Ali Jinnah, of all the dramatis personae of the nationalist movement, is the most misunderstood person in India. Addressing the Royal Empire Society London in 1949, David Gammans, a British M.P., said: "The creation of Pakistan is one of the most fantastic happenings of this age, and shows how individuals can still determine history, for Pakistan was the creation of one man— Mr. Jinnah." And yet, everybody who cares to know knows that when the idea of Pakistan was first mooted by Rahmat Ali in a meeting in London, Jinnah had rejected it straightaway as not practicable. Everybody knows that he was an ardent nationalist, a top leader of the Indian National Congress and a great political leader in his own right working for independence of India from British rule. If he changed his track in the middle to espouse the cause of a separate Muslim state, which he succeeded in establishing with aplomb, he had his own reasons for that. In his obituary of Jinnah contributed to the London weekly the *New Statesman*, another British M.P. Woodrow Wyatt wrote: "Once an ardent nationalist, Congressman, gradually, as they kept him out of leadership, Jinnah had become frustrated at the Hindu turn the Hindu majority gave to the organisation... To him it seemed that he was being squeezed out by the Congress and that his co-religionists were being squeezed out by the Hindus."

In *The Discovery of India* published in November 1947 Jawaharlal Nehru gave his own interpretation to Jinnah's change of mission: "Jinnah left the Congress not because of any difference of opinion on the Hindu-Muslim question, but because he could not adopt himself to the new and more advanced ideology, and even more so because he disliked the crowds of ill-dressed people talking in Hindustani who filled the Congress." Dr. Sachchidanand Sinha attributed it to Jinnah's basic personality trait of dominating or trying to be "the first and foremost in every walk and sphere of life" that he strode, which felt stifled by the effective appearance of Gandhiji on the political scene from around 1920 onwards. In the *Hindustan Review* of September 1949, which he himself edited, Dr. Sinha wrote: "Jinnah grasped it immediately that the predominance of Gandhiji over the Congress was to be wholly exclusive and no one could successfully compete with a leader like the new one, who was a conglomeration of asceticism, mysticism, non-cooperation, non-violence, charkha spinning, renunciation of the world, coupled with the intensely patriotic demand for the independence of India."

If Jinnah's domineering political personality could not reconcile to playing a second fiddle to anyone, not even Gandhiji, in the national movement, he cannot be faulted for that. That is the archetypal personality trait of every great leader everywhere in the world. The notable fact is that none of these estimates of Jinnah by his contemporaries, friends and foes has accused him of religious fanaticism. His espousal of Muslim separatism had nothing to do with religious bigotry or anti-Hinduism. He only wanted and worked tirelessly, with his extraordinary political skill, to have a place under the sun for his Muslim co-religionists independent of the over-powering Hindu majority in the sub-continent. Jinnah after all had a case which he knew very well as a brilliant lawyer that he was professionally. In a society where religion so overwhelmingly influenced and still influences every bit of a man's life— his food, his wearing apparel, his name, his taboos and so on— there was nothing sinful, as people in India seem to think, about his demanding and achieving Muslim separation. His intense desire for separation had basically nothing anti-Hindu about it. In any case, his concept of Pakistan was one of a thoroughly modern nation state in which all its inhabitants lived as equal citizens irrespective of their religion, ethnicity, culture, language etc. There was nothing theocratic about the nation state of Pakistan of his dreams.

What would have been the shape of Pakistan if he had lived

longer to guide its destiny is a hypothetical question, and history of nations is replete with such hypothetical questions which none can answer nor need to be answered. The important fact is that the Quaid-i-Azam who had so single-mindedly and single-handedly brought about the creation of Pakistan passed away even before the basic objectives of the new state could be formulated and given shape. As mentioned earlier, Jinnah passed away on 11 September, 1948 and the Pakistan Constituent Assembly was able to adopt the 'objectives Resolution' only in March 1949. And the 'objective Resolution' did not contain even the outlines of a constitution but only a rehash of all pious platitudes in broadest terms.

It was left to Jinnah's worthy successor Liaquat Ali Khan, the Quaid-i-Millat as he came to be called, to steer the ship of the new state through rough waters. He was the only chip of the old block, unbigoted, liberal and mature enough left in Pakistan to build up the Pakistan of Jinnah's dream. All that he could manage was to get an all-party Basic Principles Committee set up by the Constituent Assembly to draw an outline of a constitution for Pakistan. And all that he could get out of it was merely in interim report which he presented on 21 November, 1950. Even before the committee could prepare its full report, Quaid-i-Millat Liaquat Ali Khan was assassinated on 16 October, 1951.

The two giants of the Pakistan movement and founding fathers of the new state were thus removed from the scene, one by God and the other by man, in its very infancy. The extent of the vacuum created in Pakistan after their departure can be realised from the fact that Pakistan could not have a regular constitution of its own until March 1956. For nearly nine years after achieving independence, Pakistan continued to be governed under the government of India Act 1935 as suitably amended by the Constituent Assembly. The Noons (Malik Feroz Khan Noon), Nishtars (Sardar Abdur Rub Nishtar) and Daulatnas (Mian Mumtaz Daulatana) who were left to rule the roost in the country were no substitutes for the stalwarts— Jinnah and Liaquat.

General (later President) Ayub Khan had a measure of these vernacular politicians much before he pushed them out. He was to write later as he, as Pak Army Chief, viewed them after Liaquat's killing: "Before long it became apparent that none of the Prime Minister's associates was capable of filling the gap created by his death. Conditions throughout the country deteriorated rapidly and we witnessed the start of a woeful chapter in our country's history and one which was to drag on its unhappy course for several years. When I returned to Pakistan I met several members of the new cabinet in Karachi... Not one of them mentioned Liaquat Ali Khan's name, nor did I hear a word of sympathy or regret from anyone of them... It seemed that everyone of them had got himself promoted in one way or another. The termination of the Prime Minister's life had come as the beginning of a new career for them. It was disgusting and revolting. It may be a harsh thing to say, but I got the distinct impression that they were all feeling relieved that the only person who might have kept them under control had disappeared from the scene."[9]

A more forthright condemnation of the political class that assumed power after Liaquat's assassination came later from President Iskander Mirza when he abrogated the Pak constitution and assumed all powers, as a prelude to assumption of power by General (Later Field Marshal) Ayub Khan. In his Presidential order dated 7 October, 1958, Iskander Mirza said: "For the last two years, I have been watching, with the deepest anxiety, the ruthless struggle for power, corruption, the shameful exploitation of our simple, honest, patriotic, and industrious masses, the lack of decorum and the prostitution of Islam for political ends... The same group of people who have brought Pakistan on the verge of ruination will rig the elections for their own ends. They will come back more revengeful, because, I am sure, the elections will be contested on personal, regional and sectarian basis."[10] That said it all.

Anti-Ahmadi Violence

With the early disappearance of Jinnah and Liaquat, the only two leaders, who could have shored up Pakistan, vernacularisation of Pak polity began about a decade earlier than in India. And it showed in the start of a variety of sectarian violence in early 50's itself, which has kept recurring from time to time and led to the squeeze of one of the more dynamic Muslim communities from the mainstream Pakistani society. It relates to the on-again off-again violence against the Ahmadiyas—followers of a Muslim sect which has become an anathema to the Muslim clergy in Pakistan.

The tirade inevitably leading to a spate of violence against the Ahmadies in Pakistan was started by an orthodox Muslim organization known as Majlis-i-Ahrar. The Ahrar organization had a little history of its own which is highly revealing. Originally, it was a party of so-called 'nationalist Muslims' in undivided India. Although the Ahrars separated from the Indian National Congress and formed the Majlis-i-Ahrar-i-Islam at a meeting held in Lahore on 4 May, 1931, they continued to toe the Congress line right up to the time of partition. In a meeting at Delhi on 3 March, 1940, the Majlis-i-Ahrar working committee, among other things, disapproved of the idea of Pakistan. In March, 1943, the Punjab Provincial Ahrar-conference passed a resolution opposing the proposed partition of India. The Ahrar leaders repeatedly criticised the Muslim League and its leaders in most uncharitable terms and did not spare even the Quaid-i-Azam. They went to the extent of calling him an infidel-*Kafir-i-Azam* for having married a Parsi lady and not been on pilgrimage to Mecca.

These were the people who took up the cudgels against the Ahmadiya community in Pakistan soon after the birth of the new state. In a queer about turn, which has become a common feature of politics in the sub-continent, they not only affirmed their full loyalty to Pakistan but also vowed to become followers of the ruling party, the Muslim League, which also became friendly to them. Having mended their fences with the ruling party, they started virulent campaign against the Ahmadiyas through a series of Tabligh conferences held in different towns and cities of Punjab since early 1949. It was in one of these conferences that the demand for declaring the Ahmadis as a non-Muslim minority was made which was announced at a public meeting on 1st May, 1949.

Even before they had formally launched their campaign against the Ahmadis from early 1949 onwards, they had generated considerable hatred against them among the common run of Muslims, which had started surfacing. On 11 August, 1948, a Muslim Railway Employees Association meeting at Quetta was addressed by some Moulvis who poured venom against the

Ahmadis. One Major Mahmud, a young military officer who was an Ahmadi, happened to pass that way when his car broke down. That was his nemesis. A hysteric mob, seething with anti-Ahmadi poison, pulled him out of the car and stabbed and clubbed him to death on the spot. His fault was he was having short beards— an insignia of Ahmadis—and the crowd was feverishly looking for Ahmadis to bash them.

The main targets of Ahrar leaders came to be the incumbent Khalifa or chief of the Ahmadiya sect— Mirza Bashiruddin Mahmud Ahmad— and Sir Mohammad Zafrulla Khan, then foreign minister of Pakistan. To people in India, in those days, Zafrulla Khan was known only for his stout advocacy of Pakistan's case on Kashmir issue in the United Nations, matched only by Krishna Menon from Indian side. They did not know that even as he took on the redoubtable Krishna Menon with remarkable skill in UN debates, Zafrulla Khan was constantly hounded by fanatic anti-Ahmadis back home in Pakistan. He was even dubbed as a traitor to Pakistan, seeking to barter away Kashmir for Quadian in Gurudaspur district of Indian Punjab, which was the original headquarters of the Ahmadis.

As the poisonous vilification campaign continued against the Ahmadis, sporadic cases of violence and murders kept taking place. In October 1950, an anti-Ahmadi crowd waylaid one Maulvi Nuruddin and seven other Ahmadis on a religious mission, blackened their face and had them driven through filthy water to a railway station. A few days later, a Muslim youth stabbed an Ahmadis school teacher in the same area. In May 1951, an Ahrar crowd set fire to a Kacha mosque of Ahmadis and assaulted the worshippers in Samundri town of Lyallpur district. Between July and September 1952, there were many incidents of assault on Ahmadis individually in Lyallpur, Lahore, Jhang etc. By now the Ahrars succeeded in Uniting all Muslim sectarian groups against the Ahmadis. In July 1952, an All Muslim Parties convention was constituted to carry on the campaign against the Ahmadiya community.

In January 1953, the All Muslim Parties convention met at Karachi and decided to intensify the anti-Ahmadi Movement. Their main demands were: (1) Zafrullah Khan should be removed from the office of Foreign Minister. (2) Ahmadis should be declared a non-Muslim minority. (3) Ahmadis holding key posts in Government should be removed from their posts. They threatened to start 'direct action' on 23 February, 1953 if their demands were not met by then. An Action Committee was formed to conduct the 'direct action'.

The Government responded by arresting all members of the Action Committee at Karachi on 27 February, 1953. Other leading agitationists were arrested in Punjab simultaneously. These arrests provoked immediate reaction and a wave of lawlessness all over Punjab. There were riotings and violence on a wide scale in Lahore, Sialkot, Gujaranwala, Rawalpindi, Lyallpur, Montgomery, etc. The mounting wave of lawlessness became uncontrollable in the Provincial capital— Lahore. On 6 March, 1953, Army was called in and Lahore was put under Martial Law. According to Ahmadiya sources, about a hundred Ahmadies were reported to have lost their lives in course of the disturbances in 1953.

And with that, the first phase of sectarian violence against the Ahmadis abated for the time being. The period was too close to the British rule that had ceased only five years earlier and the administrative system still had the shine of the western traditions of liberalism, secularism and rule of law. Accordingly, a court of Enquiry was constituted under a special Act to go into the entire gamut of the anti-Ahmadi disturbances leading to the imposition of Martial Law. Justice Mohammad Munir, who rose to be the Chief Justice of Pakistan, was appointed the President and Justice Kayani the other member. The commission commenced the enquiry on 1st May, 1953 and took about a year to complete it. The voluminous report of the commission, which came to be called the "Munir Report", submitted on 10th April, 1954 is a veritable storehouse of information about the mountains of socio-religious and socio-political problems confronting Pakistan since its inception and dogging the country even today. The report revealed in no uncertain terms how Pakistan started deviating from the basic concepts of its founder—the Quad-i-Azam so soon after his departure from the scene. By doing so, Pakistan has landed itself in a quagmire of religious orthodoxy and sectarian conflicts from which it finds extremely difficult to emerge.

The turbulent and traumatic political developments in Pakistan during subsequent years kept the anti-Ahmadiya trouble under the carpet for nearly two decades. As so admirably brought out in 'Munir Report', there was nothing truly religious, or at any rate nationalist about the anti-Ahmadiya campaign in the first place. It was launched by a politico-religious group of leaders whose very loyalty to Pakistan ideology was suspect to start with. It gave them credibility and helped them establish their foot hold in the country as champions of pure Islam. In course of a few years, other orthodox Muslim groups also joined in giving the anti-Ahmadi drive wider support and a new legitimacy. But with dramatic happenings on the political stage—change of Prime Ministers from Khwaja Nazimuddin to Mohammad Ali Bogra to Chaudhri Mohammad Ali to H.S. Suhrawardy between 1954 and 1956, adoption of the first Pak constitution in 1956, its subsequent abrogation in 1958 and establishment of Ayub's military rule—the anti-Ahmadi movement remained dormant.

Ayub Khan's regime, lasting a little over a decade, was a period of consolidation, stability, and economic growth. Peace and order is the first priority of any regimented system and Ayub era was one of relative peace in the country, except for accumulating bitterness in East Pakistan. Ayub Khan introduced his own constitution in 1962 incorporating the system of Basic Democracy and a Presidential form of government in which the President was the real focus of power. Although by the First Amendment of 1963 Pakistan was declared an Islamic Republic, a list of Fundamental Rights was also incorporated which guaranteed, among other things, freedom of religion, culture, language etc. In any case, Ayub was himself a broad-minded person and held modernist view of Islam and Islamic ideology. In one of his few speeches relating to Islam on 3 May, 1959, he observed: "The miracle of Islam was that it destroyed idolatry, and the tragedy of Muslims has been that they rendered religion into the form of an idol."[11] With such a person at the helm, and with all powers under the system, there was no question of the anti-Ahmadi trouble coming to the surface as long as he ruled.

From Ayub Khan's ouster in March 1969 to the adoption of a new constitution in August 1973 re-establishing the Parliamentary system was a period of unprecedented turmoil in Pakistan. During this period, the country went through the trauma of a humiliating defeat in its short war with India, separation of East Pakistan, ouster of Yahya Khan and assumption of power by Zulfiquar Ali Bhutto. Such was not the time for any sectarian polemics to attract people's attention. But once Bhutto was in the saddle as the Prime Minister of Pakistan and rough and tumble of democratic polity, as known in the sub-continent, returned, the Anti-Ahmadi trouble erupted again. And to an extent, it was Bhutto's own creation.

The hallmark of Bhutto's regime was populism. He promised all kinds of things to everyone. The usual *roti, kapda aur makan* (food, clothing and shelter) to all, the stock slogan of all political pedagogues in the sub-continent, became the principal catch words in his Pakistan 'People's Party's political propaganda'. But in Pakistan as it has come to be constituted, no populist platform is complete without bringing in the sacred name of Islam. And Bhutto was not to lag behind in harnessing the sacred religion in his bid for populism. The constitution that he gave his country not only retained the name 'Islamic Republic of Pakistan' adopted for the first time by Ayub Khan through the First Amendment to his constitution, but went a step further. He declared Islam as the state religion. In the Principles of Policy, there was reference to the Islamic way of life, compulsory teaching of the Holy Quran and Islamiyat, encouragement to observance of the Islamic moral standards etc.

Once religion came to the forefront in Bhutto's scheme of populism, the anti-Ahmadi trouble, lying dormant for nearly two decades of unusual political developments, erupted again, almost with a vengeance. There were numerous cases of violence against Ahmadis in Pakistan causing loss of life and property. According to Ahmadi sources, about 75 Ahmadis were killed in violence against the community. And in keeping with his populist posture of keeping the orthodox Muslim clergy on his right side, Zulfiquar Ali Bhutto did what his predecessors had shrunk from doing earlier. On 7 September, 1974, Bhutto's Government declared Ahmadiyas as a non-Muslim minority in Pakistan.

When General Zia-Ul-Haq pushed out Z.A. Bhutto and captured power on 5 July, 1977, under circumstances which are well known, the fate of Ahmadis in Pakistan was finally sealed. For while Bhutto used Islamisation as *one* important plank of his populist platform, among others, General Zia used it as his *only and sole* support base as long as he lived and ruled. And the first and the most obvious victims of Zia's use of the orthodox Muslim clergy as his strongest allies were the Ahmadis. Being a military ruler with absolute command over the fate of his countrymen, he minced no words in telling the Ahmadis what was their place in Pakistan.

His Provisional constitutional order issued in 1981 made a clear cut distinction between Muslims and non-Muslims. It said: "A Muslim means a person who believes in the Unity and oneness of Almighty Allah, in the absolute and unqualified finality of the Prophethood of Muhammad (Peace be upon Him), the last of the prophets, and does not believe in, or recognise as a prophet or religious reformer, any person who claimed or claims to be a prophet, in any sense of the word or of any description whatsoever, after Muhammad (Peace be upon Him). A non-Muslim means a person who is not a Muslim and includes a person belonging to the Christian, Hindu, Sikh, Buddhist or Parsi community, a person of the Quadiani group or the Lahori group (who call themselves 'Ahmadis or by any other name) or a Bahai, and a person belonging to any of the scheduled castes." Zia showed them where they belonged in his Pakistan—in the group of Hindus, Christians, Scheduled Castes etc. but not among the privileged fraternity of Muslims.

With the state itself pitted against them and there being no democratic freedom to protest their persecution, the Ahmadis were at the receiving end at the hands of the orthodox Muslim groups. There were innumerable cases of harassment and persecution of individual Ahmadis both by the state and the Muslim clergy. To top it all, in April 1984, General Zia promulgated his ordinance number 20 putting severe restrictions on their religious freedom. They were prohibited from calling 'Azan' calling their places of worship as mosques and calling themselves Muslims. By one stroke of Zia's pen or fiat of the state, both of which had become one under the General's rule, the Ahmadis became aliens in their own country, their very own Islamic Republic of Pakistan.

They had become aliens in their own land for the second time since the end of the British Raj. Their original headquarters was

Quadian in Gurdaspur district of Punjab which fell on the Indian side of the divide after partition. During the partition riots, they as Muslims had to face the onslaught of Hindus and seek refuge in Pakistan. In the wake of the partition, they shifted their headquarters from Quadian in India to Rabwah in Jhung district of Pakistan where the religious head of the community stayed. Now that they were being hounded in Pakistan also, the head of the community decided to move out of the country in order to be able to preach and practice his faith in freedom. But the Zia regime was so hostile to Ahmadis that it was not an easy task.

Taking the authorities by surprise, the head of the community left Rabwah one April end evening motoring down to Karachi during wee hours of the night to catch a KLM flight for London. But a Presidential order in Zia-Ul-Haq's own hand had already reached Karachi airport directing the authorities not to allow, 'Mirza Nasir Ahmad', head of the Ahmadis, to leave Pakistan. When the Ahmadis were confronted with this order, they promptly produced the passport and flight papers which named 'Mirza Tahir Ahmad' as the person travelling by the flight. The authorities at the airport were in a quandary. They made frantic efforts to contact and check up from the higher administrative hierarchy at Karachi and Islamabad, but could not succeed as everyone was sleeping at that hour. In the end they gave up and allowed 'Mirza Tahir Ahmad' to board the flight and leave Pakistan.

No. It was not a deceptive device adopted by the Ahmadis to enable their head to get out of the country. It had so happened that in 1982 itself 'Mirza Nasir Ahmad' then head of the Ahmadi sect, had passed away. He had been succeeded by 'Mirza Tahir Ahmad' who, as the incumbent head of the community, was taking the flight to London. Evidently, Pak authorities at the highest level had not updated their knowledge about the current head of Ahmadis in Pakistan. Even dictatorships in South Asia are less efficient than their counterparts in other parts of the world. Or an act of God, as Ahmadis would say?[12]

The entire operation departure was kept so secret, thanks to the watchful eyes of General Zia, that even the Ahmadis in London did not know their head was coming until the plane reached Amsterdam. It was only in flight from Amsterdam that they were informed about the important event. They were just about in time to receive their revered religious head at London airport on 30 April, 1984.[13] Since then the head of this dynamic religious community of the sub-continent is living, preaching and practising his faith in exile in England.

For whatever reasons, the Ahmadis were among the more qualified and successful professionals in Pakistan when the new state came into being. Apart from the first foreign minister of Pakistan, Sir Zafrullah Khan, the community contributed a high percentage of Pak Air Force pilots and sizeable chunk of officer cadre in Pak Army. In an anti-Ahmadi speech at Montgomery on 15 April, 1951, one Maulvi Muhammad Ali Jullundri had said that 80 per cent of Pak Air Force pilots were Ahmadis, and branded them as potential traitors. That might have been the Maulvi's imagination, but the community did and does abound in talented people who have made their mark.

The most notable name among them is that of Dr. Abdus Salam based in America who is the only Muslim scientist born in the sub-continent to be awarded the Nobel Prize. He is the most distinguished Ahmadi hailing originally from Jhung in Punjab, Pakistan. His love for his native land was amply demonstrated when he donated Rs. 80 crores each to India and Pakistan for promotion and spread of scientific knowledge and research in the sub-continent. Incidentally, Jhung now in Pakistan has the unique distinction of producing another US based Nobel laureate—Dr. Hargobind Khurana.

The persecution and violence against such a community in Pakistan almost since its inception is only a part of the drama of violence being enacted in South Asia since the end of the Raj. If in the process a talented community of achievers, an asset in any modern society, is totally alienated in Pakistan, nobody cares. That more or less characterises the entire sub-continental society. Human resource, and indeed human life itself, is the most undervalued commodity in South Asia.

Shia-Sunni Conflicts

With the growth of sectarian orthodoxy in Pakistan, Shia-Sunni conflict was bound to erupt in a big way sooner or later.

Shia-Sunni differences are centuries old and form part of Islamic history. The schism between Shias and Sunnis existed even as the Ottoman Sultans went about conquering the whole of Asia Minor, entire Balkan peninsula, Rumanian territory at the mouth of the Danube and Russian and Mongol lands to the north of the Black Sea. The split between the orthodox Sunni and somewhat heretical Shiete sects had already become sharp by the time Sultan Mohammad II—the greatest of the Ottoman Sultans— died in 1481. His successors assumed the mantle of Sunni orthodoxy against Shiete heresy. In this capacity they waged wars against Shiete Persians and wrested the city of Baghdad and the valley of Tigris and Euphrates from the Shahs of Persia.

With such a ready-made historical background, the Shias and Sunnis of Pakistan did not have to labour hard to pick up quarrels. And if they went by the edicts of their respective Mullahs and Moulvis, it was easier to brand each other as 'Kafirs'. For different ulemas differ violently on their definition of a true Muslim. This point has been very well brought out in the exhaustive report of the Court of Inquiry into the anti-Ahmadi disturbances of 1953. Justice Mohammad Munir and Justice M.R. Kayani, who constituted the Inquiry commission, observed " Keeping in view the several definitions of a Muslim given by the Ulama, need we make any comment except that no two learned divines are agreed on this fundamental. If we attempt our own definition as each learned divine has done and that definition differs from that given by all others, we unanimously go out of the fold of Islam. And if we adopt the definition given by anyone of the Ulama, we remain Muslims according to the view of that alim but kafirs according to the definition of everyone else."

A fatwa issued by Maulana Muhammad Shafi and other teachers of Darul Uloom Deoband a long time back, came up before the Inquiry commission. It was supported by Ibrahim Ali Ch sti who had studied the subject in depth. Commenting on his views on the fatwah, the judges say: "He thinks the Shias are kafirs because they believe that Hazrat Ali shared the prophethood with our Holy Prophet..... According to the Shias all Sunnis are kafirs, and Ahl-i-Quran, namely persons who consider hadith to be unreliable and therefore not binding are, unanimously kafirs, and so are all independent thinkers."[14]

In the backdrop of such historical and ideological schism already in existence, it did not take long for Shia-Sunni conflicts to surface in Pakistan soon after its birth. A note of D.I.G., C.I.D. Punjab (Pakistan) police on the prevailing sectarian situation in 1951 autumn, as placed before Justice Munir Commission, stated " Shia-Sunni differences have been reported from different parts of the Province. The incident at village Shahpur Kanjra, where a child of 3 and a woman were killed, was, however, the first incident in which Shias became the victims of communal violence." Another note of the Police Chief of Punjab said: "At this stage, sectarian disputes took a still more ugly turn, Shia-Sunni differences began to appear and develop in several places. There was dispute about the construction of an Imambara in Krishan Nagar, Lahore, and serious apprehension of breach of peace over a tazia procession was reported from Bhakkar. In Shahpur Kanjra, about seven miles from Lahore, there was a Shia-Sunni riot in which two Shias were killed, one of them being a woman and the other a child of three."[15]

That was the beginning of Shia-Sunni disputes sprouting into skirmishes or minor violence. It was an ominous beginning though. Since then, the two communities have not looked back until they have reached a stage of no-holds-barred today. Here are a few random samples of present day Shia-Sunni killings in Pakistan.

On 14 August, 1996, a Sunni procession in the city of Karachi was attacked by some gunmen killing 12 persons and seriously wounding many others.

A few days later, on 18 August, 1996, there was a Shiite congregation at village Chak — 205 near Mailsi town in a Punjab district to mourn the death of a community member. Even as the meeting was in progress, it was attacked by a well armed group who fired indiscrimately at the gathering. The gunmen left after killing at least 18 people and wounding nearly 70 others on the spot. The Shiite spokesmen blamed a rival militant group from the majority Sunni sect of Islam for the killings. The provincial Chief Minister, Mohammad Arif Nakai, dubbed the incident as "a terrorist act," whatever it might mean.

The year 1997, the much trumpeted and lionised 50th year of

independence, opened more ferociously. On 18 January, 1997, Maulana-Zia-Ur-Rahman, senior leader of Sipah-i-Sahabah (Guardians of the Friends of the Prophet) and his deputy—Azim Tariq Rahim—were brought to the Lahore sessions court in connection with a case of murder of a Shiite leader. Just then, a massive bomb exploded outside the Sessions Court killing 25 people and injuring around 100 more. Ten of the injured succumbed to their injuries in Lahore hospital, the prominent among them being Maulana Zia-ur-Rahman himself. It was lucky that the additional sessions judge in whose court the Sunni leaders were to be produced escaped unheart, but his two stenographers were injured. The other Sunni leader—Azim Tariq Rahim— had his leg blown to pieces and was struggling for life in the hospital.

The event provoked angry reaction among Sunni groups which, in absence of any more identifiable target, got directed against Iran—the most loud and visible Shiite country in the world. A furious Sunni mob attacked and damaged the Iranian consulate in Lahore later, which evoked strong protest from Iran. Even earlier, a few days before the Lahore bomb blast, Iran had urged Pakistan to stop the anti-Shiite violence in the country. Hassan Ruhani, the deputy speaker of Iranian Parliament, had told Sahibzada Yaqoob Khan, Pakistani Foreign Minister on a visit to Iran: "we demand Islamabad to further control the terrorist groupings in Pakistan and prevent the assassination of Shias."[16]

Reacting to the event a few days later, Pakistan's caretaker Prime Minister, Malik Meraj Khalid, said: " It is imperative that the nation perceived the consequences of such secretarian polarisation and forged Unity in the ranks to eliminate the curse from the society." The usual stuff of exhortatians poured out routinely by leaders in the sub-continent after every such macabre event, multiplying by the day, without anybody stopping to take note, much less act upon. What he went on to say, at an inaugural function at Lahore Stock Exchange, was more significant. He said: " Though all such elements (arrested persons) were Muslims, yet they happened to be RAW agents, busy carrying out acts of subversion with a view to destabilise Pakistan".[17]

The allegation against RAW, the Indian counterpart of ISI, may or may not be true, but the on-going sectarian violence between

Shiite Muslims, who constitute about 15 per cent of Pakistan's population, and the dominant Sunni majority shows no signs of abatement. On 24 April, 1997, masked men on motorcycles gunned down 9 Shiite Muslims in Kharpur Tangyawala town of southern Punjab Province of Pakistan. The gunmen fired with machine-gun as soon as Zial Hussein Zargar, a Shiite embroidery shopkeeper, opened his shop, killing nine people instantly and wounding three others. In the province of Punjab alone, around 70 people were killed in Shia-Sunni violence during the first four months of 1997. And even at the time of writing, news came about five Shiite Muslims having been shot dead in Pakistan's heartland. On 3 May, 1997, some gunmen attacked a shop belonging to a Shiite Muslim in the industrial city of Faislabad killing five persons on the spot. In one week alone, ending 3rd May, 16 persons were killed in the ongoing sectarian violence.

Earlier during the last few months of 1996, hundreds of people lost their lives in this variety of Muslim-Muslim blood-letting. In this confrontation, the Sunni militants are led by Sipah-i-Sahabah Pakistan (SSP) and the Shias by two groups— Sipah-i-Muhammad Pakistan (SMP) and Tehreek-i-Jafria Pakistan (TJP), and the fight, for God knows what, goes on and on.

References

1. *Freedom At Midnight*, Larry Collins and Dominique Lapierre, 1976.
2. *Street Fighting Years*, Tariq Ali, 1987.
3. Article entitled "Communal Violence : Psycho-Social, Political and Economic Dimension" in *Denouement* Magazine, March 1990.
4. Father of Durga Das who was a village school teacher respected by all.
5. *India From Curzon to Nehru and After*, Durga Das, 1971.
6. *Communal Riots in India*, S.K. Ghosh, 1987.
7. *Lajja*, Taslima Nasrin, Penguin Books India, 1994.
8. *Freedom at Midnight*, Larry Collins and Dominique Lapierre.
9. *Friends, not Masters*, Mohammad Ayub Khan, President of Pakistan, 1967.
10. *Governments and Politics of South Asia*, by J.C. Johari, M. Nazrul Islam, W.A. Wishua Warnapala, Lik Raj Baral, Prakash Chander.
11. *From Jinnah to Zia*, Muhammad Munir, one time Chief Justice of Pakistan.

12. The event was narrated to the author by Fazal Ahmad, the Amir of Ahmadis in Bihar and a retired Police Chief of the state.
13. Fazal Ahmad worked with the religious head in London for three months beginning June, 1984.
14. Report of the Court of Inquiry into Punjab disturbances of 1953 consisting of Justice Muhammad Munir and Justice M.R. Kayani 1954.
15. *Ibid*.
16. *The Times of India* (Patna edition), dated 19 January, 1997.
17. *Ibid.*, dated 23 January, 1997.

6

Society of the Assassins

Politics of Murder

In the middle of the 11th century, an Arab religious preacher founded a highly disciplined politico-religious sect known as a "Society of the Assassins." The original Arabic word was *Hashashasin* which perhaps was derived from the addiction of his followers to hashish. The members of this intensely motivated group were supposed to kill 'bad' people on the command of their leader and considered it as their sacred duty. They believed such killing would ensure their personal salvation and usher in a new era free from all evil. The sect surfaced in Persia and Syria and existed for nearly two centuries until it was suppressed and destroyed by the Mongols in the middle of the 13 century. The words 'assassins' and ' assassination' in western languages have their root in this obscure Arabic sect.

Around nine and a half centuries have gone by since Hassan Ibn Sabah founded his "Society of the Assassins", but South Asia seems to be living in that age even today. In fact more and more so even as the people of the sub-continent approach the completion of a millennium since the birth of the society and its lesser known founder. It was not as if they have remained stuck up in the mid-eleventh century all through during these past nine and a half centuries. For around two centuries or so during the British Raj, they looked like having emerged out of that inglorious past into a more humanitarian civilized society. The astounding fact is that they started going back and lapsing into the age of the "Assassins" after the end of the colonial regime when they became masters of their own destiny. Exactly when it appeared they had all the opportunities to carve out a new future for themselves, "nearer to the heart's desire", to put it poetically, they chose to go back to the age of the "Assassins".

It had a beginning though earlier in India's protest against foreign rule. A fringe of the Indian freedom struggle in the initial stages comprised of groups of dedicated patriots who went about killing individual Britons working for the Raj in early 20th century. In December 1907, the train in which Sir Andrew Fraser, the Governor, was travelling was derailed by a bomb in a bid to kill him. In the same month, Allen, a former District Magistrate of Dacca was shot in the back but somehow survived. The most celebrated of such killings took place on 30 April, 1908 at Muzaffarpur in Bihar. On that fateful day, a horse-driven carriage believed to be carrying the English District Judge of Muzaffarpur named Kingsford was bombed. Kingsford had earlier tried cases against some terrorists as Presidency Magistrate at Calcutta, for which he was sought to be killed. As luck would have it, the occupants of the horse-carriage at the time of the fatal attack were two English ladies, Mrs. and Miss Kennedy who were both killed. Kingsford escaped because he was not in the carriage at the time. Khudi Ram Bose, who was one of the killers, was arrested, tried for murder and hanged to death in due course. He is hailed as a national hero in India today, as are many others of that kind.

In July 1909, Sir William Curzon Wyllie, Political ADC at the India office in London, was assassinated by a member of India Home Rule Society of London. In December 1909, an English Magistrate who had committed a revolutionary— Ganesh Savarkar— for trial, named Jackson, was shot dead. In December 1912, there was an attempt on the life of Lord Hardinge, the Viceroy of India, when a bomb was thrown at him while having an elephant ride at Delhi. Even as individual killings were abating in other parts of India with the spread of the Congress mass movement for independence, there was a spurt in Bengal in early 30's. Some of the notable English officials of the Raj in Bengal assassinated during 1930 and 1931 were an I.G. of Police, an I.G. of Prisons, a Divisional Commissioner, four District Magistrates and a businessman— member of the European Association. Besides, an attempt was made to shoot at the Governor of Bengal, Sir Stanley Jackson and two attempts were made on the life of the *Statesman* editor Sir Alfred Watson. And in May 1934, a more determined attempt was made to assassinate another Governor of Bengal, Sir John Anderson, at the Race Course in Darjeeling by two successive assailants.

All these individual assassinations, howsoever misguided and inhuman, had an aura of patriotism and perhaps romance about them. Their perpetrators were guided not by any selfish motives or personal vendetta but were misinspired by a worthy cause—freedom from foreign rule. Similar 'patriotic' killings were being resorted to by the Irish in their struggle for independence from Britain. The Sinn Fein, Party of Irish freedom-fighters, formed in 1918, and its militant wing, the Irish Republican Army (IRA) formed in 1919 had raised killing to the level of a concerted policy. The IRA is still doing it in the name of liberating Northern Ireland. One of its most distinguished victims was Lord Mountbatten, India 's celebrated last Viceroy and the man who played a historic role in the grant of independence to the subcontinent.

Fortunately for India, Gandhiji appeared on the nationalist scene at a time when the freedom movement was poised for a big advance. When at the peak of his mass civil disobedience campaign in February 1922 an irritate mob of agitationists hacked and burnt to death 22 policemen at village Chauri Chaura in U.P., he instantly called off the entire campaign itself bringing it to an abrupt end, much to the annoyance of his followers. He effectively rescued the freedom struggle from taking the violent adventurist course and changed its entire direction. The fraternity of patriotic "Assassins" was superseded and swarmed by the Gandhian mass movement based on non-violence. Once Gandhiji was able to assume full command, India's struggle for freedom remained remarkably free from blood spilling until the approach of independence and partition.

"The Murder Manual"

The "Society of the Assassins" had a new avtar in post-independence India in late 1960's. A left-wing extremist group of Bengal led by Charu Majumdar bestowed a new glamour and legitimacy to murder of so-called 'class enemies'. An ardent admirer of Mao Ze Dong of China, he seemed to have taken the Maoist dictum 'political power grows out of the barrel of a gun' too seriously and proceeded to formalise it in his own way. In early 1969, his radical outfit launched a campaign of annihilation of 'class enemies', which was nothing more or less than brutal murder of individuals dubbed as 'class enemies'. These included landlords, rich peasants, village moneylenders, police informers and landlords' agents who were mostly from the poorer strata. Starting from Bengal, the annihilation campaign spread to the Indian states of Bihar, Andhra Pradesh and Kerala during 1969-70. This movement will be dealt with at some length in the next part of the book devoted exclusively to the Indian scenario.

More important than the number of individual 'class enemies' killed by this outfit was the raising of the act of killing to the level of a cult. Charu Majumdar actually drew up kind of a "Murder Manual" to guide his followers in pursuit of their task. He envisaged the formation of 'murder squads' in rural areas to carry out the task of annihilation of selected targets. The constitution of the 'murder squad' was to be wholly conspiratorial and the conspiracy was to be between individuals on a person to person basis. No third member of the group was supposed to know what the other two members were doing or planning to do. The killer squads were supposed to use conventional weapons such as knives, choppers, swords, rods etc. which could be easily available in rural areas. The targets were to be selected and murders committed in a manner which created maximum impact on the rural masses. In the initial stages of the annihilation campaign, the killings were deliberately brutal and savage aimed at creating "red terror" in the countryside among landlords and better off peasants and their supporters. And all such killings of 'class enemies ' were loudly owned and acclaimed by the party's news-sheet entitled "Liberation."

Charu Majumdar openly said that any youngman (of course he had to be a Marxist) who could stab a policemen to death in the streets of Calcutta was fit to be his party cadre. Many idealistic young boys and girls were attracted to the ideology and started participating in killings of petty landlords and moneylenders in rural areas and policemen in the streets of Calcutta. In the process, an intellectual like the Vice-Chancellor of Jadhavpur University was also murdered during the peak of the annihilation campaign in Bengal. For some time the terror created in Calcutta was such that streets in many areas were deserted after dusk.

But politics of murder has its own dialecties. "Red terror" was followed by state terror on a large scale which more than matched the strength and capacity of the cadre of killers. Many bright young idealists of Bengal and other parts of the country, who had been attracted to the movement by the promise of an imminent revolution, were 'liquidated' in course of the state action against the outfit. Charu Majumdar himself died in police custody which was officially made out to be a case of death due to heart ailment, but was widely believed to be one of counter-annihilation by the state. After Charu Majumdar's dubious custodial death, the chapter of individual killings of selected 'class enemies' was closed, but the movement left an indelible mark on the politics of the sub-continent. His "Murder Manual" vanished with him, but his cult of murder not only remained intact but also got a new respectability. Wider acceptability of murder, cold, calculated, conspiratorial, even brutal, as a valid instrument of politics was one of his most important legacies to the practice of politics in India.

V.I.P. Victims: The Second Round

After the assassination of all apex leaders of South Asia, Aung San of Burma, Mahatma Gandhi of India, Liaquat Ali Khan of Pakistan, S.W.R.D Bandarnaike of Sri Lanka and Sheikh Mujibur Rahman of Bangladesh, in the wake of independence, the curtain seemed to have dropped on the dark scene. But it proved to be only an interval in the on-going drama of political assassinations at the apex. The curtain lifted again in the 80's, marking the beginning of the second round, spilling over to the early 90's.

The scene opened this time round in Bangladesh. After the ruthless elimination of Sheikh Mujibur Rahman, the founder of the Republic, in an army coup on 15 August, 1975, power ultimately passed on to general Zia-Ur-Rahman who emerged as the military strongman of the country. Under virtual martial law regulations, he assumed the Presidency of the Republic which was confirmed by a referendum on 30 May, 1977. He was formally elected as President in the election held on 3 June, 1978. But history repeated itself when President Zia-Ur-Rahman of Bangladesh was himself assassinated in another bloody army coup in the district of Chittagaon in May 1981.

Many in South Asia and the world regarded the execution of

Zulfiquar Ali Bhutto in April, 1979 also as 'Judicial murder' of the popularly elected Prime Minister of Pakistan who was toppled by General Zia-Ul-Haque earlier in July 1977. This perception and the manner in which Bhutto was hanged to death at 2 a.m. on 4 April, 1979 had a little history behind it. He took over as the President and Chief Martial Law Administrator on 20 December, 1971 as the saviour of Pakistan after its defeat in the Indo-Pak war and separation of Bangladesh. In his first broadcast to the nation, he said: "I have come in at a decisive moment in the history of Pakistan. We are facing the worst crisis in our country's life, a deadly crisis. We have to pick-up pieces, very small pieces, but we will make a new Pakistan." People had great hopes from him and he did everything, in his initial years, to build up their hopes. To endear himself to the masses he projected himself as a great Socialist and an ardent Islamist. While his socialism remained largely confined to rhetoric and tokenism, he tried to establish his Islamic credentials by declaring Islam as the State religion of Pakistan. He was the Knight in shining armour to protect and propel Pakistan to greatness.

But the shine started wearing thin sooner than one could imagine. He was found out to be not a democrat nor really a socialist but essentially a powerist. For instance, the state of Emergency which was proclaimed when Bhutto came to power in unusual circumstance continued throughout his regime. His socialist pretensions were belied when he unceremoniously dropped Dr. Mubbasir Hasan, the well-known leftist economist and one of the architects of PPP's economic platform, from his cabinet in order to humiliate him. As for his own code of political conduct, one writer narrates: "He was harsh to friends and cruel to opponents and politics was a game that he wanted to play without any reference to individuals.... One of the trusted lieutenants Ghulam Mustafa Khar had to bow down to the wishes of Bhutto and relinquish the office of the Chief Minister of Punjab. He was driven by policemen in car all day long blind-folded and then abandoned at night seventy miles outside Lahore."[1]

When such a person secured a run away victory in the General Elections held in March 1977, his PPP having won 154 out of 200 seats in the Pak National Assembly, alarm bells rang all along the political spectrum. The opposition Pakistan National Alliance (PNA) cried foul and alleged massive poll rigging. The Tehrick-e-Istaklal leader, Air Marshal (Retd.) Asghar Khan said: "We always knew and believed that whenever elections took place in Pakistan under Bhutto's regime, they would be totally rigged and utterly devoid of all ethical character."[2] A virulent anti-Bhutto agitation was launched by the combined opposition in course of which thousands of processions and demonstrations were organised all over Pakistan by political parties, women and student organizations, lawyers etc. Bhutto responded by putting hundreds of thousands of people behind the bars. It was in such a background that military— the most stable factor in Pakistani Establishment— stepped in. Bhutto's trusted Army Chief— General Zia-Ul-Haq, took over the administration of the country in his own hands and imposed Martial Law on 5 July, 1977.

It was probably under the mistaken notion of Bhutto's growing unpopularity that Zia-Ul-Haq announced to hold elections within 90 days of his taking over. But the impression was soon proved wrong. After his overthrow by the Army, Bhutto soon acquired a martyr image in the eyes of the general mass and started addressing large public meetings and rallies. That brought forth the prospect of Bhutto's return to power once again if elections were held in the near future, with frightful consequences for hundreds and perhaps thousands of those directly or indirectly responsible for his overthrow. With Bhutto's tracks record of frightening vendetta, it was a prospect which Zia and his cohorts could entertain only at the risk of their own physical liquidation. They decided to act in time and raked up an old case of murder of a political activist in which Bhutto was supposed to be involved. That enabled them to put Bhutto behind the bars pending prolonged investigation and trial.

Once having done that, Zia was in a bind. For if Bhutto was a martyr of military take-over outside the prison, he became more of a martyr inside the prison. If he escaped punishment in the murder case and came out and fought election, no one could stop his return to power. That would have meant countertrial of Zia and innumerable others for high treason and consequential punishment including death. It boiled down to gallows either for Bhutto or for Zia.

Trial of any political leader for howsoever grave a crime in such a situation under such an absolutist regime would be suspect. Trial of Z.A. Bhutto, the ousted Prime Minister, under the military dictatorship of Zia-Ul-Haq, who had ousted him, was suspect from the beginning. His conviction on the count of murder ending ultimately in his execution was only more so. Dr. K.L. Kamal writes: "Without going into legal intricacies and Bhutto trials which lasted a year and half it may be safely stated that guilty or not, Bhutto's trial was political, neither criminal nor Islamic."[3] In the circumstances, Bhutto's hanging was largely perceived as" judicial murder" outside Pakistan—just another case of a top South Asian leader being physically liquidated, this time round judicially.

It was not necessarily so perceived in Pakistan itself, not at any rate by those who knew better. Justice Mohammad Munir, retired Chief Justice of Pakistan, has made only a brief comment on Bhutto trial in a book, which by implication tells a lot. He writes: "After the longest trial in history he has been convicted of murder and sentenced to death and the appeal from the conviction has been dismissed after the longest hearing and by the longest judgement in history. He has now been executed."[4] The very brevity of the observation almost clinches the issue. The judgement and the sentence could not possibly be faulted. And Justice Munir ought to have known.

In fact the case itself, "the longest trial in history" and the long judgement, would indicate that Bhutto was not really a victim but a practitioner of the politics of murder. Bhutto's own track record of his six-year rule was hardly flattering. At the hight of anti-Bhutto agitation in June 1977, an influential PPP man from Baluchistan had alleged that Bhutto had been advised by a high party echelon to plan for large scale killings of his opponents to crush the movement against him.

In the circumstances, the alarm at Bhutto's execution was not based on presumption of his innocence of the murder charge. It was an alarm at the audacity of Zia's regime in bringing such a populist mass leader, with considerable mass base still intact, to book for his crime or crimes, even to the extent of inflicting the highest punishment. Because in post-independence South Asia, equality before law is more an exception than the rule. Especially when it comes to making politicians in power to account for their deeds or misdeeds. Bhutto's hanging raised eye brows, or was even dubbed as "judicial murder" by many, not because he was deemed innocent but because he was Bhutto, the all powerful elected Prime Minister of Pakistan ousted by the Army Chief.

If heads at the appex of power were tumbling, literally and physically, in Pakistan and Bangladesh, how could India lag behind? After all the three peoples came from the same stock and were one under British rule before August 1947. It happened in India with a bang in that grey autumn of 1984. Around 9 a.m. on 31 October, 1984, Indira Gandhi, the Charismatic Prime Minister of India, was pumped with bullets by two of her own security guards just as she stepped out of her residence to grant an interview to a team of foreign newsmen waiting in a close-by room. She fell down lump upon the ground and died. It was in retaliation for the famous or infamous "Operation Blue Star" launched by the Army in June 1984 in course of which the militant Sikh preacher— Bhindrawale— and hundreds of others were killed and the Golden Temple at Amritsar, the holiest of Sikh shrines, was considerably damaged. The inexorable logic of state violence grievously wounding the psyche of an entire religious community appeared to have caught up with India's top political leadership, more of which later. The most shocking aspect of the episode was that the Prime Minister's own security guards, those entrusted with protecting her life, themselves shot her dead. In a split second of anguished surprise, she exclaimed "What are you doing"? and fell down.

About four years later, Pakistan's all powerful military ruler, General Zia-Ul-Haq, died in a mysterious plane crash inside Pakistan. In August 1988, the V.V.I.P. aircraft took off from Bahawalpur with President Zia and some among the top brass of Pak Army on board and crashed soon after leaving no survivors. As usually happens in such disasters taking VIP lives, official investigations into the crash went virtually clueless. The crash was reportedly attributed to some mechanical fault in the aircraft, which appeared highly surprising considering the extraordinary status of the passengers it was carrying; or some such innocuous factors which carried little conviction. It was, on the other hand, widely believed that the crash was man-made aimed at elimination of President Zia-Ul-Haq physically, which it resulted in. It is another matter that not many tears were shed in Pakistan, or outside for that matter, over the tragedy.

The scene shifted back to India again in the summer of 1991. Rajiv Gandhi, a member of the charismatic Nehru-Gandhi clan which had ruled India for more than 37 years out of 42 between August 1947 and November 1989, was blown to pieces by a suicide bomber of Sri Lanka's LTTE at a public meeting on 21 May, 1991. Rajiv Gandhi had been bestowed the Prime Ministership of India, which had almost become a family legacy, after the assassination of his mother— Indira Gandhi — in October 1984, by a grieving nation still under shock. With all the goodwill of the people under his belt, he carried on his job with elan initially even though he was too inexperienced and a little too refined for the dirt and muck of political practice in India.

His in-experience told in course of time and he lost his job when his Congress party was defeated in the parliamentary election of November 1989. He was succeeded by his one-time most trusted lieutenant and Finance Minister— V.P. Singh— who until less than a year earlier was swearing his loyalty to Rajiv and yet mounted a bitter tirade against him in November elections. (Nothing unusual about practice of politics in India). V.P. Singh, the wily politician who managed to reach the top slot in course of a political career spanning less than 20 years when senior leaders of freedom movement vintage were knocking at the periphery of power, headed a makeshift Coalition Government which lasted only eleven months. Another uneasy coalition headed by a veteran politician, Chandrashekhar, an ex-socialist, ex-Congressman, ex-Janta Party and so on, came to power on the support of Rajiv Gandhi's Congress Party. This Coalition Government had even a shorter tenure of nearly four months or so. When Rajiv Gandhi felt confident enough to face the electorate, his Congress Party withdrew support to the coalition, pulling down the Government and plunging the country into another parliamentary election.

It was in course of campaigning during this mid-term poll that Rajiv Gandhi had been to Perumbdur in Tamil Nadu state down south on 21 May, 1991. At the venue of the meeting, the woman suicide bomber—a hard-core LTTE cadre—approached ostensibly to garland him and blew him and herself off with a powerful explosive device wrapped around her body. Though out of office at the time, he was definitely on a come-back trail when he was bumped off. He had encurred the wrath of LTTE by despatching an Indian Peace Keeping Force to tame the Tamil militants in Sri Lanka under Indo-Sri Lanka Accord when he was Prime Minister. The LTTE did not forgive him for that. They did not like his becoming the Prime Minister of India once again. It was politics of murder, pure and simple.

The South Asian circuit of this brand of politics was completed two years later. On 1st May, 1993, R. Premadasa, the President of Sri Lanka was bumped off in a repeat performance of Rajiv Gandhi's killing. As the President was inspecting a big May Day Parade organized by his United National Party in Colombo, a suicide-bomber approached his jeep. Even as his security men were trying to hold him, the explosive device tied to his body went off reducing Premadasa and himself to ashes.

The killing of Premadasa came as a bit of a surprise for these not quite familiar with the labyrinths of political feuds and intrigues in latter day Sri Lanka. For Premadasa was one prominent leader of United National Party who was opposed to the presence of the Indian Peace Keeping Force on Sri Lankan soil almost from the beginning. He was the one who had talked loud of Sri Lankans themselves— the Sinhalees and Tamils— solving their problems without the big brother India poking its nose. He was the one who had tenaciously worked for withdrawal of the Indian troops from Sri Lanka and openly welcomed the withdrawal when it was effected. After being elected President, he had even taken initiatives to open a dialogue with LTTE which of course did not bear fruit. In any case, President R. Premadasa was a less likely target of LTTE's mission of murder than many other prominent leaders of the country. But politics of murder has a logic of its own. Premadasa was a victim of that logic.

Head-hunting in Colombo

Of all the countries of South Asia, Sri Lanka, the most peaceful island country under the Raj, has become the worst victim of politics of murder today. It started after the shift of power from the immediate post-independence nationalist elites to the latter-day more populist vernacular politicians. The worst phase began since around mid-80's with the intensification of Tamil separatist movement in the island. Even as President Junius Jayavardhane, a chip off the old block, was trying to hold his country together by accommodating the moderate Tamil outfits and leaders, an extremist Sinhala organization had come up in the southern heartland of the country. It was kind of a Sinhala counterpart of LTTE in central and south Sri Lankan, without of course the armed teeth of the latter. It was proving to be great embarrassment to Sri Lankan political establishment playing a delicate balancing game to keep the country in one piece. The Government could not afford to ride rough shod with the Sinhala extremists for fear of alienating the vast Sinhala majority and Buddhist clergy.

It was at this stage that politics of murder came into full play in the unfortunate country. Mysterious murder squads seemed to have gone into action in and around Colombo. Mysterious murders of selected political activists started taking place with sinister regularity for some time. Only dead bodies were found abandoned in remote areas without much fuss or any clue about the killers. But victims in this round, as long as it lasted, were mainly Sinhala extremists belonging to the militant outfit referred to above. And the most prominent victim of this mysterious series of murders was its firy leader— Vijaya Veera— who was threatening to emerge as a Sinhala Frankestein to counter the LTTE. No one knew nor knows till today who killed Vijaya Veera or got him killed, but it was politics of murder with extraordinary fineness.

Once murder became a tacitly accepted instrument of politics, there was no stopping it. In February 1991, Sri Lankan's Defence Minister— Vijayaratne— was killed in a devastating explosion in Colombo, which also took as many as 38 more lives. It was one of the worst terrorist strikes by LTTE which was increasingly assuming more and yet more ruthless and brutal posture in its onslaught against the Sinhala dominated Government of Sri Lanka. There had been an earlier attempt also to blow up the Government headquarters during Jayavardhane Presidency but the attempt had failed. This time it succeeded in knocking off the Defence Minister and many others.

Two years later on 23 April, 1993, Lalit Atulathmudali a Minister in President Jayavardhane's Government and the ebullient Government spokesman during the hectic Indo-Sri Lanka parleys of mid 80's was killed while addressing a public meeting. Lalit was a young and upcoming leader of Sri Lankan's Grand Old Party— the United National Party (UNP)—cast in the mould of the old western oriented nationalist elites who had takenover from the British after independence. He represented the modern, secular and upper class traditions of the UNP coming on since the time of Don Stephen Senanayake, the first Prime Minister of independent Sri Lanka. On the other hand, R. Premadasa, also of the UNP who was elected President in December 1988, belonged to the other strata of nativist indigenous politicians rooted in the Buddhist masses. Premadasa was actually the first vernacular politician to assume the leadership of UNP and the Government of Sri Lanka. The ascendency of Lalit Atulathmudali in UNP could pose a challenge to Premadasa's leadership of the party and government. In this background, Lalit's assassination led to rumours and suspicions linking R. Premadasa— the incumbent President — to the event. Fingers were raised against the President suspecting his complicity in the conspiracy to eliminate Lalit. Premadasa of course blamed it on the LTTE. Nobody knew; nobody knows.

In less than a month, as already described earlier, President Premadasa himself was blown off by a suicide bomber on 1st May, 1993. And the game of political murder continued. After Premadasa's physical elimination, the office of President had to be filled up. Even as the country was gearing up to elect a new President, Gamini Dussanayake, a senior leader of UNP, was killed in another gruesome incident. The grand Old Party—UNP—which had ruled Sri Lanka at a stretch after dislodging Srimayo Bandarnaike's Sri Lanka Freedom Party over two decades ago, suddenly became leaderless. The party had no option except to put up Dussanayake' widow as its candidate for the top job. She contested the Presidential election as the UNP candidate and was defeated by Chandrika Kumartunga of Sri Lanka Freedom Party (SLFP), who is the incumbent President of the country today.

President Chandrika Kumartunga's own immediate family

had been victim of politics of murder twice in the past. Once it was her father SWRD Bandarnaike who as Prime Minister fell victim to an assassin's bullet in 1959. Next time round, her husband Vijay Kumartunga was killed in 1988. And news comes now that the late President Premadasa has been posthumously found guilty of her husband's murder in 1988. It seems it was politics of murder all the way, in which the distinction between killer and the killed got blurred. Everybody seemed to be killing everybody else and getting killed in the process.

And the sinister game goes on without any visible sign of stopping. On 11 February, 1997, Nalanda Illavala, a nephew of President Chandrika Kumartunga and M.P. belonging to her ruling Sri Lanka Freedom Party, was killed in Ratnapura district about 100 kilometres south of Colombo. Illavala was on his way to file nominations for his party cadres to contest local body elections when he was shot with automatic rifles. Punchi Nilame— the UNP M.P. from Ratnapura district— and Mahinda Ratnathilake, a former Mayor of Ratnapura belonging to the UNP, are the principal accused in the killing of the ruling party M.P.

To cap it all, there was an ominous grenade explosion on 3 March, 1997 near the Queen's cottage residence of President Chandrika Kumartunga at Numara Eliya, about 180 kilometres east of Colombo, where she was the main speaker at an election rally. A 17-year-old Tamil youth Sendil Kumar, suspected to be a suicide bomber, a la LTTE instantly died in the explosion believed to have been triggered by himself. President Chandrika Kumartunga told her people that LTTE whose trademark was the use of suicide bombers was planning to assassinate her. Hovering clouds of assassinations continue to darken the political horizon of Sri Lanka.

The Killing Fields of Karachi

If Colombo, the capital of Sri Lanka, has turned into a virtual land mine for political elites, Karachi, one time capital of Pakistan, has become a killing field for the laity and the elites alike. Every variety of conflict situation that the state of Pakistan is plagued with has its bloody echo in this port city. Sectarian conflicts between Shias and Sunnis, ethnic clashes between Pathans or Afgan refugees and Sindhis and above all running battles between the indigenous Sindhis and Mohajirs have all been taking their toll among the beleagured people of this commercial capital of Pakistan. At one time or the other, each one of such conflicts, sectarian, ethnic, linguistic and regional, has resulted in considerable blood-letting in this embattled city.

In regard to the more loud and open killings, the pattern is by now familiar, as in some other parts of Pakistan also. A group of motorised masked gunmen go about spraying bullets on their opponents killing quite a few on the spot and leaving a trail of bitterness around. This is avenged with equal noise and ruthlessness by the other group sooner than later, keeping up the tempo of killings and cojunter-killings. For instance, a fundamentalist group of Sunnis sprays bullets on a Shia congregation at a mosque and vice versa. Sometimes, there are firings and counter firings by armed groups in case they chance to confront each other. One thing is common among all the militant outfits. There is no dearth of firearms in possession of any group. They are all flush with AK 47, stenguns etc. thanks to the large influx of sophisticated weaponry in the wake of the Afghan civil strife. The people of Karachi have to pay in their blood for the role Pakistan played as a conduit for American arming of diverse Afghan Mujahidean groups to fight against Soviet occupation of that unfortunate country.

Of all the conflicts bleeding Karachi during the last couple of years, the one between the Sindhis and Mohajirs has been the most lethal and devastating. The Mohajirs are the Muslims who came over to Pakistan from India in large numbers in the wake of the partition. The word Mohajir itself is of Arabic origin which in simple terms means migrants or may be refugees. But it has another connotation also which makes it more respectable. History has it that when Meeca became hostile to the Holy Prophet, He moved over to Medina to carry on with His preaching's and spreading the message of Islam far and wide. All faithfuls who went over to Madina with the Holy Prophet were referred to as Mohajirs. They were more than ordinary migrants; they were sort of holy migrants. The Muslim migrants from India perhaps imagined or imagine themselves to be in the same category as those who went over to

Medina with the Holy Prophet. They pride in calling themselves Mohajirs which connotes something more than mere migrants or refugees.

They could legimately pride themselves in being the principal protagonists of Pakistan movement before partition. The fight for Pakistan was mainly carried on in the plains of northern India, and of course the eastern wing, rather than in Sindh and North West Frontier Province where the Muslims were in overwhelming majority. Sindh joined in the Pakistan movement rather late when its leader G.M. Sayed switched his loyalties over to Jinnah and NWFP had returned a Congress majority even in the Provincial elections of 1946. It was the Muslim leadership of U.P., Bihar and the rest of India which was in the forefront of the agitation for creation of Pakistan. To that extent, the Muslim migrants to Pakistan from U.P., Bihar and other parts of India could be considered among the architects of Pakistan. Quaid-i-Azam Jinnah himself was from Bombay and Liaquat Ali Khan from U.P. The migrants from India could shine in the reflected glory of the two founding fathers of Pakistan, if they so desired.

But they were no real 'Mohajirs' in the original Arabic sense referring to the faithfuls who migrated from Mecca to escape persecution. Most of the erstwhile Muslim League leaders and activists, who remained in India after partition were absorbed in the country's political mainstream by joining the Congress or other political parties. Those who opted to go over to Pakistan did so to seek new pastures for their economic betterment. The new state was beckoning them with immense career prospects and virgin resources. At its birth, Pakistan hardly had any industrial giants like Tatas and Birlas and the quantum of professional talents to man the rapidly expanding state and commercial services was severely limited. The migrants from India included those with capital to invest—the landed aristocracy and the upper middle class—as well as the professional products of the prestigious Aligarh Muslim University. The latter found it easier to compete and land with plum jobs in the new state than they could hope for in the highly competitive job market in India.

They were migrants, pure and simple, who moved over to Pakistan in search of material well being and they largely made good. In the heartland of Pakistan—Punjab—they got easily assimilated first because of linguistic and cultural affinities. They shared the same way of life and spoke the same language because most of them were from the other half of Punjab which remained a part of India. Second, Punjab was no virgin land for Muslims from India to fatten themselves economically by pioneering economic development. It had enough business and professional talents and manpower of its own so there was no question of migrants from India filling any vacuum and calling the shots. They could only mingle and share in all economic activities with the local people.

Not so in Sindh. It was a backward and underdeveloped region still mired in feudal socio-economic milieu. While the landed aristocracy symbolised by the likes to Bhuttos and Zardaris comprised the upper strata, the vast majority of people belonged to the class of 'cutters of wood and hewers of water.' The Hindus who constituted the relatively small middle and commercial classes before partition fled to India in course of the partition riots and their aftermath. The socio-economic vacuum created by almost total Hindu migration was filled by the Muslim migrants from India. Most of them were well qualified, hard-working people who came to occupy important positions in business and services in urban centres of Sindh like Karachi and Hyderabad. Karachi being the national capital of Pakistan during the first decade after independence, until Ayub Khan shifted the capital to Islamabad in Punjab, provided ample scope for their vertical and horizontal expansion.

As they prospered and proliferated in Sindh, particularly in Karachi, the Sindhis became more and more jealous of their growing prosperity which they felt was at their own cost. In course of time they became an eyesore not only to the Sindhis but to other indigenous ethnic groups also including Punjabis. It is said that one of the factors which prompted Ayub Khan to shift the capital from Karachi to Islamabad was to free the Pak establishment from the strangle hold of the migrants. In any case, they came to acquire a distinct identity of their own, somewhat separate from the native Pakistanis, some kind of a recent incarnation of the Tamils in Sri Lanka. In the run of the mill politics of the country, their Indian roots began to be touted sometimes even to cast suspicion on their loyalty to Pakistan. They on their part combined to emerge as a significant political block in the name of the Mohajir Quami Movement (MQM). The MQM claims to speak for Pakistan's 22 million Mohajirs or migrants from India and aims at securing their rightful place in the country of their adoption. Their numbers largely concentrated in Sindh, has endowed them with enough muscle to assert themselves politically, particularly in Sindh. That stands at the root of their running feud with the native Sindhis which has assumed bloody proportions in course of the last few years.

In their struggle to find a place under the sum in their second home, commensurate with their numerical and economic strength, they have been at the receiving end both under the military and democratic regimes. The military rulers from Punjab who thrived on concentration of power in their hands never liked a possible rival power centre in Sindh. And the democratic regimes of the two Bhuttos— the father and the daughter— thrived on native Sindhi vote bank based on hostility to the outsiders. In the bargain the Mohajirs took to arms against what they called 'Sindhi Chauvinism'. This brought about violent clashes and running battles between the Mohajirs represented by the MQM and native Sindhis represented by the Pakistan People's Party (PPP) of Zulfiquar Ali and Benazir.

The Mohajirs' woes multiplied manifold when Benazir Bhutto of the PPP came to power at the end of General Zia's regime. They were hounded both by the PPP and the government of the day. A large number of criminal cases were started against MQM activists, large numbers were arrested and large numbers died in police custody and encounters. Altaf Hussen, the top leader of the MQM, had to take refuge in London where he was living in exile till the time of writing. According to MQM sources, about 1000 of their party functionaries fell victims to extra judicial killings during the last few years of PPP rule in Pakistan and Sindh. More than that number were killed in frequent gun battles between the PPP and MQM ranks in the streets of Karachi.

In course of time, a splinter group led by Haqiqi broke away from the parent MQM and started on a hostile course. The parent

MQM leaders claim that the break-away Haqiqi group was a creation of the government with a view to splitting and check-mating the Mohajir Movement. Whatever be the truth, there were violent clashes between the principal and break-away MQM groups themselves causing considerable loss of life. Sporadic clashes continue even though the parent MQM is now sharing power with Pakistan Muslim League in a coalition government in Sindh. A newspaper columnist sums up "Away from the vanity estates of Clifton lies the 'other Karachi' where violence is often the order of the day and rival factions of the MQM are still engaged in slugging it out in broad daylight."[5]

In the midst of regular shootings, gun-battles and cross firings between warring sectarian, ethnic and factional groups, macabre custodial deaths and fake police encounters involving the common cadres, the killing fields of Karachi also had their toll of some prominent personalities. In the first week of May 1993, Azim Ahmad Tariq, the incumbent president of MQM was shot dead at his residence in Karachi. Perhaps the most gory of such open killings which shook even the sluggish conscience of Pakistani people took place in September 1996. Murtaza Bhutto, the lone surviving son of Zulfiquar Ali Bhutto, brother of the then ruling Prime Minister Benazir Bhutto and head of a break-away group of PPP opposed to his sister Benazir, was shot dead along with seven of his men by policemen as he approached his residence in Clifton. (The police claimed it to be a case of encounter with his armed men, which incidentally may go down as an epitaph on the demise of what was once the time-honoured institution of law and order.)

The unabashed killing of Murtaza Bhutto by an arm of the state itself ostensibly hastened the dismissal of Benazir's Government by the President of Pakistan in the autumn of 1996. Her ill-famed husband— Asif Ali Zardari— has been accused of conspiring to get Murtaza physically eliminated. To cap it all, Benazir herself has now been accused to complicity, along with her Government's Home Minister Nasrulla Babar, in the murder of two close relatives of Altaf Hussen, the MQM Chief in exile. By a queer twist of destiny, Benazir, the erstwhile glamourous Prime Minister of Pakistan, is being investigated for a kind of political murder for which her husband is also currently being investigated and her father was once investigated. That almost epitomises the overpowering sway of politics of murder over Pakistan and perhaps the whole of South Asia as the sub-continent approaches half a century of independence from British rule.

To complete the record of Karachi killings, it is estimated that over 2000 people were killed in ethnic, sectarian and political clashes in 1995 and nearly 1000 in 1996 in the city of Karachi alone.

References

1. *Pakistan—The Garrison State*, Dr. K.L. Kamal, 1982.
2. *Bhutto: A Political Biography*, Salman Taseer.
3. *Pakistan—The Garrison State*, Dr. K.L. Kamal, 1982.
4. *From Jinnah to Zia*, Justice Mohammad Munir, Retired Chief Justice of Pakistan, 1981.
5. Dina Vakil in *The Times of India* (Patna Edition), dated 25 April, 1997.

SECTION II

THE PERSPECTIVE

7

Free Trade in Terror

Free Terror Area

Fifty years ago, every school Atlas depicted South Asia as one compact block comprising India, Burma and Ceylon painted green or yellow or whatever as the most precious constituent of the British overseas Empire. Today it is five countries on the map—India, Pakistan, Bangladesh, Myanmar (Burma) and Sri Lanka—painted in different hues. There is nothing intrinsically unusual or wrong about that. Throughout recorded history, maps of diverse areas and territories have been drawn and re-drawn all over the world peacefully or through wars or otherwise, and the process continues. History knows no full stop. There is no finality in the affairs of man and his world, but India, Pakistan and Bangladesh have to exist and stay as separate, distinct and independent states in their own way and own right. No one should have any illusions on that. What is unusual is the distances the South Asian countries particularly India, Pakistan and Bangladesh, have travelled from each other during the last 50 years in spite of their geographical proximity. The present generation of their citizens would hardly know that their parents and grandparents could be as much at home in Karachi as in Calcutta and could just as easily travel from Dacca to Lucknow or Delhi to Lahore. An artist or singer or actor could live at Lahore and make his mark on the stage or film-studios of Calcutta or Bombay and vice versa. An average Indian or Pakistani or Bangladeshi today would find it difficult to imagine it was so only 50 years ago and could ever be so once again. Highly surprising in this jet age when any one can hop over from Dacca to Delhi to Lahore twice over in course of 24 hours. Even as distances are shrinking, being measured in Units of time rather than miles, and being reduced from days to hours, the people of these countries are drifting wider and wider apart.

Economics is one compelling factor which has induced

countries in one geographical area to come closer together. The benefits in terms of enhanced economic prosperity acruing from European Common Market, launched in the 60's, have driven the perpetually feuding and warring countries of western Europe into a kind of union which would have been unthinkable even 30 years ago. Nearer home, economic benefits have joined the ethnically, religiously, linguistically, politically diverse peoples of South East Asia into a kind of Union (ASEAN) which has become the envy of all developing countries. This latter grouping particularly, with its remarkable success story, caused ripples, if not waves, even in the sluggish waters of South Asian political stream. The political elites of South Asia may lag behind in everything worth aspiring for in the world today, but not in showing that they also ran. Nearly twelve years ago, they decided they would also enter their august name in the fashionable register of regional groupings. They sat down one fine morning and gave themselves a big name— South Asian Association for Regional Cooperation (SAARC) to proclaim they had also arrived.

Promoting economic cooperation, cultural relations, tourism, poverty alleviation, good-neighbourliness etc. have all been there on SAARC agenda since its inception. But through all these years since it came into being over a decade ago, it has meant nothing more than addition of one more pompous name to the catalogue of regional economic groupings proliferating in the world. One is reminded of its existence only through telecast of a little footage about one or the other country, may be about its fauna and flora, on the TV once in a blue moon. Or of course through its annual meets at various levels— at the levels of Secretaries, Ministers and Summit— held with monotonous regularity in one or the other of the seven countries it comprises of — India, Pakistan, Bangladesh, Sri Lanka, Nepal, Maldives and Bhutan. The meetings begin and end with nothing more than the usual bon-homie among the dignitaries of the seven countries, the usual warm rhetoric and touting of the usual platitudes. What more could be expected of a grouping the two most important members of which— India and Pakistan—were hardly even on speaking terms still yesterday?

They met at the summit level for the ninth time at Male — the capital of Maldives— in May 1997 with a promise of achieving something more concrete. One of their major 'achievements' was the decision to set up an 'eminent persons' group to assess the performance of this 'august' association since its birth. That was quite in keeping with a practice familiar in the affairs of state or public administration. If you have no work to do or do not intend doing anything, you appoint a committee to go into this or that.

But that was only one part of the task they performed at Male. The more important achievement of SAARC Summit of May 1997 was the decision or promise to form the South Asian Free Trade Area (SAFTA) by the year 2001. They had been talking of SAFTA for sometime in SAARC forums and even had fixed a deadline of achieving it by the year 2004. By advancing the deadline to 2001, the SAARC leaders seem to have given notice that they are more serious about their job now. For the core of a regional grouping, as in the case of European Union or ASEAN, is economic and commercial integration. SAARC would have any meaning only if the seven countries are able to integrate economically through formation of Free Trade Zone or something approaching that in the near future.

But their declaration at Male to establish SAFTA by 2001 carries little conviction. They have travelled so far away from each other that their coming together in some kind of an economic Union within such a short time frame appears a remote possibility. Here again, the track record of the two major countries — India and Pakistan — has been not very encouraging. In regard to closer economic cooperation, both India and Pakistan have been looking in other directions rather than towards each other. India has been bending over backwards to join the ASEAN and somehow gain entry into the charmed circle of Asia Pacific Economic Cooperation (APEC). It has now cast its eyes on another much wider integration with the littoral countries of the Indian Ocean which could link it to Australia and many countries in Africa. Pakistan, on the other hand has been forging links with Economic Cooperation Organization joining it to Turkey, Iran and other 'Islamic' States of Central Asia.

It is a queer way of looking at things, which has come to be the trade mark of SouthAsian countries. While economics is superceding politics all over the world— at least the world that counts— in SouthAsia Politics still overshadows and eclipses economics, which makes for neither good politics nor good economics. There are people in Pakistan, not confined only to the orthodox fringe or the clergy who feel that any economic integration with India would undermine the ideological structure and finality of the 'two-nation' principle. They seem to be still living in the pre-1947 era when the 'two-nation' theory was being hotly debated in the sub-continent. For them time has stood still for 50 years even though Pakistan has emerged as a viable and powerful nation state during this period. With such a frozen mind— set at least in one major constituent of SAARC and ethereal politico-economic outlook generally in others, ushering in of Free Trade Area in South Asia at the beginning of the 21st century may be a tall order, if not a pipe dream.

They may or may not be able to herald the much talked about South Asia Free Trade Area by the year 2001, but one thing they have achieved without talking about. They have over the years worked overtime to establish a *Free Terror Area* in South Asia without much fuss. The one commodity which the South Asian countries trade in freely is terror or terrorist violence. Neither national frontiers nor any 'trade barriers' stand in the way of free exchange of terrorist violence between and among the countries of this region. It is a trade in which every country of the region—big and small—is absolutely free to contribute its ware without anybody in any country batting an eyelid. It is a trade in which there are no surpluses or deficits and no balancing of accounts. It is a trade in which every country indulges in according to its capability and clout. It is SAFTA par excellence, with a difference.

Bangla-India

On 20 May, 1997, the Prime Minister of India, on a visit to Assam, says matt-of-factly that terrorism in North-East India was being encouraged from across the border. He only promised to talk to Bhutan "at the diplomatic and other levels" to prevent terrorists active in North-East India from getting shelter there. India's North-East has been a happy hunting ground to terrorist violence almost since the birth of the Republic. It started with Naga tribals on the extreme north-eastern fringe bordering Burma demanding succession and rising up in arms against the Union of India in early fifties. Since then it has been a constant factor in India's political life.

From Nagas to Mizos to ULFA (United Liberation Front of Assam) to Bodos to militant tribals in Tripura, it has been an unbroken chain of terrorist violence rocking the whole of North-East India. And all the militant and terrorist outfits have all the time been getting shelter, support and even training beyond the borders of India. Initially it was East Pakistan, on permanently hostile terms with India, which sheltered, trained and 'exported' them to India. There was a brief respite with the birth of Bangladesh during Sheikh Mujib's regime, but that proved to be only an interregnum. With the overthrow of Sheikh Mujib, it was traffic as usual on the terror front, with North-East India primarily, but not exclusively, at the receiving end.

And what is the face of terror in the North-East of India? Here is the latest from Tripura, a tiny state (province) perched on the borders of Bangladesh. In the wee hours of Sunday, 16 February, 1997, a marauding horde of tribal militants descended upon two villages of Khowai sub-division of Tripura, set fire to all the houses, pumped bullets into dazed villagers trying to flee and hacked many of them with sharp cutting weapons. By the time the mid-night swoop on sleeping, unsuspecting villagers ended, at least 27 persons lay dead, with several bodies mutilated beyond recognition. Thousands of non-tribals were rendered homeless. Earlier in the middle of December 1996, tribal terrorists had committed a carnage at Kalyanpur of Tripura. Between December 1996 and February 1997, about 60 persons were killed in Tripura in attacks by tribal militants and violence between tribals and non-tribals.

Terrorist assaults and killings of villagers and personnel of the armed forces continue unabated in other north-eastern states (provinces) of India, particularly in Nagaland and Manipur. In Nagaland, groups of Naga militants keep on attacking and killing Kuki tribemen and ambushing patrolling parties of the armed forces in the rugged terrain of the region. In Manipur, another tiny state (province) of the area, 20 armed militants ambushed a convoy of Border Security Force personnel in Thoubal district on 22 May, 1997. The convoy was intercepted on a national highway linking Imphal, the capital of Manipur, with Moreh, while carrying ration from a local Army headquarters. Eleven Border Security Force personnel, including an officer, were killed and three others injured in the ambush. The entire region is in the throes of multi-dimensional terrorist violence.

On the otherside of the border in Bangladesh, violence continues between Chakma tribals and Muslim Bengalis in the Chittagong Hill Tracts. A large number of Chakma tribals from Bangladesh have escaped to India and are sheltered in refugee camps in Tripura. They are engaged in a running fight against the Bangladeshis in Chittagong Hill Tracts which was once the Chakmas' home. The Chakma tribals have formed a militant force called 'Shanti Bahini' which keeps on conducting guerrilla attacks on Bangladesh armed forces in Chittagong Hills Tracts. In February 1997, the Shanti Bahini militants based in Chakma refugee camps in Tripura, India, ambushed and killed four men of Bangladesh armed forces in course of their on-going fight.

For numerous reasons, historical, geographical, economic and others, the "Seven Sisters" (provinces) of north-eastern India— Arunachal Pradesh, Assam, Manipur, Meghalaya, Mizoram, Nagaland and Tripura— have for long remained the most lucrative 'market' for South Asian trade in terror. The erstwhile East Pakistan and later Bangladesh has long remained a prominent 'exporter' of terrorism to this 'market'. The ever multiplying terrorist groups operating in the area of the "Seven Sisters" — ULFA, Bodo Security Force, Nationalist Socialist Council of Nagaland (NSCN), Mizo National Front (MNF), Peoples Liberation Army (PLA). The All Tripura Tribal Force (ATTF) and National Liberation Front of Tripura (NLFT)— have all been patronised by East Pakistan and Bangladesh at one time or another. They are still receiving help and encouragement from Pakistan's Inter Services Intelligence (ISI) based in Bangladesh in the shape of training, false passports, weapons, safe sanctuary and even funds. With free flow of terror from across the border, the dance of death and destruction goes on unchecked in India's north-eastern backyard.

India-Sri Lanka

India is a big country which can live with inflow of terror from its neighbours into one corner of its territory or another. But the free terror regime in South Asia has totally devastated the beautiful little country on the southern tip of the region— Sri Lanka. It was considered not long ago as the island paradise on the threshold of another economic success story in Asia. With flourishing rubber, tea, coconut, fishing and tourism industries, it had the potential of turning into another Korea or Taiwan. But in less than two decades since early 80's, it has slided down politically to the level of Lebanon or Cambodia, thanks to the dumping of terror on this placid land. Sri Lanka has been the worst victim of free trade in terror rampant in South Asia.

One writer has summed up: "Terrorists with guns and bombs abound. With thousands killed with guns and bomb blasts every year, Sri Lankans are locked in a hopeless war with themselves. Corpses flow down the rivers, hang from the trees, smoulder by the roadside. Roar of gunfire and sound of bomb blasts can be heard throughout the day and night."[1] And the chief exporter in South Asia of the merchandise-terror-to Sri Lanka has been India. It is bitter a irony of South Asian scene that the biggest country of the region, ever so vocal against trans-national terrorism in all international fora, has itself been the principal source of 'export' of terror to one of its most peaceful, innocuous neighbours.

The Sinhalese majority and Tamil minority had lived together peacefully for centuries since long before the British established their rule over the island. It is absolutely wrong to think that Tamil migration to Sri Lanka took place only or mainly during the days of the British Empire which had both India and Sri Lanka under its canopy. It has been going on since long before the British set up their empire over the region. In fact, above 12 per cent of Sri Lankan's population consists of native Sri Lankan Tamils who were there long before the coming of the British. Only 5.6 per cent of the population comprises Tamils of Indian origin who migrated to Sri Lanka during the time of Pax Britannica. The issue of Indian Tamils living in Sri Lanka had been coming up from time to time during the British Raj days also. Quite a large chunk of Indian Tamils living and working in Sri Lankan were kind of "stateless" citizens at the time of independence. The question of their legal status was discussed across the table occasionally between the respective Governments of Ceylone and India during the British period and also after independence. It remained a diplomatic and negotiational issue as long as Sri Lanka was ruled by the old elite represented by the United National Party.

It was only after S.W.R.D. Bandarnaike formed his Sri Lanka Freedom Party on the populist platform of Sinhala language and Buddhist nationalism that Sinhala-Tamil co-existence received a sever jolt. The strain in their relationship showed in violent clashes between the two communities in 1956 and 1958, but the uneasy co-existence continued. When a dove like Lal Bahadur Shastri was the Prime Minister of India, there was even a pact between the Governments of India and Sri Lanka over the long pending issue of Indian Tamils living in Sri Lanka. In terms of this pact—about 500,000 Indian Tamils of the "stateless" variety were to be repatriated back to India. Many in the Indian political establishment were critical of Shastri's gesture to Sri Lanka, but those were different times. The issue remained subdued during the first decade of Indira Gandhi's Prime Ministership of India which incidentally more or less coincided with Srimayo Bandarnaike's Prime Ministership of Sri Lanka. The two ladies enjoyed good personal relationship which helped in keeping the issue under the carpet.

Somewhere along the line, the relationship soured after Srimayo's Government was replaced by the UNP's Government. The UNP changed the constitution and adopted the Presidential system with Junius Jayavardhane as President. And India started playing the usual sub-continental game of supporting and encouraging Sri Lankan Tamil militants. With the Dravidian Tamil political parties in saddle in the neighbouring Indian province of Tamil Nadu, it was easy to provide shelter and other facilities to Tamil militants creating havoc on Sri Lankan soil. They could easily cross over the Straits, mingle with their fellow Tamils, set up training camps, and launch assaults on the fragile Sri Lankan administrative set up in northern and eastern Sri Lanka.

With one or the other Dravidian political parties in power in the Indian State of Tamil Nadu, jealously nursing their Tamil vote bank, Sri Lankan Tamil militants had all the opportunities to train and acquire arms to carry on terrorist attacks on Sri Lankan administration and Sinhalese minority in Jaffna province of northern Sri Lanka where Tamils are in majority. The 'benign' government of India at the centre looked on approvingly, both to keep Sri Lankan Government under sheath and also cultivate the Tamil vote bank for the ruling political party at the Centre. One writer observes: "Long before Pakistan took advantage of the unrest in Punjab and Kashmir and supported the Sikh and Muslim terrorists with supply of arms and training bases, we had initiated manipulations by taking advantage of the unrest among Sri Lankan Tamilians."[2]

But for India's support and encouragement in the initial stages, the deadly Sri Lankan Tamil outfit—Liberation Tigers of Tamil Elam (LTTE)— would not have acquired the armed muscle it has today to carry on the savage civil war that country in going through today.

It was a horrific spectacle to find all the top LTTE leaders whose hands were red with Sri Lankans' blood, enjoying the warm hospitality of Government of India at Delhi at the peak of Indo-Sri Lanka talks during Rajiv Gandhi's regime. It appeared in those few days as if LTTE was more a wing of Indian Establishment, or rather of India's top intelligence agencies, than a Sri Lankan political outfit fighting for the cause of Sri Lankan Tamils. Rajiv Gandhi signed the accord with President Jayavardhane of Sri Lanka, hoping that the LTTE would follow the course prescribed by their Indian patrons, give up the demand for a separate Tamil state and take to peaceful ways. When it refused to oblige, India had to despatch the ill-fated Indian Peace Keeping Force in terms of the accord to tame the 'Tigers' in their own den.

The IPKF operations not only failed to tame the 'Tigers' in Jaffna, but also invited their wrath against the Government and leaders of India. As often happens, the genie patronised by India earlier, under the misconceived notion of playing an effective role in settling the affairs of its southern neighbour, grew into a Frankestein. When it turned against its erstwhile patrons themselves, it ended up liquidating Rajiv Gandhi himself physically. In the bargain, it also annihilated a veteran moderate Sri Lankan Tamil leader— Amritlingham. As of now, the LTTE is engaged in a bitter struggle for survival against sustained Sri Lankan military onslaught in the jungles of northern and eastern Sri Lanka painting the entire territory red with human blood.

Pak-India

It is the terror trade between Pakistan and India which is in real boom. For all its ferocity and ravages, the Indo-Sri Lanka terror trade pales into insignificance before the booming Pak-India trade in terror. It goes on and on without any let or hinderance, without any balancing of accounts, irrespective of surpluses and deficits, relentlessly, endlessly. It is not dependent upon grant of MFN (Most Favoured Nation) status by one country to another or mutually to each other. It is free for all between the two countries in the arena of terror, and mutuality or reciprocity is taken for granted by both sides without murmur or fuss.

On 12 March, 1993, a series of high powered bomb explosions rocked the city of Bombay (now Mumbai)— India's commercial capital—from south to north leaving a trail of death and destruction. For nearly three hours, 13 big blasts tore through the heart of the city, devastating the Bombay Stock Exchange building, killing nearly 300 persons and injuring about 1500 of innocent Bombayites. In course of this terrorist strike, a lorry filled with high explosives was blown up through remote control in the congested central Bombay locality of Dongri causing extensive damage to life and property. Besides killing and maiming several persons on the spot, the explosion destroyed many shops, houses, buses, cars, taxies etc. near the site. Bombs also exploded in the building of Air India— India's internation air carrier— and rooms of prestigious hotels Sea Rock and Centaur in Juhu and Santacruz. It was one of the most demonstrative and destructive terrorist actions even by the sub-continental standards.

From all accounts—tenacious investigations by police, explosive experts, national and international intelligence agencies, tell-late evidence etc.— the serial blasts in Bombay could be traced to the elite Pak intelligence agency — ISI (Inter Services Intelligence), which has been known to be working over time to export terror to India. The explosive used in the Bombay blasts was RDX which is very expensive and difficult to obtain in India. Investigation revealed that the first batch of RDX landed at Dighi, a few hundred miles south of Bombay, as early as 9 January, 1993. More of this high explosive arrived from outside between 9 January and 9 February, 1993. Meanwhile some men from Bombay underworld were recruited by the planners of the blasts and sent abroad for training in bomb explosion. After the entire consignment of explosives was transported to Bombay and all preparations were completed, the date was fixed for the final act on 12 March, 1993. And between 7 March and 16 March, all the key participants in the plot fled Bombay along with their families.

It was a copybook terrorist act meticulously planned to the minutest detail and equally meticulously executed to telling effect. The entire project — Operation big blast as one may call it— was scripted, directed, and launched by Pakistan's star agency—ISI. The principal agents were Bombay's Tiger' Memon and his family who fled Bombay before the D day and, above all, Dawood Ibrahim, Bombay's notorious underworld don based in Dubai. Dawood Ibrahim is now believed to be right in Pakistan, under the protective wings of the ISI.

Pakistan's nodal agency for export of terror to India is ISI. The agency has spread its tentacles to wide areas across the Indian territory as far away from Pakistan as north-eastern India. From its bases in Bangladesh it guides and operates terrorist actions in India's north-eastern states now in the grip of widespread terrorism. It has its field station in Sylhet in Bangladesh for directing terrorist operations in India's North-East. It operates in northern sub-Himalayan region of India through its Nepal connection.

During the peak of Sikh terrorism, the ISI had established its foothold in the northern hill regions of U.P. And through its religious veneer, it has also succeeded in extending its net as far south as Hyderabad (India), once the capital of Nizam's princely state. The agency plans to turn Hyderabad into a major operational base in South India to bring it under the ambit of Pak inspired terrorism. There were four bomb blasts of relatively minor intensity in different nerve centres of the city during latter half of 1993. There were two bomb explosions in two city centres on 12 August and another at Secunderabad railway station on 12 September 1993 in which Pak agents were suspect.

The Indian counterpart of ISI is RAW (Research and Analysis Wing) which is supposed to trade in terror with Pakistan. As a super intelligence agency of India handling international intelligence and counter espionage, its role is well defined and known. But unlike ISI, nothing much is known in India about Raw's transnational activism in the arena of terror trade. Every time masked gunmen spark off sectarian violence in Pakistan by firing indiscriminately on religious congregations of one sect or another, the Pak authorities blame it on India's RAW. It may be Shiite Muslim militants firing at Sunnis or vice versa in Punjab (Pak) the Pak officials promptly name RAW. It may be Mohajir extremists shooting at Sindhis in Karachi, the unseen hand of RAW is always suspect in the eyes of Pakistani people and government. In all recent killings and counter-killings of Shias and Sunnis in Pakistan, the invisible 'foreign hand', meaning India, is invariably held responsible. Benazir Bhutto, when in power, had been most vocal in this regard. She saw Indian hand even in the high powered blast that rocked cricketer turned into politician Imran Khan's prestigious cancer hospital in Lahore a few years back. Unidentified masked gunmen shoot at MQM headquarters in Karachi on 26 May, 1997 killing two persons on the spot and fatally wounding two others. Here again, India's RAW in suspected to have engineered the shooting, this time using the rival Haqiqi faction of MQM which is carrying or running battle with the official group.

Terror in Punjab

That would only show that the game can be played by both sides. The trade in terror cannot be entirely one-sided. But in this macabre trade, Pakistan has undoubted advantage and is way ahead of India. It has a huge trade surplus over India. Since around the mid 80's, thanks to India's monumental political blunders, Punjab became a highly 'lucrative market' to Pakistan for 'export' of terror. India almost handed over the Punjab 'market' on a platter to Pakistan to dump terror at will. And Pakistan gratefully accepted the opportunity to go the whole hog in its drive to 'export' terror to India's Punjab. For almost a decade beginning early 80's and specially since the "Operation Blue Star" in June 1984, it was an entirely one-way traffic of every conceivable variety of terror into India from Pakistan through the Punjab route. The inglorious "Operation Blue Star" opened the flood-gates for onrush of surging waves of terrorism into India originating in the fountain springs in Pakistan.

At its peak, terrorism in India's Punjab was the bloodiest and most lethal that the modern world has witnessed in peace time anywhere. The terrorist blood letting in West Asia over the Palestinian question, which erupted in a big way in the 60's and keeps recurring from time to time, pales into insignificance before the terrorist bloodbath in and around Punjab from mid 80's onwards. In Amritsar, a powerful bomb was detonated on a crowd of Hindu shopkeepers who had assembled in front of a Shiva temple to pray after closing their shops. The blast killed 22 persons instantly and injured many more. Terrorists set off three major bomb explosions in crowded localities at Kurukshetra in Haryana, Tilak Nagar in west Delhi and for the second time in Amritsar on three consecutive days. Over 70 persons perished in these blasts and another 175 injured, many of them seriously. On 10 and 11 May, 1985, over 100 transistor bombs exploded in the slum colonies of Delhi, killing 85 persons, including children fiddling with the killer transistors at one go.

There were numerous instances of passenger buses in Punjab being stopped mid way by armed terrorists, the Hindu passengers being a segregated and killed. In some cases, the Hindu passengers were made to get down at gun-point, taken to a lonely place and gunned down in cold blood. It was not necessarily an exhibition of Sikh anger against the Hindus as such. The two communities still lived side by side in rural Punjab in reasonable harmony. Their parents had jointly fought communal battles against Muslims who constituted the state of Pakistan. The older generation of Punjab Sikhs still had bitter memories of partition holocaust in which they were one with Hindus in their common suffering. The Pakistani patrons of Sikh terrorists who resorted to such open, selective killings of Hindus aimed precisely at erasing those memories and splitting Hindu and Sikh minds beyond repairs. The idea was to provoke a Hindu backlash in wide areas across Punjab to plunge India's vital border state into utter turmoil of large scale Hindu-Sikh riots. It was Pakistan's answer to India's role in the separation of Bangladesh from the original state of Pakistan. Or may be, Pakistan was trying to turn the table on Hindus and Sikhs who had jointly faced and fought the Muslims at the time of partition It is another matter that the plan did not succeed.

In Delhi, bomb blasts in buses and other crowded localities have since continued taking innumerable lives. There were several attempts at causing derailment of railway trains by planting bombs on railway tracks in Punjab. In February 1993, some Punjab terrorists were arrested at Delhi railway station who confessed to have been trained by Pakistan's ISI to bomb civilian targets in India's capital. A month earlier, a more deadly and spectacular plan of terrorist action in Delhi was foiled and uncovered. It was a plan to cause a series of major blasts targetting important public installations in Delhi on the occasion of India's Republic Day celebrations on 26 January, 1993. The idea was to 'impress' John Major, the incumbent British Prime Minister, who was to attend the celebrations as the chief foreign dignitory. Four hard core terrorists— Sukhjit Singh alias Sukhi, Bolwinder Singh Cheema, Jaspal Singh Pala and Paramjit Singh Giani—spilled the beans when they were arrested by Delhi police just in time. They had all been assigned the task of letting off terror in Delhi on or around the Republic Day. They all belonged to the dreaded Punjab terrorist outfit, the Khalistan Commando Force (Panjwar group), operating from Pakistani soil. Incidentally Wassan Singh Zafarwal, leader of another group of Khalistan Commando Force, was also based in Pakistan and was carrying on depredations in India's Punjab from his safe hide-out there. Most of over a dozen Punjab terrorist groups like Babbar Khalsa, Kirtani Jatha, Bhindrawale Tiger Force etc. were operating from their bases in Pakistan, with active support and encouragement from Pak Establishment.

The Pakistan factor in Punjab terrorism was evident and visible. Repeated hijacking of Indian Airlines flights to Lahore and Karachi by Sikh terrorists in the 80's was one of the indicators of their Pakistan connection. Immediately after "Operation Blue Star", an Indian Airlines Airbus carrying 255 passengers on a scheduled flight from Srinagar to Delhi was hijacked to Lahore on 5 July, 1984. The hijackers— all Sikh terrorists— were not exactly given political asylum in Pakistan, at least not officially, but were not repatriated to India either to face legal action. They seemed to be welcome guests in Pakistan. Again on 24 August, 1984, seven Punjab terrorists hijacked an Indian Airlines flight from Delhi to Srinagar with 79 passengers on board. The aircraft was refuelled at Lahore taken to Karachi and finally to Dubai. After a few days of hectic negotiations, the UAR authorities handed over the hijackers to Indian officials to be flown back to India for trial. The contrast in treatment of the hijackers by Pakistan and UAR authorities was too glaring to escape notice.

A more overt clue about Punjab terrorists being trained by Pakistan in distant lands came to light from an unexpected quarter. In late 80's the Soviets, then in occupation of Afghanistan, carried out a raid on an Afghan Mujahideen camp at Patkia in Afghanistan. Among those killed in this raid were some Sikh terrorists belonging to "Dal Khalsa". Documents seized in this raid revealed the fact of training being imparted to this terrorist outfit in Afghan territory, courtesy Pakistan. Above all, the US House of Representatives' Task Force on Terrorism and unconventional warfare confirmed in its voluminous report about Pakistan's involvement in terrorist activities in Punjab and, of course, Kashmir. In fact, the secret code name of Pakistan's meticulously drawn agenda of promoting terrorism in India is K2 implying Khalistan and Kashmir.

Some of the notable victims of Punjab terrorist killings in course of the 80's were Lala Jagat Narain, the veteran Punjab editor, Jatheder Santokh Singh, President Delhi Gurudwara Prabandhak Committee, A.S. Atwal, D.I.G Police, Amritsar who was killed just when he came out of the Golden Temple after offering prayers, Sant Harcharan Singh Longowal, President of Akali Dal, M.L. Manchanda, Station Director, All India Radio, Lalit Makan and his wife, son-in-law and daughter of Dr. Shankar Dayal Sharma who later became the President of India, General (Retd.) A.S. Vaidya, the ex-Chief of Indian Army, besides of course the doyen of them all— the reigning Prime Minister of India— Indira Gandhi. Later in early 90's Maninderjit Singh Bitta, a minister in the Congress government of Punjab who also subsequently became the President of Indian Youth Congress, narrowly escaped an attack on his life but lost his legs in the bargain. He survived another bomb attack outside the Youth Congress headquarters in Delhi by a few seconds on 11 September, 1993. The last major casualty of terrorist action in Punjab was none other than the ruling Chief Minister of Punjab himself— Sardar Beant Singh— during whose regime terrorism was ruthlessly suppressed and controlled. He was blown to pieces, along with others, in a severe bomb blast triggered off by remote control on 31 August, 1995. The dreaded Punjab terrorist outfit Babbar Khalsa International was found involved in this killing and its Chief—Wadhwa Singh was based in Pakistan.

The overall outcome of decade-long outrage in Punjab was the killing of over 11,000 ordinary men, women and children in terrorist actions and related violence. In addition, 62 media persons, 27 election candidates, 1587 policemen and 133 members of policemen's families were also done to death by terrorists. There were also innumerable cases of kidnappings, rapes, bank robberies, bomb explosions etc. With increasing lumpenisation of terrorist cadres, bank robberies, kidnapping and gang-rape came to be common features of terrorist action in Punjab countryside. Of these, kidnappings, rapes and forced marriages of young girls, often to more than one terrorist, proved to be the most traumatic forms of outrage for the victims and their families. In many cases, kidnapped girls were kept as captives for a few months and then abandoned when found pregnant.

On 16 August, 1990 two terrorists abducted Kulwinder Kaur, an 18-year-old girl from a farm house in Raoli village of Jallander district. They told her family members they wanted to verify if the girl was of "loose character" which if found true would attract punishment to be meted out by women terrorists. They went to another farm house and tried to abduct another young girl—Jaswinder Kaur—on similar plea. When the girl refused to go with them, she was beaten up and shot dead. On being rescued subsequently, Kulwinder Kaur told the police how she and another girls abducted earlier were sexually assaulted by their abductors day and night, besides acting as beasts of burden as they moved from one hideout to another. They were forced to act as kind of 'comfort girls' for the terrorists fighting their 'holy war' against the state. One rich farmer had to pay Rs. 5 lacs to terrorists as price for sparing his only daughter from their 'services.' Innumerable stories of such ravished and abandoned girls and women came to light as terrorists beat a retreat in face of mounting police assault during early 90's.

Mountains of arms and ammunitions of the most sophisticated

kind—obviously a gift from Pakistan—were recovered by armed forces as they tightened their grip over terrorism in Punjab. The haul between 1981 and 1992 included 3232 A.K. series rifles, 4893 pistols/revolvers, 1086 grenades, 2274 mines, 1639 guns, 1486 kg of explosives, besides 745 rocket launchers and nearly 350,000 assorted ammunitions. This vast arsenel of death and destruction was a measure of the unhindered 'export' of terror by Pakistan to India's Punjab.

Mayhem in Kashmir

Agar Firdous Barrue Zamin Ast, Hamin Asto, Hamin Asto, Hamin Ast (If there is paradise on earth, it is here, it is here, it is here). Thus exclaimed the famous Mughal Emperor being enchanted by the celestial beauty of Kashmir on visiting the land. That was some centuries ago. This writer had his first encounter with Kashmir valley, enclosed by four high mountain passes— Banihal, Razdan, Zozila and Tangdhar—in 1954 autumn, as a fledgeling IPS officer fresh from training ironically on a mission of keeping peace in that peaceful land.[3]

Two lines scribbled in his diary on that momentous day in course of a brief stop-over between Quazigund— the gateway to the valley — and Srinagar, jealously preserved till this day, read:

Gazab ki bulandi hai yahan ke zarre zarre me,
Kaise Khush Kismat hain is Zamin Pe Basne wale.

(Every bit of it is endowed with fantastic sublimity, how blessed are the natives of this land.)

No one would say that about the hapless people of Kashmir valley today. While contemplating the Kashmir scene today, a poet's oft-coated words come to mind: "How much it grieves my heart to think, what man has made of man." One would only like to rewrite the second line as: "What man has made of Kashmir."

The straight, tall poplar trees with white trunks and green tops, rows and rows of them along the highway from Quazigund to Srinagar, the fabulous cliffs and gorges all along the route from Kud to Banihal to the gateway, which overwhelmed the author to pen those lines impromptu, are still there. The vast planes inside the valley still boast of the Nishat, Shalimar and Chashmeshahi gardens, which could be a marvel of colour for human eye to feast upon if in full bloom. Narcissuses still grow wild spreading their fragrance and red Chinar leaves still lend colour to the landscape. The greenish waters of Dal Lake and Jhelum river still wash the edges of Srinagar habitat and anchor floating wooden abodes of variegated colours, sizes and shapes, somewhat suggestively called 'house boats'. Floating little velvet cushioned boats known as 'Shikaras', which once carried romancing couples through the waters, still dot the water front of Srinagar. The majestic Whullar Lake, the largest fresh water lake in Asia, still winds its way through the valley for miles upon miles. The high altitude plateau of Pehalgam and hill tops of Khilenmarg, Sonemarg and Gulmarg are still covered with vast white sheets of snow in winter, which could be a sheer delight for any snow-lover from any part of the world. Above all, the omnipresent snow clad high mountain peaks, which beckon you wherever you are in the valley, make it literally a paradise on earth the Mugal Emperor so eloquently pronounced.

Nothing has changed in Kashmir physically, in the sense of its sylvan setting and natural beauty, and yet nothing is the same in Kashmir today. What was once a paradise on earth has turned into a veritable hell for its inhabitants. Terror, with heavy inflow from Pakistan, has swarmed the land as in no other part of the subcontinent. Fundamentalist Muslim groups like Jamait-e-Islam in Kashmir and outside the country call it *Jehad* (Holy Crusade). Pakistan and pro-Pakistan outfits in Kashmir call it *Junge Azadi* (Fight for Freedom). Indians call it Pak-inspired militancy or trans-national terrorism. The Indian armed forces view it as low-intensity conflict with Pakistan or low key war launched by Pakistan against India on the soil of Kashmir. Whatever it is or is not, the common denominator is the blood spilling of simple, innocent, entrapped people of the valley. They are the guineapigs to be sacrificed at will for every variety of ideologies and strategies—religious, national, military—of Pakistan, India, and may be others also.

Hordes and hordes of young men from Indian Kashmir are lured, coaxed, cajoled, motivated and taken across the border willingly, unwillingly, at gun-point and trained in terror tactics in camps spread over Pakistani Kashmir and even beyond. After some rudimentary training in handling arms, grenades, explosives and in modes of guerrilla warfare, besides plenty of motivation to sacrifice their lives in the cause of 'jehad', they are hurled back into the cauldron that Kashmir has turned into. As they are sneaked into the Indian side of the line of control in Kashmir, they are hounded like dogs by the ever watchful Indian security forces guarding the line. Many of them perish on the LOC itself while trying to cross over. The media in India coldly report and keep on reporting week after week, month after month, routinely, dutifully, 5 or 7 or 10 Pakistani infiltrators or terrorists shot dead by security forces on the border. Pak media perhaps do not even report that. No one in either country sheds any tears for them, except their near and dear ones in Kashmir if they come to know. Many of them never come to know. For Indians, they are just so many 'enemy agents' or Pak trained terrorists killed in encounter with security forces; for Pakistanis; no more than fodder for their cannons pointed at India or Indian part of Kashmir.

Those who manage to sneak into the Indian side, with their Kalashnikovs, grenades or explosives, are always on the run from one hideout to another with the Indian security forces ever on the look out for them. When traced and confronted, they may indulge in some fire-works with their newly acquired weaponry, but almost invariably end up being shot dead or captured by security forces. As long as they remain in hiding, committing one terrorist act or another, killing some one here or exploding a grenade there, they are a constant threat to their hiders who may be their family members or friends or associates. And once the armed forces catch up with them, as they invariably do in due course, it is not only the end of the game for them but also spells disaster for their shelterers. The amateur terrorists may succeed in inflicting some casualties on the armed forces, but in any armed confrontation face to face they predictably lose out to professional soldiers. And once there is shooting or grenade lobbing inside a street or a house, no one can prevent innocent passers-by or harmless house-holders— men, women and children— being killed.

Many are trapped in crossfire between the armed forces and militants holed up in their hide-outs in crowded localities. No operation by any armed force anywhere in the world against terrorist groups in civilian localities can be surgically clean and pin-pointed. The gun knows no distinction between the guilty and the innocent. Even among the sharp shooters, there is only a rare one who shoots straight into the bull's eye. Others go about spraying bullets all around killing people at random. No terrorist outfit, indigenous or imported, can match the ferocity of state terror. It may not be intended or planned by the Indian state in case of Kashmir terrorists, but it is incidental in the kind of operations the armed forces are carrying on in Kashmir.

There is more to it than simple matching or overmatching of terrorists' arms with police or army's arms. Even inside Kashmir, terrorism has become a two-way traffic independent of the armed forces. Numerous Kashmiri youths once used as cannon fodder by Pak terrorist machine returned to the valley disillusioned and devastated. Their families suffered deprivations and ravages of various kinds, they lost their career, best years of their youth, their everything, without gaining anything. Their bitterness and desperation came in handy for the state agencies to organize them into a counter terrorist outfit in the valley. A good number of once pro-Pak terrorists who are captured by or surrender to the security forces are encouraged to join this outfit to counter the terror unleased by their original sponsors. In cold terms it means killings and counter killings between what have come to be known as pro-Pakistan and pro-India groups of terrorists operating in the valley.

Of course the pro-Pakistan or Pro-Azadi (independence) groups far outnumber the counter groups whose number may be limited to one or two. As terrorism lingers in Kashmir, terrorist groups keep on multiplying, splintering, organising and re-organising, each vying with the other to call itself by one pompous name or another. Some of these groups profess the cause of independent Kashmir, others desire merger with Pakistan and all of them swear in the name of Islam. Some of the more active and known groups are Jamaat-e-Islami, Hizb-Ul-Mujahideen, Jammu and Kashmir Liberation Front, Muslim Janbaz Force, Al Jehad Force, Mahar-e-Azadi, Al Faran, Islamic Jamaat-e-Tulba, Tehrik-e-Harkat-e-Kashmir, Mutahida Jehad Council, Jamait-ul-Mujahideen, Al Mustafa Liberation Fighters, Tehrik-e-Jehad-e-Islam, Ikhwan-ul-Musalmeen, Dukharan-e-Millat (women's group) etc. etc.

Whose blood they are spilling anyway? They indulge in occasional pyro-techniques in different parts of India through their Pak connection and the ISI's wide network in India, like bomb blasts in Delhi and elsewhere. They caused a major blast through remote control device on the occasion of the Jummu and Kashmir Governor K.V. Krishna Rao's address at India's Republic Day Parade in Jammu. The Governor narrowly escaped, but some others lost their lives. Some stray Kashmir militants are arrested at Delhi, Bombay and even as far south as Hyderabad from time to time while on their mission to spread terror in India as a whole. For instance, Gowher Ameen Meer, a Kashmiri student of Nizamia Tibbi College Hyderabad, was arrested by police and admitted to be working for a Kashmiri terrorist group. His task was to recruit Muslim youngmen to be trained in terror tactics for action in India. On 25 June, 1993, another Kashmiri youth Zaffar Iqbal hailing from Poonch district— was arrested elsewhere. He admitted to have received 20 days training in Pakistani part of Kashmir in March 1993 and sneaked into India for terrorist acts like setting off explosions at public and crowded places. Earlier on 5 February, 1993, yet another Kashmiri— this time a woman belonging to the women terrorist group called Dukharan-e-Millat— was arrested. Identified as Ayesha Firdous Indrabi, wife of Ashiq Hussain Fak, too of Rajbagh Srinagar, she was linked with a conglomeration of several pro-Pakistani militant groups known as Tehrik-e-Hurriat Kashmir.

But by and large, their terrorist acts have remained confined to Kashmir valley itself. Here also, very few non-Muslims are among their victims, whose numbers can be counted on fingers. Two Swedish engineers working at Uri Hydro Electric Project, an Indo-Swedish joint venture in Kashmir, were kidnapped from their work place in Tanmarg on 31 March, 1991. The idea evidently was to disrupt this vital development project rather than causing real physical harm to the Swedish nationals. While they succeeded in delaying the execution of the project by years and hogging international headlines, the two Swede engineers anyhow managed to escape from captivity. The most sensational act against foreign nationals in Kashmir was the kidnapping of five innocent western tourists in July 1995 by the terrorist group Al Faran. While one of the captive tourists was killed and his dead body cynically exposed to public gaze by the terrorists, the remaining four still remain in captivity at unknown destinations. The incident attracted international attention— a core objective of all terrorist actions— with intense diplomatic efforts by the U.S., Britain and other concerned countries to get their citizens freed, without any success so far. It was one of the lasting regrets of Wisner— the last U.S. ambassador to India— that he could not succeed in getting the hostages released before his departure from India.

Their Hindu victims are also few and far between, a surprising reality in view of the fanatical Islamic stance of most of the terrorist groups, and yet not so surprising because few Hindus are left in the valley. And many Hindus were kidnapped or killed by militants in Kashmir not because they were Hindus but as symbols of the state or the Established authority. On 6 April, 1990, H.L. Khera, General Manager Hindustan Machine Tool watch factory in Kashmir was kidnapped along with his security guard Charanjit Lal while travelling in car in a Srinagar locality. Later Khera's dead body was found abandoned in a lane opposite Fire Services Headquarters, Srinagar, on 10 April, 1990. On 2/3 May, 1990, Prof. Kundan Lal Ganjoo of Wadoora Agriculture College was reported kidnapped from his home in Sopore. His dead body was recovered from river Jhelum on 7 May, 1990. On 8 August, 1990, D.N. Chaudhari, manager of Precast Cement Factory, Pampore, was kidnapped from his office and killed. His dead body was recovered by police on 11 August, 1990 at Phulwama.

Many other Hindu officials employed in Kashmir in diverse capacities were kidnapped by diverse terrorist outfits and subsequently released in exchange for members of their groups held in custody by the authorities. Kidnappings of K. Durai Swami, Executive Director, Indian Oil Corporation, Northern Zone, Ms. Rajinder Kaur, Assistant Director, Central Silk Board, Sohan Lal Khosa, Branch Manager, New India Insurance Company, K.C. Gupta, Manager, Punjab National Bank etc. come under this category. They were all kidnapped in 1991 and subsequently released in exchange for release of militants by the authorities. Also kidnapped in September 1991 were Ms Khem Lata Wakhloo, a former Minister of J and K and her husband Dr. O. N. Wakhloo who were subsequently rescued in an Army operation.

But in regard to kidnappings also, the Muslim victims far outnumbered their Hindu counterparts. On 23 March, 1990, Mir Mustafa, a former MLA of J and K, was picked up while travelling in his car and taken to some unknown destination. Two days later his dead body was recovered by police from Batmaloo locality of Srinagar. The most notable of such terrorist acts was kidnapping and killing of Professor Musher-ul-Haq, Vice-Chancellor of Kashmir University and his private secretary, Ab Gani, by a student militant group in April 1990. They were kidnapped on 6 April, 1990 and their dead bodies were found lying at Padshai Bagh, Srinagar, on 10 April, 1990. On 16 June, 1991 Raza Beigh, SHO Sophia Police Station was kidnapped along with three police guards while on way to Srinagar. The police guards were released but Raza Beigh was hanged to death and his dead body thrown in river Jhelum.

A large number of close relatives of important Kashmiri Muslim dignitaries were kidnapped and subsequently released after much negotiation, bargaining and war of attrition between the authorities and terrorist groups concerned. The most sensational case of this kind was the kidnapping of Dr. Rubaiya Sayeed, daughter of the incumbent Home Minister of India, on 8 December, 1989 at Srinagar while returning home from hospital. The case had created much sensation throughout the country in view of the high position her father was holding. For the terrorist group involved, she was a prize catch and they succeeded in securing the release of five of their cadres before releasing the lady from their capitivity. In July 1990, Farooq Ahmad Shah, son of a Deputy Commissioner Ghulam Abbas Shah, was kidnapped from Srinagar and released later after much effort.

There was a spurt in kidnappings of Kashmiri Muslim notables during 1991 and 1992. Some of these were Hassan Mir, a former Law Minister of J and K, Tassaduq Hussain, a close relative of prominent Congress leader and serving Civil Aviation Minister of India, Ghulam Nabi Azad, Mohammad Ayoub Wagay, son-in-law of former Speaker of J & K Assembly Wali Mohammad Watoo, Ms. Nahida Imtiaz, daughter of an important Kashmiri politician Prof. Saifudin Soz, now a Minister in Government of India, Dr. Mustafa Aslam, son-in-law of Kashmir Congress President Ghulam Rasool Kar. All of them were released after varying periods of captivity on varying terms and conditions virtually dictated by the militants.

Some of the notable Muslim officials of Kashmir so kidnapped and released during the period were Hafizullah Dar, DIG Police Srinagar, Bashir Ahmad Shah, Director Defence and Labour, Ghulam Hassan Zia, Assistant Director Door Darshan (TV) centre Srinagar, Zahoor Ahmad, Director SKIMS Soura, among others.

The only notable terrorist action against Hindus still left over in Kashmir took place recently in March 1997 even as the elected government led by Dr. Farooq Abdullah was in saddle. On the midnight of 21/22 March, 1997, about 15 armed terrorists swooped on Sangrampur hamlet, about 32 kilometres from Srinagar, still inhabited by at least 600 Kashmiri Pandit families who have not migrated to India in the wake of rise of militancy in Kashmir valley. Masqueradings as "pro-India" militants, they called out male members from their houses, took them some 50 metres away and showered bullets killing them on the spot. This measured action was significant in the background of the Indo-Pak Secretary level talks scheduled at Delhi. The Kashmir Chief Minister Farooq Abdullah reacted sharply and asked the Indian government to seek a firm assurance from Pakistan to stop aiding and abetting terrorism in Kashmir.

Leaving aside such rare and exceptional instances, the brunt of ravaging terrorism in Kashmir is being borne by the Muslims of Kashmir themselves. It is the Muslim population of Kashmir which is the worst victim of eruption of the most virulent form of terrorism in the valley since around 1989-90. Caught in the cross-fire between the 'imported' terrorists and state armed forces, they are at the receiving end of both the terrorists 'actions and the armed forces' counteraction. The militants kill them if they give information to state authorities about their where-abouts and movements. The security forces harass them if they don't. The terrorists force them to close their shops and stop work when they give a call for 'bund'. The armed forces intimidate them not to heed the 'bund' call and keep going with their work and business. If there is an armed confrontation between the two opposing forces in the streets, the common people are caught in the middle and in many cases suffer as many causalties as the combatants on either side. In a regular war between two armies, the soldiers on the two sides confront, target and kill each other and get killed. The most cynical aspect of the low key or proxy war between Pakistan and India in Kashmir is the devastation and killing of non-combatants, the ordinary men and women of Kashmir. In a sense, the militants themselves are unsuspecting victims of this proxy war. Kashmiri Muslims are picked up in the prime of their youth, given a few weeks 'or months' elementary training across the border and pushed into Indian Kashmir to fight unequal battles with superior and professional armed forces of India. In the process, they are hounded and killed like rabbits while their distant sponsors remain safely ensconced within the borders of their country.

The same news column which flashes the killing of seven Kashmiri Hindus in Sangrampur hamlet also routinely reports killing of seven militants, two security men and three others. The killed militants are obviously the pick of Kashmiri youth and the abstract 'others' ordinary citizens of Kashmir. It has been going on for the last seven years with no end in sight. The tragedy of Kashmir is that its proclaimed Islamic redeemers are seeking to redeem it through remote control by spilling the blood of Kashmiri Muslims themselves. It is their blood that is painting the valley red and sprinkling over to the snows in the mountains around. According to one estimate, about 40,000 civilians, terrorists and soldiers were killed or wounded in course of terrorist violence in Kashmir between 1989 and 1996. Only a totally callous society which has absolutely no regard for human life can put up with destruction of life on such a vast scale for so long, more so when it shows no signs of abating.

References

1. *Terrorism: World under Siege*, S.K. Ghosh - 1995.
2. *Law and Terrorism and Crimes in India*, S.H. Subha Rao.
3. "There were minor disturbances in the Kashmir Valley in the wake of arrest of Sheikh Abdullah—the symbol of Kashmir's accession to India—in 1953. Armed police forces from several states including Bihar were sent in Kashmir to maintain law and order. The author was one among three Bihar officers who were deputed to Kashmir with the force and spent nearly seven months in the valley doing really nothing but savouring the beauty of the place. Because Kashmir in 1954-55 was more peaceful than the most peaceful state in India today."

8

To What End?

Kashmir Terrorism

Unlike in case of Punjab, Pakistan had made no secret of its help and encouragement to the terrorists in Kashmir. Benazir Bhutto, as Prime Minister of Pakistan, repeatedly asserted Pakistan's commitment to give all "moral material and political support" to militants in their struggle against the established authority in Kashmir. The terms "moral" and "political" are vaguenesses, which could mean anything or nothing. But to leave no one in doubt, she emphasised Pakistan's commitment of "material" support to the militants in Kashmir loud and clear, which in the context of the type of activities they were indulging in, meant nothing less than supply of arms and ammunitions to carry on with their terrorist acts.

And it showed in no uncertain terms in the big haul of all manners of weapons and equipment from captured terrorists by Indian forces in Kashmir. Between mid-1989 and mid-1993, the arms and equipment recovered included 8802 Kalashnikov Rifles/ Carbines, 11,126 handgrenades, 17,328 detonators, about 4400 bombs and explosives, 2848 pistols/revolvers, 1795 anti-tank mines, 486 rocket-launchers, 520 LMG/GPMG = UMG, besides 10.7 lac rounds of ammunitions. Many times more of all these remained and still remain with the terrorists to carry on with their proxy war in the valley, and with everflowing ceaseless replenishments from across the border. Also captured during this period were 20 radio-controlled devices and 178 wireless tele-communication sets. Pakistan also set-up clandestine communication network within the valley over and above its elaborate network in Pakistani part of Kashmir to guide and control terrorist operations.

The U.S. intelligence agencies in their own periodical reports on global terrorism have from time to time pointed to Pakistan's support to terrorists active in Kashmir. The latest in the series is the U.S. State Department's annual report on global terrorism. It refers to the terrorist operations against Indian security forces and civilian targets in Kashmir carried out by Harkat-ul-Ansar, a major terrorist outfit based in Muzaffarabad, Pakistan, in course of the last year. The Kashmiri ultra group Al-Faran, which has held four western hostages since July 1995, is linked to this super terrorist outfit. According to the U.S. report, this supra-national militant organization has spread its tentacles to not only Kashmir but also Burma, Tajikistan and Bosnia. Moulana Saddatullah Khan, leader of this organization, defines its goal as helping armed struggle against non-believers and anti-Islamic forces across the border. In respect of operations in India, its proclaimed objective is to secure Kashmir's accession to Pakistan.

Not that Pakistan is unduly concerned about American certification of its involvement in Kashmir terrorism. Its firm resolve to take over Kashmir from India is there for everyone to take note of and any means of achieving the objective is good enough. After all it has fought wars with India in the past over the issue. Out of the three Indo-Pak wars since independence, two were fought on the issue of Kashmir alone. If, for a change, Pakistan chooses to fight a proxy war this time through its surrogates in Kashmir, what is there to fuss about? In any case, what is there to hide about it?

Incidentally, in both the first and second Indo-Pak wars over Kashmir in 1947-48 and 1965, Pakistan came very near succeeding and taking over Kashmir, but missed the target very narrowly. On the first occasion when prompted by Pak Establishment Pathan and other tribal raiders from the north-west as well as Pakistani soldiers disguised as tribals broke into Kashmir in late October 1947, Kashmir was virtually a no-man's land between India and Pakistan. Maharaja Hari Singh, the ruler of the princely state of Jammu and Kashmir, was under intense pressure from Pakistan to accede to it in view of the predominantly Muslim population of the valley region and its contiguity with that state. Even before he could decide on the issue of accession to Pakistan or India, the raiders broke loose into Kashmir making mince meat of the ramshackle forces of the Kashmir Raj. The only stable political factor in Kashmir at that time was the personality of Sheikh Abdullah who had emerged as a towering leader of Kashmiri people in course of a longish struggle against the princely order during British Raj. His long association with Nehru in this struggle helped to clinch the issue in favour of India. After hurried tripartite consultations involving the Maharaja, Sheikh Abdullah and Government of India, Kashmir formally acceeded to India with Sheikh Abdullah as the *de facto* ruler and India intervened militarily to stop the raiders from completing their occupation of the valley.

But before the formalities could be completed and Indian troops could move in, the Pakistani raiders had a field day in Kashmir valley. The vastly outnumbered, ill-equipped rag tag forces of Kashmir Raj were no match to Pakistani soldiers disguised as tribal raiders who kept advancing towards the capital Srinagar with lightning speed. Even after India decided to intervene in defence of the Maharaja, it had no means to send its troops speedily except by air. There was no all-weather road link between the rest of India and Srinagar with Muzaffarabad going over to Pakistan after partition. The tenuous air link with the valley was solely dependent on one single little airport at Srinagar. The Pakistani raiders, assembling at and starting from Muzaffarabad, had an open and obstacle-free road link to Uri, Baramula and Srinagar airport before they could expect some resistance from Maharaja's forces on entering the city. And the speed with which they were cruising along merrily without any resistance from the non-existent Maharaja's forces, they could have easily taken over the Srinagar airport at least a day or two earlier than when they actually arrived within its striking distance. And if they did actually capture the airport, which was waiting to be captured, it would have been impossible for the Indian troops to land in the valley.

But the raiders were interested in 'other good things of life' also, besides securing Kashmir for Pakistan. There were plenty of 'attractions' on the way, the virgin nuns in the church at Baramula and the beautiful girls and women of Kashmir, apart from the material goods of the local inhabitants. They let themselves go and indulged in looting and rape at lib in the manner of a conquering army gone berserk. That delayed their advance towards Srinagar airport considerably. And yet they were hardly a few miles away from the airport when the first contingent of Indian troops landed there. The troops had to engage the raiders almost from the moment they landed. The Indian air force carried out sorties after sorties non-stop landing more and more troops. There were heavy casualties on both sides, but ultimately professional soldiers carried the day and succeeded in chasing the raiders away from the airport and saving the capital Srinagar for India.

With the joining in of regular Pakistani troops subsequently, the conflict was prolonged and the war dragged on for over a year until India took the matter to the U.N. Security Council and cease-fire was brought about in 1949. With easy road communication from the planes of Pakistan to Kashmir valley, Pakistan enjoyed a great strategic advantage in this war. But Indian military genius, among other things, largely offset that advantage. General Thimayya of India created a record of sorts when he got tanks and armour dismantled into parts, transported by air to Srinagar, assembled on the ground and then deployed against the Pakistani forces. Durga Das was to write later: "The warfare in Kashmir proved a blessing in disguise from the national point of view. It not only trained our officers and jawans to plan operations and work in cohesion but also threw up men like Srinagesh, Thimayya and Kalwant Singh whose daring and exploits marked them for future leadership. If the Army gave India Kashmir, Kashmir gave India its Army."[1]

Referring to this abortive Pakistani campaign in Kashmir in his famous autobiography nearly two decades later, Pak President Ayub Khan wrote: "Then there was the fighting in Kashmir. It started as an irregular campaign. Soldiers and officers were out on their own with little direction from headquarters and with considerable responsibility placed in the hands of junior officers,"[5] Ayub Khan had ample opportunities to make amends for the rather disorganised, slip-shod first Kashmir war, launched by Pakistan on the morrow of independence, when he came to be the President of Pakistan. He waited for seven long years, putting some order into the fractitious politics of Pakistan, introducing and implementing his system of 'Basic Democracy', and ensuring stability and economic growth, before embarking upon Pakistan's second Kashmir war. And he did it at the peak of his power after winning over Ms Fatima Jinnah, the venerable sister of the Quaid-e-Azam, in the bitterly fought Presidential election of January

1965. (Of course only over a hundred thousand 'Basic Democrats' spread over West and East Pakistan were entitled to vote in this election.)

On the other side of the fence, the indomitable founder Prime Minister of India, Jawaharlal Nehru, was no more on the scene, having passed away on 27 May 1964. Politically, India was going through a lean period with the little known little man of Indian politics—Lal Bahadur Shastri—in the saddle as an uneasy Prime Minister after nearly 18 years of Nehru's undisputed rule. Considered a dove in foreign affairs, humble, meek, assailed by Ms Vijay Lakshmi Pandit, Nehru's celebrated sister, as a "prisoner of indecision", Lal Bahadur Shastri was the least likely Indian leader to cope with a determined Pakistan's well-organized military bid to take over Kashmir. Yet Ayub Khan took no chances. He tested Shastri's guts through a calculated and controlled Pak offensive in the Runn of Kutch early in 1965 summer. Shastri bought peace by entering into an agreement with Pakistan over the Runn issue rather than confronting it head-long. Pakistan could not think of a more opportune moment to strike and annex Kashmir. President Ayub Khan recognized the opportunity and decided to act.

And act he did in the manner of a perfect professional General that he was, in late July 1965. Equipped with heavy American Patton Tanks, the Pak Army crossed the cease-fire line in the Poonch Sector on the southern fringe of the valley in commanding strength. Every move was planned with consummate skill in utter secrecy so as to take the Indian Army by surprise. And the Indian Military high command was actually taken by surprise when heavy Pakistani armour suddenly erupted in Chhamb-Jauria sector of Jammu, India's Chicken's neck' which served as its only narrow link with the Kashmir valley. It was a calculated, well planned and executed Pak Army move, probably masterminded by President Field Marshal Ayub Khan himself, to cut off India's only road link to Kashmir valley. According to Indian intelligence reports, the Pak military strategy further was to go down the Beas, penetrate the Ferozepur area in Indian Punjab, capture the road leading northward from Delhi and thereby completely choke the lifeline to Kashmir.

It was a measure of Pak Army's meticulous planning or Indian

General Staff's poverty of thinking that the Indians had not expected any major Pakistani thrust in the Chhamb— Jauria sector. Once the unexpected happened, panic buttons were pressed and Indian Air Force vampires went into action straffing the confidently advancing Pak armour. But the Pakistani Juggernaut seemed invincible and kept advancing in this most vulnerable sector, which is almost indefensible at any time for geographical reasons. If the Pak armour had succeeded in sapping the tenuous road link to the valley in this sector, the Indian troops would have been trapped in Kashmir in the same manner as Pakistani troops were trapped in erstwhile East Pakistan six years later. The only outcome would have been the surrender of Indian troops and occupation of Kashmir valley by Pakistan. Ayub Khan had very nearby succeeded in achieving what Pakistan has been seeking to achieve since its creation— annexation of Kashmir.

But his Indian counterpart, Prime Minister Lal Bahadur Shastri, had other ideas. Pushed to the wall, the "Big Little Man", as he came to be called in India after the event, decided to strike at a point where Pakistan least expected a military strike by India. It was Pak high command's turn now to be taken by surprise. They had primarily planned for a limited localised war in Kashmir, with only incidental spill-overs in the Punjab, by crossing over the uneasy cease-fire line which was not so sacrosanct after all. But Shastri signalled the Indian Army to cross the more sanctimonious international border in Punjab and attack Sialkot and Lahore. This could have had grave international repercussions and drawn India and Pakistan into a bigger, generalised war, which India's Foreign Minister, Swaran Singh, kept cautioning till the last hour.

With Indian troops advancing right up to the Ichhogil canal, a few miles from Lahore, and the peripheri of Sialkot, the complexion of the war changed completely. Pakistan did counter attack by moving its caravan of formidable Patton tanks in Khem Karan area of Indian Punjab. In any face to face confrontation, the American Pattons could have easily wiped out the smaller Indian tanks. But the tall and thick standing crops in the Khem Karan area provided a convenient cover to the Indian armour to hide and attack when the Pattons were sighted as sitting targets. The war ended in 21 days with India gaining a little territorial advantage in Kashmir by occupying the strategic Haji Pir Pass. The cease-fire on the ground was formalized by the Tashkent Agreement between India and Pakistan brought about through Soviet mediation. Both countries reverted back territorially to the pre-conflict position, which meant India giving up the Haji Pir Pass back to Pakistan.

The third Indo-Pak war of December 1971 was of course fought on the issue of Bangladesh and conflicts in Kashmir on this occasion were only incidental. But from Tashkent to Simla Agreement to the current terrorist phase of the dispute, nothing has changed in the respective positions of Pakistan and India in regard to Kashmir. It is a harsh reality on the ground which has to be reckoned with. In fact nothing has changed since Pakistani raiders entered Kashmir in late October 1947 and the Maharaja of the princely state hurriedly acceded to India so India could come to his rescue. India accepted the accession of Kashmir "provisionally" subject to some kind of confirmation by the people of Kashmir. The UN resolution which brought about the cease-fire in the first Kashmir war revolved round the twin proposition of vacation of occupied Kashmir by Pakistan and holding of a plebiscite to ascertain the wishes of the people. Pakistan's charge against India of blocking a plebiscite in Kashmir is countered by India's charge of Pakistan refusing to vacate the part of Kashmir occupied by it. When Pakistan demands ascertaining the wishes of the people as promised by India at the time of accepting Kashmir's accession, India touts successive democratic elections in the state returning parties and governments which repeatedly confirmed Kashmir's accession to India.

The dull and tormenting debate goes on endlessly, tiringly, monotonously in every forum ever since Krishna Menon of India and Zafrullah Khan of Pakistan exercised their respective debating skills in the UN Security Council. (Krishna Menon once fainted in course of his marathon presentation of India's case in the Security Council.) Nearly 50 years of conflict and blood-letting in Kashmir has not brought about an iota of change in the postures and attitudes of Pakistan and India towards Kashmir, towards each other. They fought three bloody wars, the first two exclusively on Kashmir, but at the end of it all it was back to square one. The stalemate continues.

Can the input of terror bring about a significant change in the tangled Kashmir situation? Pakistan at least tends to think so, or else it wouldn't have done all that it has been doing in recent years to export terror to India. But even Pakistani Establishment couldn't be so naive as to believe the militants in Kashmir could one day stage an armed coup and capture power. There is no power vacuum in Kashmir, as happened in Afghanistan after Soviet withdrawal, nor is Kashmir another Ziere (Congo) or Kashmiri militants anywhere near Laurent Kabila's forces. In any case, there is no despot like Mobutu Sese Seko in Kashmir waiting to be overthrown out by a Laurent Kabila. Kashmir is governed by the biggest country of South Asia which has a well organized modern system of governance internally backed by a powerful army externally.

On the other hand, terrorism of any variety resorted to for any cause has its own pitfalls and, in a way, contains the seeds of its own destruction. In an article on terrorism, the author wrote seven years ago (in March 1990): "Society will tolerate terrorism only so long as it is no more than a nuisance. Once in security spreads and terror becomes a real danger, cry goes up for more repressive measures, irrespective of price to be paid in terms of human rights. Once the might of the state is in full swing, terrorism cannot survive."[3] And this is exactly what happened in case India's Punjab terrorism which is as good as finished now. The process may be a little prolonged in case of trans-national terrorism originating from outside the country's frontiers, but it cannot sustain itself from 'imported input' for long.

The only significant contribution that terrorism can possibly make towards achievement of a political goal or objective is by attracting wide attention of the people concerned towards the objective. In case the goal or objective is in danger of being lost sight of or forgotten, terrorism helps to keep it alive or in focus. That is why terrorist groups all over the world take special pains to loudly publicise their acts of terror. Their targets are also selected with an eye on their publicity value. A bizarre terrorist act of this nature in the heart of America that shook the whole nation took place on 19 April, 1995. After 9 a.m. on that fateful day, a high explosive bomb erupted from a Ryder rental van and rolled through the nine-storied Alfred P. Murrah Federal Building in the Oklahoma city reducing it to debris. All the nine stories collapsed into the building's basement, taking a toll of 168 innocent lives besides injuring 850 others. It was demonstrative terrorism of the most cynical kind resorted to by a miniscule militant group little heard of in America, except in the counter-terrorism section of the F.B.I, meant to draw attention to the group's even less known cause.

And it did draw a complacent American nation's attention with a big bang, as not even the bombing of New York's World Trade Fair Building earlier by Muslim fundamentalists had done. The US News & World Report summed up: "unlike previous terrorist attacks, the fireball that engulfed the Murrah building on a quiet spring morning as Americans went about their normal routines consumed more than its victims. The World Trade Centre bombing largely failed to shake the presumption of most Americans that in their own homes, in their own cities they were safe, far from the violence plaguing the rest of the world. New York was a seething, violent place, a place of too many immigrants, too many misfits. It was, in other words, foreign, not so Oklahoma city. It is the nation's heartland, a locus of normalcy far removed from the nastiness and nuttiness of New York and Los Angels."[4]

The US President Bill Clinton even called for a national day of mourning and visited Oklahoma city with the first lady Hillary Clinton to lead the nation in a memorial ceremony. (Forget about South Asia where such bomb blasts and killings hardly cause ripples in the political establishment and go largely unwept and unsung. Except for hogging the newspaper headlines for a day or two, they go largely unnoticed also and are easily forgotten.)

The instant American reaction was to attribute the Oklahoma bombing to Islamic extremists, as the New York's Trade Centre bombing came to mind. Being on a visit to Atlanta and Columbus in Georgia, USA in May 1995, the author was told about menacing threats received by many Muslims living in that area of dire revenge immediately after the Oklahoma tragedy. In the circumstances, it was lucky that within 24 hours the news went round that a white man, and not an immigrant Muslim fundamentalist, was behind the heinous crime. It was a rare fortuitous circumstance that the main culprit— Timothy Mcveigh — was caught by a Highway Patrolman on a routine check-up of speeding vehicles. Mcveigh was detained by the Patrolman not for the colossal crime he had committed but on twin charges of driving an unregistered car and carrying an unregistered hand-gun. It was after sometime, with high profile F.B.I sleuths and forensic experts descending on the scene, that Timothy Mcveigh was found to be the principal Oklahoma culprit.

Investigations revealed Mcveigh's close association with a right wing extremist group in US known as the Michigan Militia. Many such militia groups were reported to have sprung up in many parts of America during the 90's which were opposed to nearly every act of the Federal government from gun control to crime control. Many called upon America to leave the United Nations which they considered as a global conspiracy to subvert the US constitution. Probably it was to highlight such crazy demands and ideas that Timothy Mcveigh committed such a ghastly act of terrorism. After nearly two years of trial, Timothy Mcveigh was found guilty of conspiracy and first degree murder by a US court and sentenced to death by a federal jury in June 1997. The Oklahoma tragedy is a telling illustration of the basic characteristic of terrorism — wanton destruction of innocent human lives unconcerned with the cause it is supposed to promote.

In case of Kashmir, the only worthwhile purpose of terrorist violence from Pakistan's point of view could be to keep the issue alive and bring it to the attention of the world. Implicit in this course of action is Pakistan's belief that foreign powers, particularly the US and Britain, would somehow intervene and help secure what it considers its rightful objective in Kashmir. Which in concrete terms would mean securing the Kashmir valley for Pakistan on the basis of its overwhelming Muslim population. The irony of the situation is that in spite of all talks about freedom from colonial rule and 50 years of independence, South Asians still seem to be looking up to one foreign power or the other as final arbiter of their destiny. It was as if the British were still there to allocate territories on the sub-continent between India and Pakistan on the basis of one criterian or another. They find themselves incapable of solving their territorial disputes by themselves, which would necessarily involve some give and take in a spirit of mutual accommodation. More of it later.

For Pakistan, this kind of dependence on foreign powers, particularly the US, to secure its objectives in Kashmir had some relevance till the end of the 80's. It could look up to the US, the number one Super Power in a bi-polar world, to support and prop up its case over Kashmir, just as India looked up to the Soviets. But there has been a sea change in the international situation with the end of the cold war. In the Uni-polar world with US emerging as the sole Super Power, it has no need any more to cultivate allies and satellites in distant corners of the globe. Even before the formal disintegration of the Soviet Union, as the cold war was inexorably coming to an end, Peter Galbraith, the Chief South Asia Policy Advisor to the US Foreign Relations Committee in 1990, observed that "the basic point is that the cold war is over, particularly as regard to South Asia." He went on to elaborate that India and Pakistan could no longer play the US and Soviet Union off against each other for their own benefit. Because the US and Soviet Union, in the words of Peter Galbraith, "are not in the business of trying to solicit clients in that part of the world any more."

A wrong parallel is sometimes drawn between the eruption and efficacy of terrorism in the Israeli-Palestinian conflict in West Asia and Indo-Pak dispute over Kashmir. Historically, Palestine was home to both Arabs and Jews, who had common ancestory, but unlike many Arab states in existence, the Jews had no home state of their own. Since the close of the 19th century, Jews spread all over the world had been demanding a 'state of Jews' in Palestine where their ancestors hailed from and which was a mandated territory under Britain. Their demand received a great impetus in 1917 when the British Foreign Secretary Balfour's Declaration favoured the establishment of a Jewish national home in Palestine. Later during the 30's, Nazi atrocities against the Jews earned world-wide sympathy for them and the holocaust added moral urgency to the quest for a Jewish state.

It was in this background that Britain, which had mandate over Palestine, announced its intention to withdraw from Palestine in 1948 and turned the issue over to the UN. By a resolution in November 1947, the UN announced partition of Palestine into an independent Jewish state of Israel, an independent Arab state, and an international city of Jerusalem. While the partition plan was totally rejected by the Arabs, Britain unilaterally ended its mandate on Palestine in May 1948. On the same day, the Jews proclaimed the establishment of an independent state of Israel. The next day, Arab states of Egypt, Jordan, Syria and Iraq attacked Israel but were beaten back. The Arabs fought the second Arab-Israeli war in 1956 but Israel again emerged victorious. It was the third Arab-Israeli war of 1967 which proved most disastrous for the Arabs. In this war Israel made considerable territorial gains at the cost of the Arabs by occupying the West Bank of Jordan river, the Gaza Strip and Golan Heights.

Up to this point, terrorism did not emerge as a factor in the Arab-Israeli dispute. The Arabs fought wars against Israel because a Jewish state in the midst of Arab land was an anathema to them. Right from Israel's birth in May 1948, they were dead opposed to the idea, but terrorism did not come into play. The Palestinians became aliens in their own land, they were outraged, but did not resort to terrorism. It was only after Israel made substantial inroads into established Arab territory by occupying the West Bank, Gaza Strip and Golan Heights and started settling Jews in occupied territories on a large scale that terrorism burst forth in a big way. That meant Israel's attempt to change the population composition of occupied Arab lands. Nothing like that has happened in Kashmir. The Kashmir valley was not captured by India from Pakistan by altering the status quo as in the case of the West Bank, Gaza Strip and Golan Heights. Kashmir has been with India right from the time the independent states of India and Pakistan came into being. And there is no question of changing the population composition of the valley in India's favour. Article 370 of Indian Constitution still guarantees special status to Kashmir in India's federal set-up.

Although there was a spurt in international terrorism beginning in 1968, the nature of terrorist acts in West Asia or elsewhere was very different from what is happening in Kashmir. The acts were scattered, sporadic, more demonstrative than actually destructive. There were hijackings galore, kidnappings of diplomats, political leaders, businessmen, exploding of booby trap cars, spate of parcel-bombs in widely scattered areas across the world rather than intensive, localised killings and massacres of civilians confined to a single territorial area as in Kashmir from day to day. There were such token acts as seizure of the French Embassy at the Hague in 1974 and shooting of eleven Israeli sportsmen in the Munich Olympic village in 1972. One of the more sensational international terrorist acts of the 70's was massacre of 26 passengers at the Israeli airport of Lod by Japanese terrorists allegedly financed by Arab countries. But these major incidents were one-time acts, hardly ever repeated, aimed at creating an impact and drawing world's attention to the Palestinians' case against Israel.

And yet, the world at large, or the powers that mattered in world affairs, took not much notice of the Palestinian question as long as the terrorist phase lasted for about two decades. During this phase, in spite of occasional terrorist fireworks by the Arabs, the Super Powers did nothing except firefighting when open hostilities broke out between the Arabs and Israelis, as in 1973. In stead of heeding to the Palestinians, the US actually weakened them by weaning away Egypt, the most powerful Arab State of the region from their ranks. In September 1978, Egypt and Israel signed their momentous accord at Camp David USA through the good offices of President Jimmy Carter of America. The only effective part of Camp David Accord was Israel's agreement to withdraw from Sinai which it had captured from Egypt in war. After this was compiled with and Sinai restored to Egypt, the latter signed a Peace Treaty with Israel in March 1979. Egypt thus became the first Arab state to officially recognize and acknowledge the Jewish state in Arab land 31 years after it came into being. As the flagship Arab state which had been in the vanguard of Arab crusade against Israel in the past, its defection to the other side considerably weakened the Arab position vis a vis Israel.

But the Camp David Accord did not result in the US relenting in its tough stand against Palestinian terrorism. It had branded Palestinian Liberation Organization (PLO) as a terrorist outfit since the outbreak of terrorism in West Asia in late 60's and continued to do so for a decade after Camp David. The PLO leader Yasser Arafat, so much respected in the Third World and a conspicuous presence at NAM gatherings, remained a *persona non grata* with the US till almost the close of the 80's. So much so that till as late as 1989, the US administration had denied visa to Yasser Arafat, the PLO Chief, to visit New York for addressing the UN General Assembly. And that at a time when the PLO Chief's status as the most authentic mouthpiece and apostle of the Palestinian cause had come to be recognised by the world community. It was a measure of world's recognition of Yasser Arafat's status as the leader of Palestinians that a session of the UN General Assembly was held outside America to enable him to address it.

America started dealing with Yasser Arafat only after the PLO renounced terrorism and accepted the state of Israel. The US decision to have direct dialogue with the PLO Chief on the Palestinian issue was one of the most pleasantly surprising developments in the long drawn Arab-Israeli conflict situation in the Middle East. But it came after 20 long years of Quarantine in which the PLO was kept because of its terrorist antecedents or links. Far from promoting or expediting a solution of the Palestinian question, terrorism considerably hampered and delayed the solution and prolonged the agonies of the Palestinians.

It was only when terrorism by and large ended in the Middle East or at least PLO categorically disassociated itself from it, that the world took up the Palestinian question with any amount of seriousness. And with the evaporation of the Soviet block, it was the US, the lone Super Power which had shunned the PLO till the other day, which single-handedly brought about Palestinian self-government at least in part of the Palestinian territory. Warren Christopher, the US Secretary of States during President Clinton's first term, paid many more visits to West Asia to bring this about than any of his predecessors had ever done any time before. And in spite of set-backs and hiccups, the US has kept up its efforts to shore up what has come to be known as the 'West Asia Peace Process' to a more stable position.

But that should not lead to an impression that the lone Super Power would be similarly interested in mediating in Indo-Pak dispute over Kashmir. If US has intervened effectively in bringing about a working settlement on the Palestinian issue, it is primarily because of its own vital interests in that region. West Asia is vital to the US because of its oil and so is lasting peace in West Asia. Right from Camp David to Israeli-Palestinian peace initiatives, US has been as much, if not more, motivated by its oil interests in the

Middle East as by anything else. The same cannot be said about South Asia. After the end of the cold war and block system in international relations, South Asia is no more than a land mass or human mass in a part of the globe. South Asians, or Pakistan and India to be precise, should have no illusions on that. As one Columnist put it rather bluntly and cynically, if the entire South Himalayan region went beneath the sea, the Americans and Europeans would be content with shedding only humanitarian tears. It would not make any difference to their overall global interests. If India and Pakistan would themselves not solve the Kashmir question, nobody else would do it for them.

Perennial Strife

If terror in Kashmir is a cynical exercise in futility, terror in the rest of the sub-continent is a callous or rather ridiculous exercise in frivolity. If terror is the wrong and self-defeating mode of securing the goal of its perpetrators and sponsors in Kashmir, it has no goals at all to achieve in the rest of South Asia. Unless, of course, weakening one's neighbour in a general sort of way or keeping it in a state of turmoil is in itself considered a goal. The countries of South Asia seem to believe in the dictum 'your neighbour's weakness is your strength' or otherwise, it is impossible to understand or explain the kind of terror trade they have been indulging in at the cost of each other.

There is no nation in the world which is not composed of historically, ethnically, religiously, linguistically, culturally diverse peoples, even nationalities in the narrow meaning of the term. Even a small supposedly compact nation like Britain consists of the Scottish, Welsh, Anglican protestants, Roman catholics, besides Africans, Asians etc. There are diverse sub-national groups in almost every nation state of Europe like Prussians, Austrians, Bavarians in Germany, Sardinians, Sicilians and Romans in Italy, Castilians, Aragonians and Christianised descendants of Moors in Spain and so on. But the European nations do not go about fomenting ethnic, religious or any variety of sub-national troubles or disturbances in each other's territory. They fought two world wars among themselves in course of the 20th century, but they have not been in the business of exporting terror or creating internal conflicts in other countries by exploiting sub-national diversities in peace time.

In Canada, there is a strong separatist sentiment among the French-speaking people of Quebec, who constitute a preponderant majority of the population of the province. They consider themselves culturally different from the English-speaking majority of the Canadian nation. It is perhaps rooted in the historical rivalry between the English and the French in North America in which the English came out victorious. Yet Canada's big neighbour— the USA—has never tried to play the Quebec card or engineer trouble in Quebec to tame Canada or keep it under its thumb. Of course, the French Quebecans themselves have never been bothered by their history to settle scores with the English Quebecans in violent clashes and conflicts. Instead, in the run up to the last referendum on the issue of separation held in the autumn of 1995, they were debating at what price investors from Tokyo to New York would continue to lend money to an independent Quebec nation. No wonder Quebec finally voted against separation, even though a majority of the French Quebecans were for it.

The practice of transnational trouble-making was a bi-product of the bi-polar world that emerged at the end of the Second World War. The cold war that ensued between the two Super Powers—the U.S. and Soviet Union led to a no-holds-barred tussle between them across the board. In a bid to win friends and influence people across the world, they freely indulged in creating troubles against established regimes in different countries to bring them under their sphere of influence. It was basically a conflict of ideology between communism and anti-communism. The western powers chose to call it a clash between communist totalitarianism and 'free world', but that was hypocritical. In their bid to contain and stall, if not stamp out, communism, they proped up all kinds of absolutist and dictatorial regimes in different parts of the globe. Blind anti-communism or anti-Sovietism itself became an ideology for the western block in pursuit of which they went about exporting strife and violence in countries susceptible to communism.

As the leader of the western block and number one Super Power, the US did it on a wide scale extending from Latin America to Africa, Middle East and South East Asia. At one time or another,

Chile, Congo, Angola, Mozambique, Nicaragua, El Salvador, Afghanistan, Cambodia etc. were all victims of transnational civil strife and violence emanating from the cold war. As soon as the 'foreign hand' behind the internal conflicts in these countries was withdrawn with the end of the cold war, all the violence and bloodshed ended in no time. Peace returned to Nicaragua, El Salvador, Angola, Cambodia etc. after years of raging and tearing internal violence. Afghanistan is the only notable exception where the rival Mujahideen groups, once actively propped up and armed by the US against Soviet occupation, are still fighting it out in the rugged terrain. If Afghanistan has been devastated in the process, it is nobody's concern, not of the US in any case. The Soviet Union, of course, does not exist now.

But all the ravages were caused by the Super Powers, notably the US, in third countries for a cause. For America, no human sacrifice across the globe was too great in furtherance of its ideology of anti-communism. It was this ideology which landed its conscripted soldiers to fight a savage war in the inhospitable terrain of Vietnam for nearly a decade which it had to lose ultimately. It was this ideology which prompted it to actively aid and abet the *contra* rebels in Nicaragua against the Sandistian government backed up by the Soviets, Khmer Rouge (ironically an ultra Marxist gang) and their allies against the Hun Sen government supported by Vietnam in Cambodia, Unita rebels against the pro-Soviet regime in Angola and so on. It was this ideology which gooded it to indulge in its gross misadventure against Fidel Castro's regime in Cuba.

After the overthrow of the pro-American rightist dictator Batista by pro-Soviet leftist Fidel Castro in Cuba, a large number of Cuban refugees fled to the neighbouring coastal areas of America. The US Central Intelligence Agency (CIA) located them in Florida and Guatemala and started training and equipping them for an eventual clandestine invasion of Cuba to overthrow Fidel Castro. In mid April 1961, some 1400 Cuban refugees nursed, trained armed and funded by the CIA, were landed in the Bay of Pigs to start kind of a civil war inside Cuban territory against Castro's regime. As it turned out, the half-baked 'exported' fighters were no match to the Cuban armed forces and were mopped up by the

Castro regime within 48 hours. The "Bay of pigs" faisco, which had been planned earlier, caused much embarrassment to Kennedy at the start of his Presidency and helped Fidel Castro to emerge as a hero in the eyes of Cubans.

It was the ideology of anti-communism which turned a traditionally isolationist country like America into a principal interventionist country, promoting strife in state after state, during the post-war period. Which ideology is motivating the new nation states of South Asia to sponsor and encourage internal strife in each other's territory? What induces India, Pakistan, Sri Lanka and Bangladesh to gloat at and support internal disturbances and terrorism in their neighbour's land? If they are blindly copying the USA and doing to South Asia what US did to the world during the cold war regime, where is the cold war in the sub-continent and for what cause?

South Asia is swayed by a destructive negative ideology, like the anti-communism of western powers earlier, without any cause, just for the sake of it. For Indians, it is anti-Pakistanism and for others, particularly Pakistanis and Bangladeshis, it is anti-Indianism. Any internal turmoil or strife, however destructive of life and property, in India is good news in Pakistan and vice versa. The greatest sacrilege for any political party or leader in Pakistan, and to a lesser extent in Bangladesh, is being soft towards India on any issue. The same more or less is true of the Indian psyche in respect of Pakistan at least, if not Bangladesh. This kind of meaningless *anti-ism* has completely distorted the practice of politics among leading nations of the sub-continent, even though they were parts of one whole under the British Raj. To promote or at least support and encourage internal strife and troubles in each other's territory seems to have become an accepted part of diplomacy among the countries of South Asia.

Some people loosely talk of a cold war between India and Pakistan. That amounts to utter trivialisation of the term itself. 'Cold War' was a specific situation in international relations which came to prevail in the context of the bi-polar world emerging after the Second World War. It was so termed because it had the potential of developing into a 'Hot War' involving the whole world. At its peak, the cold war came very near becoming hot war over one or the other major issue dogging the relationship between two power blocks. It was so when in June 1948, the Soviet Union began the blockade of Berlin—which lay 100 miles inside the Soviet zone of occupied Germany—with a view to driving America and other western powers from their zones of Berlin. Since then, the cold war regime moved from one flash point to another over repeated crises on the Berlin question, Suez crisis, Vietnam and Cuba.

By far the most dangerous crisis of the cold war arose over Cuba in October 1962 when it came closest to turning into hot war. The Soviets set-up missile bases in Cuba—right in America's backyard—and despatched ship loads of nuclear missile to its ally. The US demanded dismantling of missile bases in Cuba and imposed a naval blockade of that country. The imminence of a possible confrontation and clash between the US and Soviets in the high seas sent shock waves throughout the world, which shuddered at the prospect of a nuclear holocaust. Ultimately, after days of acute tension and hectic parleys, the Soviets called back the ships and agreed to dismantling of missile bases in Cuba. The inevitable nuclear logic of mutual destruction drew back the two Super Powers from the precipice and the world heaved a sigh of relief.

That was cold war all about which, in the ultimate analysis was rooted in the ideological conflict between communism and anti-communism. It would be naive to describe any major or minor dispute between the two countries anywhere in the world as a state of cold war between them. It is ridiculous to term the dispute between India and Pakistan over whatever it may be as something of a cold war. Dispute over one issue of another is a common feature of international relations. It is difficult to conceive of any two independent nation states which do not have a dispute over one matter or another at any point of time. To term any such dispute between two countries as a state of cold war between them is an exercise in absurdity.

In case of India and Pakistan, the only ostensibly insoluble dispute which has kept them apart since independence is in regard to Kashmir. The sacredness imparted to it on both sides and the drum-beating, sabre-rattling and rabble rousing associated with it have blown the Kashmir dispute out of all proportions. Pakistanis have invested Kashmir with the holiness of a second Jerusalem or another Mecca worth fighting a 'Jehad' for. Indians have attached to it the sacredness of the holiest of the holy cows not to be touched with a barge pole. It is neither.

Referring to the 'Jehad' call for securing annexation of Muslim populated Kashmir valley to Pakistan, an Indian Muslim columnist writes: "This is preposterous. Seceding from India and joining Pakistan simply means leaving a country inhabited by 130 million Muslims and joining one with 100 million Muslims".[5]

That should set the records straight. Islamic Republic of Pakistan has 100 million Muslims but 30 per cent more than that number of Muslims—130 millions— live in India. Out of these, only three million Muslims live in India's part of Kashmir valley. If some one talks of 'Jehad' to liberate three million Muslims of Kashmir from India, what about the remaining 127 million Muslims in India? Would anybody talk of a "Jehad" to liberate them?

Shorn of all populist rhetoric and politico— religious pedagogy on the part of Pakistanis and Indians, the dispute over Kashmir is no more than an ordinary territorial dispute between the two countries. Not that either country is short of territories to administer. One wished India and Pakistan administered the territories they already have better rather than fussing and fighting about additional territory in Kashmir or anywhere else. It is undoubtably a hang-over of the partition. It was a mere chance that Jammu and Kashmir happened to be a native state ruled by a Maharaja under the overall control of the British as the 'paramount' power. If it had been a part of British India, Mountbatten and Radcliff would have just drawn a line to democrat the boundary between India and Pakistan in that region and that would have been the end of the matter. If it happened in Bengal and Punjab, it would have just as well happened in Jammu and Kashmir too.

When Bengal and Punjab were partitioned in 1947, there was dispute over the capital cities of Calcutta and Lahore. The Radcliff Award gave Calcutta to India and Lahore to Pakistan and everybody accepted it without a whimper. The state of Jammu and Kashmir comprises of Hindu majority Jammu in the south and Buddhist majority Ladakh in the north with the Muslim majority Kashmir valley in the middle. Even according to the religious yardstick, Jammu and Ladakh would have been awarded to India with a connecting link through the Kashmir valley. Radcliff would have simply drawn a line on the map of Kashmir valley allotting Srinagar, with its considerable Hindu population, and of course the northern passes for access to Ladakh to India and Baramula to Pakistan or something like that. It would have been just like Calcutta being awarded to India along with the narrow north Bengal link to Assam while partitioning Bengal and drawing the boundaries of East Pakistan (now Bangladesh). And everybody would have accepted it as the international border.

What Radcliff would have achieved by using his pen to draw a line on the map, India and Pakistan have not been able to achieve in 50 years— a solution to the so-called Kashmir dispute. In the process, they have bled Kashmir through three bloody wars and are bleeding it now through a corrosive bout of terrorism or proxy war. By giving it an oversize dimension in their relationship, they have converted this simple little dispute into a mega issue to keep on a course of perennial confrontation and strife. With both India and Pakistan having ill-concealed nuclear capability of sorts, with perhaps a few vintage bombs in their basements, and newly acquired missile capability, indigenous or imported, they have exposed the teeming millions of South Asia to mutual destruction.

With the present frozen mind-set of Indian and Pakistani people, no solution to the Kashmir problem can be expected in the foreseeable future. With the sky-high populist postures on both sides, no Government in India can afford to hand over any part of Kashmir to Pakistan on a platter. And no Government in Pakistan can survive if it gave up claims on any part of Kashmir. It is an international stalemate of the century set to spill over to the next century. In the arena of politics among nations, there are and always have been many instances of seemingly interminable disputes or territorial claims and counter-claims between two countries—hanging fire for what would appear to be ages. But they know better how to live with such disputes and yet do business or at least avoid grievously hurting each other with remote controlled violence and terrorism in each other's territory.

Hong Kong and Taiwan belonged to the "Heavenly Kingdom" of China since the time of the Manchu dynastic rule beginning

1644, or before. With the decay of the "celestial Empire" and its mounting humiliation at the hands of western powers and Japan during the 19th and early 20th centuries, both the territories on its outer fringes slipped out of Chinese hands. Hong Kong was ceded to the British by the Treaty of Nan-King in 1842 after China's humiliating defeat in the First opium war. Since then it remained a British colony for over 150 years until its restorations to China in this 50th year of British withdrawal from South Asia. It remained outside Chinese domain for 48 long years after China emerged as a power to reckon with in 1949. All these years China kept asserting its firm claim over Hong Kong without yielding an iota over the issue. But it never tried to 'export' terror or violence to Hong Kong which it could have easily done with the large ethnic Chinese population in the land. China had an additional ground to destabilise Hong Kong, if it wanted to, because it practised unabashed capitalism right in the face of Mao's die-hard communism. But Mao's China chose not to do so. And all these years, Hong Kong continued to prosper under its free market capitalist economy until it grew to be one among the economic giants of East Asia.

Even more telling in this regard is the case of Taiwan (Formosa) which was a part of the Chinese Empire till 1895. China fought a disastrous war with Japan over the issue of Korea in 1894-95 and was roundly defeated. It was in the wake of this decisive defeat that China ceded that island of Formosa (Taiwan) to Japan in terms of the Treaty of Shimonoseki concluded in 1895. By the time Taiwan reverted back to China after Japan's defeat in the Second World War, China itself was plunged into a bitter civil war between the Kuomintang forces of Chiang Kai Shek and communist Armies of Mao Zedong. As the Kuomintang armies were routed by the communists on the Chinese mainland, Chiang Kai Shek fled to the offshore island of Taiwan and set-up his own Government there under American protection. Since the day Mao established the People's Republic of China on the mainland in October 1949, China has claimed Taiwan as an integral part of the People's Republic under illegal occupation of the Kuomintang 'clique'.

For nearly 48 years, the two Governments of China (mainland) and Taiwan have been on bitterest of terms. Until early 70's it was Kuomintang Government of Taiwan which occupied the seat meant for China as a permanent member of the UN Security Council. It was only after the Sino-American rapproachment during Nixon Presidency that mainland China replaced Taiwan as the fifth permanent member of the UN Security Council. Even with such a background of inbuilt hostility, China never thought of 'exporting' violence and terrorism to Taiwan. And all through while Mao's China went about its own communist way, even blundering through the 'great leap forward' and "Cultural Revolution", Taiwan kept marching along the capitalist road to prosperity absolutely unhindered by the 'Big Brother.'

That would actually be an understatement in respect of the emergence of what may be called the 'Taiwan Phenomenon' of the 90's. Along with South Korea, Hong Kong and Singapore, Taiwan has emerged as one among the four economic miracle-makers of Asia Pacific region. The four tiny Pacific Rim countries have grown into world's leading exporters of manufactured goods. By early 90's the four economic giants together with Japan accounted for over 10 per cent of the world trade in manufactured goods, approaching the US share of around 12 per cent. The tiny foursome have come to be the fastest growing economies in the world registering growth at a level twice that of the global mean.

That is only one part of the 'Taiwan phenomenon'. The other more significant part from the stand point of our analysis here is the collapsing wall between China and Taiwan. In 1987, bilateral trade between Taiwan and China, which can legally be conducted only through third countries, amounted to about 1.5 billion dollars. Five years later in 1992, bilateral trade through Hong Kong alone was estimated to exceed 6 billion dollars, with the total estimated at around 10 billions. In 1987, less than seven thousand Taiwanese visited the Chinese mainland. In 1992, the number was estimated at over one million. Taiwanese light industrial and processing companies were estimated to have invested above three billion dollars in China between 1987 and 1992, most of it in the "special economic zone" or 'capitalist' area of communist China across Kowloon Bay from Hong Kong.

But that is another Asia, the achieving and performing one, the one that has not only caught up with the developed nations of the west, which had a heady start with the Industrial Revolution of 18th and 19th centuries, but is beating and surpassing them in this late 20th century age of Technological Revolution. That Asia is geographically not so far and yet socially, economically and technologically so very far from the cesspool of socio-economic stagnation that South Asia has come to represent. It is a part of Asia where all manners of anachronistic, outmoded non-issues become the most important issues of multiple conflicts and confrontations. It is an Asia where any dispute appearing totally irrelevant in any modern society—religious, ethnic, regional, linguistic and what have you— is good enough to trigger of violence and terrorism. It is a part of Asia where everybody in stead of looking and moving or at least inching forward is looking more and more backwards in time and history. South Asia has become a land of perennial strife, conflicts and violence because it is in conflict with history itself. How come? The succeeding chapters will explore.

References

1. *India From Curzon to Nehru and After*, Durga Das, 1971.
2. *Friends not Masters*, President Mohammad Ayub Khan of Pakistan, 1967.
3. "Terrorism Violence", the author in *Denouement* magazine March, 1990.
4. U.S. News & World Report, dated May 1, 1995.
5. *Mindless violence, not 'Jehad'*, Sultan Shahin, *The Hindustan Times* (Patna edition), dated 15 March, 1997.

9

March of History

From Tribe to Nation State

From the time the homosapien (the human kind) started living with others of his kind, he needed some sort of a social organization to make community life possible. The earliest social organization to knit man and man together was tribe. The tribe emerged to bring about some order in the conduct and activities of its members as the primitive man advanced from root-picking, fruit-gathering and hunting for a living to agriculture which needed a settled or partially settled life. Although the primitive human kind remained partly pastoral for a long time, his taking even to rudimentary agriculture required some kind of fixed abodes. That meant living together in communities on fixed locations which necessitated some kind of sharing and regulation of the activities of community members. The tribe came up to perform the regulatory function and command obedience of its members. Though purely need-based and utilitarian in origin, in course of time every tribe became an over-size entity with a special sanctity attacked to it. Legends and myths grew around tribes through thousands of years of sway and they started commanding absolute loyalties of their members. Tribes or group of tribes also developed their own superstitions and beliefs, totems and taboos, diverse and distinct, and often clashed violently when coming into contact, usually for acquiring land or other means of subsistence.

Living under nature in its raw form, the primitive man must have been struck by wonder at the vastness of his natural surroundings and fear of the unknown early in his evolution. The roots of rudimentory religion lie in the primitive man's sense of wonder and fear as is evident from his worship of nature and natural objects. It was reflected in the worship of fire, rain, trees, animals and so on. Right up to the time of the Hellenic civilization, the westerners were by and large worshippers of nature or pagans.

The ancient Greeks and Romans are known to be Pagans. (Incidentally, Nehru was so enamoured of them that he often prided in calling himself a Pagan.)

To start with, regulatory decisions binding on members of a tribe were taken by each and all members as a collectivity, but this became too cumbersome and unpracticable as numbers grew. This in due course led to one among them, usually the ablest, being accepted as the chieftain who exercised all regulatory powers over other members of the tribe. Initially the tribal chieftains were chosen or elected by the members in consideration of their capabilities and suitably for the task. Some emerged as chieftains by cowing down or subjugating others by virtue of their physical or mental prowess. Through passage of time, the office of tribal chief became hereditary and started passing from father to son. That gave birth to dynastic monarchy or kingship as the premier institution of social regulation and control in any society.

The transformation of tribal chieftainship into dynastic monarchy is well illustrated in the origin and development of the oldest known Chinese ruling dynasty known as the Xia dynasty. The Hoang Ho civilization of China—one of the oldest in the world—originated in the settlement of central Asian invading tribes on the banks of river Hoang Ho more than 4000 years ago. The chiefs of this tribal settlement used to be patriarchs chosen by members of the tribe, but a few centuries later one of the chiefs named Yao designated himself as the emperor. Even then Yao was not succeeded by his son but chose his successor with the yardstick of his suitability for the job. It was only later that the emperorship started passing from father to son giving birth to the Xia dynasty—the first dynastic monarchy in ancient China.

Revealed religion as a major reforming and unifying force in human society, taking tribes and Kingdoms in its sweep and uniting these under its wing came much later. The most pervasive of these were Buddhism originating in the 6th century B.C., Christianity at the start of the Christian era and Islam in the 6th century A.D. Buddhism was born in India and in its hey day spread to large parts of South and East Asia and fringes of West Asia. Christianity and Islam both originated in West Asia— about 700 years apart— and spread to vast areas across the world. As all religions are meant to, Buddhism, Christianity and Islam acted as great redeemers of humanity, each in relation to its own time and social context.

Christ preached his gospel of humanism at a time when the mighty Roman Empire had degenerated into an oppressive dispensation. His ideals of equality, love and compassion had great appeal for the oppressed and deprived sections of the Roman society. As the Empire decayed and degenerated further, the attraction to Christianity became so great that the believers were ready to endure persecution and even die for it. And while Rome as an empire was destroyed by North European 'barbarians'— the invading tribes of Goths, Franks and Vandals— in the 5th century A.D., Romanism was demolished by Christianity.

In course of one thousand years from the birth of Christ and advent of Christianity, the religion spread to the whole of Europe from the Russians and Poles in the East to the Irish in the west and from Finns and Scandinavians in the north to Spaniards and Italians in the south. The European society as a whole came to be known as "christendom". By the time Christianity spread to Russia in the 11th century A.D., Europe was split into two Christendoms— the Eastern Christendom based at Constantinople embracing the Russians, Balkan peoples and Greeks known as the Orthodox church and western Christendom based at Rome known as the Catholic church comprising the rest of the European peoples. Christian Europe lived under two parallel authorities independent of each other but working in close alliance and commanding equal allegiance of all Christians—the church and the Empire. The church was supreme in matters spiritual while the Empire was the supreme temporal authority. This coexistential arrangement between the church and state continued in Europe more or less till around the beginning of the 16th century.

Meanwhile, there was another revolution in the sphere of religion in west Asia which was to change the course of history. It was the advent of Islam in the deserts of Arabia with the birth of a new prophet, the Holy Mohammad, in Mecca in the year 570 A.D. The simplicity and directness of its meassage "there is no God but Allah and Mohammad is his Prophet" worked wonders among the utterly confused religious situation of the Arab people.

They were kind of nomadic people living in perpetually feuding clans who travelled to Mecca once a year to worship 360 idols as their gods. What Islam did to their lives is aptly described by Jawaharlal Nehru: "It is strange that this Arab race, which for long had lived a sleepy existence, apparently cut off from what was happening elsewhere, should suddenly wake up and show such tremendous energy as to startle and upset the world. The story of the Arabs, and of how they spread rapidly over Asia, Europe and Africa, and of the high culture and civilisation which they developed, is one of the wonders of history."[1]

The rise of Islam— another revealed religion with the finality of its message— not only halted the spread of Christianity further, but largely wrested western Asia and northern Africa from its fold. With a new proselyting zeal and military conquests, the Arabs carried Islam right into south European territory of Spain. Alarmed at the rising tide of Islam, the Eastern and Western Christendom joined hands together to stop the advance of the Arab champions of the new religion and started the "crusades" against Islamists towards the end of the 11th century. The Arab Muslim advance into Asia Minor and south-eastern Europe was effectively checked.

The later Middle Ages were rocked by recurring religious wars between the adherents of Christianity and Islam inspired by missionary proselytizing spirit of the two religions. Between 12th and 15th centuries, hordes after hordes of Christian monks and 'crusaders' fought to wrest the Near East from Islam. The Christian 'crusades' not only failed eventually, but helped to revive and arouse the forces of Islam to mount another more successful assault on Christendom. This time round, it was the more vigorous Ottoman Turks who took up the cudgels on behalf of Islam with all the zeal and energy of relatively new converts.

The Turks were a tribal people hailing from the steppes of Turkestan in central Asia who had migrated and settled down in Asia Minor. They had adopted Islam from the Muslim people among whom they had settled in their new homeland. The chieftain of one of these Turkish tribes settled in Asia Minor named Osman assumed the title of Amir of the Turks about the year 1300. It was after him that the Turks who launched the second wave of Muslim conquest from 14th to 16th centuries came to be called the Othman or "Ottoman Turks". And it turned out to be a real big wave which threatened to submerge the heart of Christian Europe. The tidal wave of Ottoman Turks not only restored the whole of Asia Minor to Islam but ended up conquering the entire Balkan peninsula and capturing Belgrade and Budapest by the first half of the 16th century.

But the Ottoman wars against Christian Europe finally ending in the first half of the 16th century turned out to be the end of the series, the last of the big religious wars of history. Not only because the Turkish surge exhausted itself and abated, but more importantly because the European's at this point in history had other more important things to do than engaging themselves in rolling back the Muslims. The process which was to take the Europeans far ahead of the rest of the world for centuries to come had begun in the 15th century itself. Referring to the state of the non-western world, primarily Asia, in the 15th century, Vera Micheles Dean writes: "For a variety of reasons, recorded in history, this vast land stopped developing politically, economically and socially around 1400, just about the time that the western nations started on a period of extra-ordinary growth with the age of exploration and colonial expansion, the Renaissance, the Reformation, the English, French and American Revolutions, and the Industrial Revolution."[2]

While the Ottoman Turks were totally absorbed in their Islamic zeal and went about conquering West Asia and South Eastern Europe, the west Europeans were bugged by more material motives to embark upon a different course altogether. Prior to the 15th century, people living in distant parts of the world knew very little about one another. Occasional forays into distant lands by stray travellers like the Chinese Fahian and Hiuen-Tsiang lay burried in history. Around the 15th century, ignoring the religious fervour of rampaging Ottoman Turks, the west Europeans set upon the uncharted course of exploring the world. And more remarkably, the people of some of the smaller countries of western Europe did it. The result was an unprecedented spurt in geographical discoveries which in course of the next two centuries not only knit the world together, but also reshaped it beyond recognition.

In 1488, the Portuguese captain Bartholomew Diaz reached

the southern most tip of Africa which was named as the "Cape of Good Hope" by the King of Portugal. Another Portuguese Captain Vasco da Gama rounded the Cape in 1497 and landed at Calicut, India, in 1498. The Christian Missionaries accompanying the Portuguese merchants in the ship established themselves at Goa on the Indian Coast. In 1517, European merchants and missionaries reached as far east as Canton in China and that marked the beginning of European inroads into the Far East. In 1542, they also entered Japan.

The example set by the Portuguese King in sponsoring explorations was also followed by the Spanish king. He sponsored and funded the voyage of Christopher Columbus aimed at finding a new route to India and China. Columbus was an Italian who believed that Asia lay to the west of Europe. Accordingly, he sailed westwards along the Atlantic from a Spanish sea port in August 1492. When he reached a land mass in October 1492, he believed he had reached an island off the coast of Asia. After sailing around other islands (the Caribbeans Islands), he returned to Spain in 1493, still believing he had reached the Asian coast. Three times Columbus went back to the scene of his discovery, carrying merchants and missionaries, looking for the wealth of India and China mistakenly. It was only gradually that the peoples of Europe realised that the landmass across the Atlantic discovered by Columbus was not Asia but a new world, which later came to be known as 'America'.

The first voyage of columbus was quickly followed by similar voyages by other Europeans. In 1500, a Portuguese fleet bound for India ("Indies"of the explorers) by way of Cape of Good Hope was driven westward by strong winds and currents along the narrowest stretch of the Atlantic. It reached the eastern most part of what is now known as South America. The Portuguese captain landed there and named the land as "Brazil".

In 1513, a Spanish explorer named Balboa crossed the Isthmus of Panama and discovered the "Great South Sea", which we now know as the Pacific Ocean. There is a story behind the name. In 1519, a Portuguese Captain named Magellan serving under the king of Spain, proceeded to explore the whole route from Europe to America and America to Asia. In course of his voyage, he ploughed across the vast expanse of the rather smooth and placid ocean to which he gave the flattering name of "Pacific". He finally reached the archipilago which was later named as the Philippines.

Thus by the middle of the 16th century, when the Ottoman Turks were resting on their oars after conquest and Islamisation in a limited part of the known world, the Europeans had discovered a much bigger world as their playing field. They had gathered considerable knowledge of the size and shape of the world. They knew of the general location of oceans and major continents. They had discovered two great new trade routes by the sea—the eastern route around Africa to Asia and the western route to America. As a result the European commerce was going through a veritable revolution.

But geographical discoveries were only a part of the far reaching changes sweeping across Europe during the 15th and 16th centuries. A whole way of life—economic, social, political, traditions, beliefs etc.—which had seen little change for well over a thousand years went through a rapid transformation in course of just a century and a half. In the economic sphere, capitalism emerged to replace the dying and outmoded feudal or manorial economy."Intellectual quickening", also referred to as "Renaissance", was stirring the minds of Europeans away from superstitions and crippling religiousity to a new rational outlook. Politically, the most import development was the emergence of the nation state system or nationalism which overshadowed and superceded all other collectivities claiming people's loyalties. The basic inspiration from which all these revolutionary changes flowed was material betterment.

In its evolutionary process, the European society needed fresh institutions and ideas more suited to the state of development it had reached in the 16th century than the older institution of religion. It required another more pervasive and this—worldly institution to satisfy its urges and aspirations. It needed a political state which was quite different from the politico-religious Holy Roman Empire or the Ottoman Empire. Although each nation state was centred round a core of nationality based on commonality of language, culture, tradition, heritage etc., but the most important uniting force was the common economic interests of the fast growing sections of the population.

Medieval craft guiltes in small towns and feudal stranglehold in the countryside were proving too localistic and restrictive. The rising class of merchant capitalists and traders looked more and more to their respective national governments for protection and support both against restrictive feudal particularities at home and competition abroad. New interest in the pagan culture of ancient Greece and Rome aroused by the "Renaissance" inspired the belief that satisfaction was better than sacrifice, gratification of human desires better than abnegation preached by religion. Vast economic opportunities opened up by the discovery of America and new ocean routes to South Asia and the Far East beckoned to be exploited. The people of Europe needed an adequate political instrument to enable them to do so. The institution of nation-state admirably filled the bill.

Nationalism was thus another utilitarian, need-based political organization emerging in Europe in course of the 16th century, as tribe and kingship earlier, across the world. It was and is only a stage in the evolution of socio-political institutions to meet the changing needs of human society. There is nothing more sacred or sanctimonious about it; nothing less either. For the process of human and social evolution has not come to a full stop. It never does. If there is one unchangeable law of social evolution, it is change itself.

One major obstacle to the evolution of full-fledged nationalism in the 16th century and earlier was the tradition bound supranational institution of the Christian church. When printing was invented, America discovered and Copernicus was born, vast majority of Europeans were Christians. Those who lived in central and western Europe were members of the Catholic church, those living in Russia and majority in the Balkan peninsula belonged to the orthodox church. But in the year 1500 and onwards, European society was undergoing a sea change. The 'Renaissance' generating a new admiration for the pagan values of ancient Greeks and new learning had begun to fast erode purely religious ideals. It fostered the ideals of human satisfaction and happiness and promoted adventures in pursuit of these. The artist, the ruler, the sea captain and businessmen were pursuing careers which were more exciting than sainthood. Above all, humanist scholars of the age like

Erasmus and Thomas. More highlighted the evils that had crept in the functioning of the established church at the time.

All these factors coupled with advancing economic nationalism made the demand for radical reforms of the existing church irresistible. The result was a religious upheaval in 16th century Europe which goes by the name of the great 'Reformation'. Three main reformist groupings labelled as Lutherans, calvinists and Anglicans, with a number of splinter groups rose up to challenge the established church. The radical 'Protestants' as the reformist groups were broadly referred to, revolt against the Catholic church shook the foundations of the religious order in Europe, which removed a major obstacle in the way of full growth of the nation state and nationalism. In fact Reformation was both fanned by growing nationalism and also fanned the spirit of nationalism to consolidate itself.

The most important impact of Reformation was the dethroning of religion from the dominant position it occupied earlier in the sphere of politics. The thousand years old belief that political unity of a country or kingdom depended on religious unity, which had led kings and emperors to compel their subjects to conform to one religion, took a severe beating. In the centuries that followed the Reformation, it steadily dawned upon the Europeans that tolerance of religious differences was not only not destructive of national unity but also positively strengthened it. The Reformation paved the way for the eclipse of the theocratic polity of earlier centuries in Europe and ushering in of modern, religion-neutral or secular polity which is the essence of nation state system or nationalism.

One last encumberance of emerging nationalism in Europe during the 16th century was its association with monarchical absolutism. Nationalism grew up initially in the apron-strings of kings and monarchs in England, France, Spain, Portugal, Scandinavian countries etc. But this was only a transitional phase suited to the interests of the dominant merchant class in the period of transition from feudalism to capitalism. In due course when full-fledged capitalism or capitalist mode of production arrived in Europe during the 17th and 18th centuries, monarchical absolutism became a fetter in the way of advancing capitalism based on freedom of enterprise and competition. This was manifest in parliamentary struggle against royal absolutism in England during the 17th century and in France and the rest of Europe during the 18th and 19th centuries. It was the French Revolution which finally freed nationalism from the apron-string of monarchy and ushered in the era of Republican nationalism.

Colonialism and Post-Colonialism

Colonialism was nothing more than a part of the process which transformed Europe beyond recognition, socially, economically, politically, intellectually, geographically etc., beginning the 15th century. The outstanding fact of modern world history is that of all the diverse peoples inhabiting distant parts of the world, like the Chinese, Indians, Africans, Caribs, Mayas etc. it was the European alone who set about exploring distant regions of the globe since the 15th century onwards. Equipped with mariner's compass and navigation charts based on knowledge of the Pole star, people of small countries of Europe like Portugal, Spain etc. sailed across the high seas across the world. They not only discovered the new world and new ocean routes to South-East Asia and the Far East, but also established contacts with placid peoples and civilisations of Asia and Africa in course of the next three centuries.

There was nothing ethereal, spiritual or racial about it all as some people are apt to believe. On the occasion of the anniversary of the sub-continent's independence in August 1995, Arvind Kala, an Indian columnist wrote: "Independence Day is usually the occasion for looking back with resentment on the 200 years the British ruled over India. What India and the rest of the third world must ask, however, is why the west was the conqueror and not the conquered in the colonial game." And then he proceeds to provide the answer: "The answer is that the third world did not possess the adventurousness of white men, who crossed oceans in leaky boats to discover and colonise vast land masses they did not know anything about. The people of the third world remained stuck to their shores, living in primitive huts and subsisting on marginal agriculture.....Undaunted by adversity, a succession of white pioneers in primitive boats battled storms, attacks of scurvy, and mutinous sailors to conquer the world. Thanks to this dynamism, European colonial powers controlled 85 per cent of the world's land mass by 1935."[3]

The answer begs many questions. What propelled the "White pioneers" to their extraordinary "adventurousness" only during and after the 15th century? If "this dynamism" was in their blood or colour of their skin, why it manifested only after the year 1400? Why this sudden outburst of energy after one and a half millennium of sleepy existence as the rest of the peoples of the world? What the columnist has furnished as the answer to the question put by himself is actually a statement of bare fact and not the answer, a statement of what exactly happened and not how and why it happened. A more adequate answer has been sought to be provided in the author's book *India: Twilight At Midday (Untold Story of a Sick Society)* published less than a year ago.[4] It need not be repeated here except for affirming that it was the indomitable urge for material betterment, shorn of any religious or spiritual hang-over of the past, which goaded the Europeans on to their epoch-making adventures of geographical discoveries. Nothing more, nothing less.

From their adventurous voyages across the high seas and visits to distant lands, the European adventurers returned with ships laden with commodities like spices, silks, cottons, precious stones etc. and made huge profits by selling the merchandise in fast expanding urban centres of Europe. What eventually made them the masters of the countries of Asia and Africa was the political advance they had made in their own countries. It was the political institution of nation state which clinched the issue in their favour. Britain, France, Spain and Portugal had become nation states while the rest of the world was still in the prenational stage of mere dynastic, religious, regional kingdoms or tribal regimes. They became the colonial rulers and Asia and Africa their colonies because they had arrived in the modern world while the others were still politically in the Middle Ages.

Vera Micheles Dean aptly sums up:"Before the 1600's there were no divergences of a fundamental nature between the living standards, the cultural achievements and the political theories of Henry VIII in England, Peter the Great in Russia, a wise Chinese emperor or, in India, the Hindu ruler Ashoka or his Muslim counterpart Akbar....But with the coming of modern industry, the rapid development of science, the growth of towns, the rise of the middle class, *and the emergence of the modern nation-state*, the west forged rapidly into another era while the rest of the world continued to live in an earlier time."[5]

Commercial penetration was whole-heartedly aided by rising nationalism of European countries to thread the medieval kingdoms of Asia and tribal societies of Africa into the imperial network. Initially as nationalism was growing under the wings of monarchy, the large trading companies of European countries were actively patronised by the kings and monarchs of the respective countries. The English monarchs Elizabeth and James I held shares in the East India Company and relied upon it for financial and even political support at home. The British and French monarchs fought the 'Seven Years' war (1756-1763) as two nation states across the board in America, West Indies and India. In all these areas, the British decisively defeated the French, who were driven out of these countries except for a few pockets. In India, it was Robert Clive who clearly out-manoeuvred and vanquished the French commander Duplex to confine the French to the tiny pockets of Pondicherry and Chandernagar. All this while, the Indians were a bunch of native princes—Peshwas, Nizams, Sultans, Rajas and Nawabs—who could not be expected to stand up to a fully-fledged nation state that England had grown into.

The advent of Industrial Revolution, first in England and then in other countries of Western Europe, further accelerated the process of establishment of colonial empires. The Industrial Revolution brought about a quantum jump in production of commodities by European nations which far exceeded their national capabilities. To maintain and expand their scale of production, the European nations were eternally hungry for sources of raw materials and markets to sell their products. This is exactly what they secured by establishing colonies and bringing vast areas of Asia and Africa, still subsisting on the medieval modes of production for use and primitive agriculture, under their sway. The Industrial Revolution enabled the westerners to make use of man-made energy to produce goods and commodities for sale while the old countries of Asia and Africa were still dependent upon energy of drought animals and human muscles to produce for use. As a result, by the end of the 19th century, Europe spread its imperial tentacles over non-European peoples across the globe.

So much so that by late 19th and early 20th centuries, colonies became a kind of status symbol for European powers competing for supremacy among themselves. One of the major grievances of resurgent German nationalism before the First World War was that Germany did not have her share of the non-European colonies to which she was entitled in accordance with her stature in the hierarchy of European nations. By the time she could join the scramble for colonies after German unification in 1871, most of Asia and Africa had been parcelled out among the old European nations like Britain and France. The Germans felt left out in the cold and, in preparing for war at the beginning of the 20th century, they were seeking for themselves "a place under the sun"—the sun of imperialism. It is a measure of the seriousness of the German grievance that in late 1911, a leading British pacifist—Noel Buxton—and his associates felt that Germany could be accommodated in the 'Cabinet of nations" (of Europe) by making some colonies available to her as a token of good-will to avoid war.[6]

But what happened after 1945? The same colonies which had acquired so much glamour for the imperial countries as to lead to wars among them went off in a bunch, detached from the once mighty European nations like a satellite from a rocket. How come? That brings up the billion dollar question left unanswered in the opening chapter of the book. The answer might explode many of the myths and illusions assiduously built and nurtured in the erstwhile colonial countries, particularly in South Asia, after independence and may therefore be rather unpalatable. But it can be avoided no longer and has to be furnished to restore the perspective.

It would be naive to assume that the colonies were given up by the victorious imperial countries in fulfilment of the professed war aims of the Allied Powers or any such pious platitudes. Political events—national or international—do not emanate from altruistic considerations. Nor did the urge for freedom in the colonial countries or nationalist movements in many of them count for much. Many of the colonial countries which were granted independence were not even stirred by any movement worth the name. At best, the nationalist movements, wherever organized in a sustained manner as in India, constituted only a contributory factor in the achievement of freedom.

The simple, and perhaps not very palatable, truth is that the colonies were set free at almost one go because it was not worthwhile to hold them any longer. The very factors which had brought them under imperial subjugation had undergone a complete transformation. The colonies were allowed to be independent because in the post-war situation, they had become economically counterproductive for the war-ravaged nations of Europe. It was no longer worthwhile to hold on to the colonies in far flung areas of Asia and Africa with the help of armed forces. The game (of colonialism) was no longer worth the candle.

The erstwhile colonies had lost their relevance as markets for the surplus industrial products of Europe, for the simple reason that there were no such surpluses to market in the immediate post-war years. With the European industry crippled by war and so much pent-up or postponed demand within war deprived Europe itself, they were not then in the business of sticking out their necks in search of markets in widely scattered and impoverished colonies. They no longer needed the colonies as profitable outlets for surplus investment capital because they had no such surplus capital to invest. The war ravaged nations of Europe were themselves suffering from acute shortage of capital to rebuild their devastated economies. The US had to come to their rescue with massive financial assistance through the Marshall Aid Plan to enable them to stand on their feet again. Nor had they any surfeit of manpower—technical or otherwise—to 'exploit' the locals. On the other hand, when they started their economic recovery in the 50's, there was considerable movement of skilled and unskilled manpower from the ex-colonies to the ex-imperial countries.

With national consciousness and restlessness growing in the colonial territories of Asia and Africa, keeping up the empire, devoid of the economic benefits, as an empty ornamental showpiece with military power was just not worth it. It would have meant additional unproductive and unnecessary economic burden which they would rather do without. Britain was the first to recognise the logic of the situation. It went about the task of shedding the load in an orderly fashion, even in a hurry. The French and Dutch dithered for sometime to their cost, and had to do it the hard way.

What the peoples of Europe needed after the devastations of the Second World War was not the beating of the hollow colonial drum but fulfilment of their pent-up material needs and economic betterment. The people's choice or preference was made unmistakably clear by the people of Britain, the biggest colonial power before the war, when they voted out the great empire-lover-Winston Churchill— right at the moment of his greatest glory—Allied victory in Second World War. After shedding their colonial load, the ex-imperial countries of Europe set-up on the task of economic recovery, with increasing economic integration in the spheres of capital, technology, market etc. And West European economy went through an unprecedented growth and prosperity during the 50's and 60's. The post-war economic boom in Europe would have been the dream of the best days of colonialism in the pre-war period. If the economies of the ex-imperial countries were booming and leading them to new, unprecedented levels of prosperity, without the colonies, why should they have bothered to keep up with the old outmoded system of colonialism? In the post-war economic situation, the colonies had become an unnecessary encumbrance, kind of a millstone round their neck, and they got rid of them as easily as they had come to acquire them in earlier centuries. Europe and the world had entered the *post-colonial era*.

The Post-Nationalist Era

The end of colonialism, which was after all only an outgrowth of acquisitive nationalism, also symbolised deep erosion of the cult of nationalism itself. The same forces of economism which had led to the emergence of nation states in western Europe in course of the 16th-17th centuries drove the same people out of the nationalist straight-jackets. Increased material well-being and prosperity of the European peoples were no longer possible within the limited parameters of national boundaries. Their efforts for economic betterment had to be integrated and dovetailed into each other's with close economic linkages. The emergence of MNC's (Multi-National Corporations) around mid-1950's revolutionised the concept, magnitude and scale of corporate production. The MNC, in the words of Alvin Toffler, "May do research in one country, manufacture components in another, assemble them in a third, sell the manufactured goods in a fourth, deposit its surplus funds in a fifth, and so on."[7]

Such 'invisible' collaboration among the investers, entrepreneurs, managers, technicians and workers across national frontiers led the European economy to a scale of growth which could not have been conceived of even at the peak of imperialism. The trans-nationalisation of the economy led ultimately to the evolution of European-idea or the Euro economic entity symbolised by the European Economic Community (EEC). In the process, the compelling forces of economic trans-nationalisation struck at the ideology of nation state or nationalism itself in the very soil where it had sprung up first. It was Europe, or western Europe to be precise, which gave the institution of nation-state or nationalism to the world, and ironically it is in western Europe itself that its eclipse is most visible.

The European idea, or the vision of a United western Europe, emerged in the thoughts of the French writer Jean Monet and others in the 50's originally in the gloomy background of a sharply divided Europe in two hostile camps. It was a bi-product of the intense hostility between Eastern Europe dominated by the Soviet Union and western Europe under the American umbrella feeling constantly threatened by the Soviet might. But the idea could not make much headway as long as it was related only to the threat perception of west Europeans and was confined to the security aspect alone. The concept of west European unification took off only when it found expression in economic terms. It was the coming up of the European Economic Community in the 60's which really started the process of European Unification.

The EEC made a modest start in the 60's with its practical agenda of a common market. But the economic benefits accruing from the common market were so great and palpable that such bitter historical adversaries as France and Germany came together to reap those benefits. The traditionally and endemically Euro-sceptic British also, in spite of initial hesitation, could not resist the temptation and joined the common market belatedly. The process of economic integration went on its own momentum until around the 70's when it received a temporary setback. The global oil crisis leading to sky-rocketing petroleum prices and stagflation, unemployment etc., that characterised the world economy, did act as a brake. Governments in Europe, as elsewhere, responded to the changed economic situation by pursuing nationalist economic strategies. This stalled the process of European Unification for sometime but did not end it.

The west European nations took off in the 80's from where they had left in the 70's and have since not looked back. They have gone on advancing from one mile stone to another on the road to unification until they have come to have a European Parliament, a bureaucracy and so on at Brussels. A significant advance was reached with the adoption of the Single European Act of 1985 which called for a fully integrated common market for the 12-member nations of western Europe by 1992. It envisaged the eventual establishment of a Central Bank of Europe, a common currency, co-ordinated tax rates etc.

As the deadline of 1992 approached, the 12 nations met at Maastricht to take stock. And in December 1991 came the momentous "Treaty on European Union" at Maastricht which stretches much beyond a mere economic Union which the Single European Act was all about. Maastricht Treaty is about a political Union of the historically world's most intensely nationalistic countries of western Europe who not only gave birth to the institution of nation-state but also fought two mega wars of nationalism in the 20th century.

Maastricht provides for complete economic union with a common currency, central bank, coordinated tax structures, elimination of internal barriers to trade etc. But more significantly, it envisages a common foreign, security and defence policy, cooperation on immigration policy, uniformity in welfare measures relating to health, education, treatment of workers etc. and such other spheres as environment. It virtually creates a sort of European citizenship. What more is needed to signify the near end of the much glorified institution of nation-state or nationalism as known to the world? And that also in the most developed, lead continent which shaped the destiny of the world during the last four centuries. Analysing the sweeping impact of Maastricht, "The Economist", London, observed: "It cites, in one way or another, just about every goal and policy with which a modern national government could concern itself."[8]

Not that nationalism is already dead in western Europe. When Maastricht was floated for ratification by the people of the 12 nations, many cried wolf. In the first referendum for ratification of the treaty held in Denmark, the Danes voted 'No' by a slight majority. In an interview to a columnist, Neils Astrup, a 79-year-old doctor of Copenhagen, who celebrated the Danish 'No' with an old bottle of Champaign, said he would not like even his great grandchildren to unite with the Germans. Alan Minc, a French economist, saw in the "continentalisation" of Europe the ghost of German domination over both western and eastern Europe from the Atlantic to Urals.[9] The Danes and British are still not reconciled to the image of their monarchs disappearing from the common European currency.

Such old fashioned nationalist stirrings and outbursts of Eurosceptics in the 12-nation combine notwithstanding, the Juggernant of United Europe keeps rolling along merrily. The unification process keeps going along the lines of the famous Leninist dictum 'one step backward, two steps forward.' The 12 nations cannot think of back-tracking on it because the economic imperatives are irresistible. A commentator on the event summed up: "The Eurosceptics have plenty to point to. The biggest reason for thinking that they will be confounded is that the EC is, amazing to relate, bound together by the market forces, rather than in defiance of them."[10] And market economy is the new magic formula, the new panacea for all their economic ills in the eyes of every country in the world. It is marketism all the way. Countries ranging from China and India to Russia and Poland are all hurtling their way to marketisation. All roads; it seems, lead to the market. The notorious Maoist dictum "power flows through the barrel of a gun," which at its worst could lead to outright political banditry as in many parts of India, has now been superseded by a new principle—power flows through the channels of the market.

And for good reasons. Nationalism and imperialism in their developed form were the products of the Industrial Revolution based on fossil fuels. To maintain and expand the massive scale of production, made possible by the Industrial Revolution, the old nationalist imperial countries were eternally hungry for fossil fuels to run their machines, raw materials to feed the machines and markets to sell the products. In course of the last three decades, the old Industrial Revolution has been superceded by an over-powering Technological Revolution. And it is the free play of market forces operating through the mechanism of price which has ushered in the Technological Revolution. Market economy fosters individuals and corporations to initiate and promote technological innovations which enable them to out-price and out-sell others and thereby reap large profits.

Reliance on high technology has not only rendered the colonies and their later version—blocks-redundant, but also made rigid national frontiers particularly in economic sphere, irrelevant. It is the capacity to convert technological developments into saleable products which are cheaper and better than what others can offer, that is the principal goal of all developed economies today. A captive market secured by force of arms or any ideological tie-up like nationalism, communism, Third-Worldism etc. is a poor substitute for the power to compete successfully in the much wider market of the world. It is this realisation among the much developed nations of western Europe that is erasing the national frontiers and bringing them together into an extraordinary union verging on a new supra-national political entity.

For the United Europe of Maastricht concept would be the largest trading block in the world. Elimination of boundaries and internal barriers to trade would make it the world's largest single market. Tremendous competitive benefits would accrue to the united countries from contemplated economic rationalisations which include enhanced savings and investment opportunities, greater mobility of capital, dovetailing of technologies and economies of scale. These could enable the 12 united countries to compete more successfully in the international market now dominated by American and Japanese multi-nationals. The stakes are too high and none of them would like to be left out from the anticipated economic bonanza, in spite of occasional noises made by Eurosceptics in Britain and some smaller partners of the combine.

References

1. *Glimpses of World History*, Jawaharlal Nehru.
2. *The Nature of the Non-Western World*, Vera Micheles Dean, 1957.
3. *The Telegraph*, Calcutta, dated 16 August, 1995.
4. *India: Twilight At Midday (Untold Story of a Sick Society)*, Shashi B. Sahai, Gyan Publishing House, New Delhi, 1997.
5. *The Nature of the Non-Western World*, Vera Micheles Dean, 1957, Emphasis ours.
6. *The Abolition of War: The Peace Movement in Britain*, Meith Robbins.
7. *The Third Wave*, Alvin Toffler.
8. *The Economist*, London, dated 11-17 July, 1992.
9. *La Grande Illusion* (The Grand Illusion), Alan Minc.
10. Nico Colchester in *The Economist*, London, dated 11-17 July, 1992.

10

Societies in Regression

The Left Overs

As elaborated in the chapter preceding, man has travelled a long way since he started living in his tribe catering to all his social needs. From tribal societies to nation states, he has covered a long distance in time extending over thousands of years. In between, dynastic kingship and religion defined and guided his life as pivots of political organization until nationalism emerged and superceded them all. In course of the inexorable evolutionary process, the human society is now at the point of breaking new grounds and advancing into the post-nationalist era. The old-fashioned nation-state system is proving unequal to the rising human aspirations for material betterment or higher and still higher standards of living. This has resulted in search for and thrust towards new supra-national regional identities, like the European Union or ASEAN, which may eventually emerge as the principal politico-economic entities of the future.

But this is not true in equal measure of all the diverse peoples inhabiting the globe. Although all peoples of the world are living and interacting with one another at the same point of time, it does not mean that all are mentally living in the same century. Perhaps it was so in the static times of the ancient and middle ages right up to around five hundred years ago. The English, the Russians, the Chinese and Indians were on the same wavelengths during the reigns of Henry VIII, Peter the Great, the Ming and early Mugal rulers respectively. But no longer so after that. The Christopher Columbuses and Vasco da Gamas and later the Hargreaves's, Arkrights and James Watts's changed all that. Time started moving faster and faster after the discovery of America and invention of the steam-engine. Only those who were instrumental in accelerating the speed of time and adaptive in reaping its benefits kept pace with it. The others were just left behind.

The process has gone on unabated since then with the speed of time assuming supersonic proportions. Some among those lagging behind recognized the change, made efforts and caught up with time. But others were not stirred, did not know what was happening and remained static and stuck up in their stagnant moorings. The result is that though inhabiting the earth at the same time, large segments of humanity today are still living mentally in pre-16th century world and some even in the neolithic age. *They are the left-overs of history.*

Most of the countries of Asia and Africa which were colonial territories before the end of the imperial regime belonged to this category when they became independent. Basically, they were no more than conglomerations of diverse collectivities, tribal, racial, religious, linguistic, regional etc., particularly in Africa. They had not reached the stage where membership of the state which governed them could foster a sense of authentic national identity. Most of them did not rest upon a 'political society' in the modern sense. Disposition to accept the legitimacy of the state which came to govern them, its personnel, laws and rules was not great because they lacked the affirmative attitude towards the norms of political behaviour. The mass of the people still lived in and subscribed to the old sub-cultures of tribe, caste, community, religion and region which commanded their primary loyalties.

On the face of it, the situation appeared different in South Asia. The founding fathers of the newly independent states of India, Pakistan and Sri Lanka belonged to the peak period of the nationalist era. They had received education which was metropolitan in its source and content. The Indian political elites had conducted a prolonged agitational movement for freedom from colonial rule, often borrowing the idioms and rhetoric from the nationalist movements which had swept across Europe in post-Napoleonic era. When they succeeded the British after independence, they worked overtime to mould their diverse peoples into compact national identities with a passionate zeal. For their traditionally splintered indigenous societies, nationalism was the most integrative ideology to keep their people together and they did everything to promote it. It was true of India, Pakistan and Sri Lanka alike.

In spite of separation of the Muslim majority provinces in the West and East, Indian leaders continued to build up Indian nationalism independent of religion. India continued to have a very sizeable Muslim population and Muslims continued to occupy very important positions in public life and public services and contribute to national endeavours in every sphere. In Sri Lanka, the first nationalist political party comprising all sections of the population was formed *after* independence in the shape of the United National Party. In Pakistan, its founder proclaimed it in most emphatic terms to be a fully modern nation-state making no distinction between its citizens on grounds of religion.

But the nationalist elites were a class apart, quite distinct and wide apart from the vast majority of people in their respective countries. By virtue of their westernised education and political training in principles of modern nationalism emanating from the west, they had fully arrived in the modern age. But not the vast majority of their compatriots who were deeply sunk in the pre-modern, pre-national milieu of medieval and ancient times. There was a wide hiatus between the nationalist elites of India, Pakistan and Sri Lanka and their countrymen in general. While the Nehrus, Jinnahs, Senanaykes and Bandernaikes belonged to the 20th century, many among their followers lower down and certainly the masses at large belonged to the medieval times in their socio-political attitudes, beliefs and behaviour. The wide gap between the nationalist elites who succeeded the British and their people was the biggest stumbling block to sound nation-building in South Asia after independence.

The Regression Syndrome

In the situation they were faced with, the nationalist elites had only two options. They could either bring up their peoples, who were left-overs of history, to modern times or go down themselves to their levels to bridge the gap and keep the people in good humour. It was a stern choice between uncompromising, unadulterated modernism and populist obscurantism. As long as the top leaders were around, they strained their utmost to bring their people up by every possible means. But it was a stupendous task and has rarely succeeded in history. Mustafa Kamal Attaturk tried to do it in Turkey and though he made significant gains in his life time, Turkey is still struggling between modernism and religious fundamentalism. In India and Pakistan, as soon as the founding fathers disappeared from the scene, their successors opted for the second, easier course of courting the masses by going down to their level of obscurantism. In Sri Lanka, one of the first generation elitist leaders himself, as described earlier, chose to arouse the pre-modern loyalties of religion and language in an exercise in populism which eventually cost his own life.

As the second generation politicians of South Asia started courting the masses by pampering to their pre-modern and primordial sentiments, all the labours of the top nationalist elites at the dawn of independence were set at naught. These societies, in stead of consolidating the gains of national independence which came on a silver platter to them, started moving backwards in time to their medieval or pre-national past. A process of virtual *de-nationalisation* began which slowly and steadily started tearing the slender fabric of new-born nationhood apart. Once the process of blacksiding started, it became competitive. Every political outfit started vying with every other in stooping down to fan up the narrow anachronistic sentiments of the masses in order to curry favour with them and strengthen its political support base.

It started with substituting everything associated with the British rule by indigenous concoctions often going to absurd lengths. As long it was confined to substitution of tokens and symbols like names of places and institutions, often digging deep into the past to cook up an equivalent which was really not there, it was all right. The competitive craze for rubbing off every trace of British connection brought about drastic changes in the dress code, manners and etique of public figures and public servants. Politicians in power from different regions started putting on outragiously uncouth and divergent robes in public to flaunt their religious, tribal, caste or regional identities and divergences, making solemn state functions look like fancy dress shows. That was also all right.

But the backsliding went much beyond such harmless exhibitionism of particularities and divergences. It started severely damaging the very fabric of the system itself when basic norms and standards of political society began to be tampered with and destroyed. Like when a notorious dacoit and outlaw accused in law courts of mass murders was nominated by a leading political party as its candidate and elected member of the Indian Parliament on caste votes. Or when the Chief Minister of a state in India charged with naked corruption involving plunder of around Rs. 10,000 millions from the state treasuries boldly proclaimed that he would continue to rule the state from within the prison house. His only claim to clinging onto power violating all norms and codes of political conduct in a modern political society was that he was elected a member of the state legislature by his castemen from one among over 300 constituencies inhabited predominantly by them.

Distancing from the British connection could not go further. If that was the sole criterian of independent national identity, Indian nationhood has reached the pinnacle of 'glory'. For in Britain, a minor misdemeanour on the part of a politician is enough to send him packing off the stage. In June 1997 the ruling British Labour Party promptly suspended its senior member—Bob Wareing—from the parliamentary party because of allegations he had not properly registered a financial matter. Another British Labour MP, incidentally of South Asian or Pakistani origin to be precise, is facing suspension from the party pending further police investigations for an alleged electoral malpractice. The MP Mohammad Sarwar, a multi-millionaire of Pakistani origin, is alleged to have paid 5000 pounds to a rival candidate in the May elections to buy off support. For the people of South Asia familiar with the range, sweep and scale of electoral malpractices, this would appear to be a harmless bit of deviation no one would bat an eyelid at, not to think of taking any notice. There can be no greater evidence of complete independence from the British.

That is perhaps the finer and more subtle aspect of backsliding to the pre-British times when the sub-continent was a congeries of regional feudatories often based on religion, caste, community etc. Beverly Nichols, the roving British journalist referred to earlier, wrote in early 40's: "After all, Indian history, until the arrival of the British, was a record of unbriddled despotism..... nobody but the most purblind nationalist could claim that India, as a whole, was a modern country. Some of it was still in a period corresponding to that of Peter the Great: some of it was Elizabethan, some of it was unabashedly medieval: it was, in fact, a whole buch of historical anachronisms".[1] His ostensibly anti-Indian outbursts, smacking of the "White-man's burden" theme, evoked a storm of protest at the time, but in the condition of the sub-continent today, they linger ominously. For the entire sub-continent seems to have lapsed into the same "bunch of historical anachronisms" which Nichols attributed to India's past. South Asia is afflicted with what may be termed as some kind of a `Regression Syndrome.'

The more pernicious and cruder aspect of this backwards march or regression relates to the lapse of the sub-continent into a state of ceaseless violence verging on barbarism. The splintering of South Asian society into all manners of pre-national identities has generated every variety of constant conflict against one another. There is communal violence, sectarian violence, caste violence, tribal violence, ethnic violence from one to the other end of South Asia all the time. Everyone is busy fire-fighting, in the process turning the states of the region more and more into police states, but no more. Everyone has learnt to live with this state of perpetual violence without a murmur as if it was the most natural thing to happen, like sunrise and sunset. It has come to be an order of sorts, kind of a *violent order*.

In its earlier, less lethal manifestation, J.K. Galbraith termed it, India in fact, as a "functioning anarchy." Today some call it 'subaltern upsurge', some `heaving of the bottom', some `a million mutinies', some even `class war.' It is nothing of the sort. The kind of violent order that has come to characterise South Asia is nothing more than manifestation of regression of South Asian societies into their pre-national, fractured past. It is the ugly face of Regression Syndrome that South Asia is gripped with. Basically, it is the product of mismatch between the technological advance, gadgetry and political institutions of the 20th century, and pre-modern, medieval or ancient mindset of these societies.

The more the relapse into the past, the more fissures appear in them. The more they try to resurrect history in a bid to establish their distinct identity, the louder becomes the clamour to right historical wrongs. There is an increasing tendency on the part of the splintered peoples to settle old historical scores invariably culminating in chronic violence. While the achieving peoples of the world are looking in their front to the future, the South Asians are looking at their back to the past. Search for ever widening material prosperity and higher standards of living is leading the west Europeans, and even the ASEAN countries nearer home, to greater integration, both economic and political. But in South Asia, the *pastomania* of its peoples is leading them to more and more disintegration, not only among the countries of the region but within each country. While economics is superceding politics in other regions of the world, bringing in greater material prosperity, politics is not only eclipsing economics but fractious polities severely retarding economic growth in South Asia. With what results? But first a fleeting view of the state of regression in the leading countries of the sub-continent.

Pakistan: From Nation-state to Nizam-i-Mustafa

Pakistan was born as a fully modern nation-state as conceived by its founder M.A. Jinnah. So as not to leave anyone in any doubt about the complexion of the new state, the Qauid-i-Azam made his conception of Pakistan very clear right from the beginning and repeated it as long as he lived. His first authentic definition of the state he founded single-handed was contained in his first address to the Pak Constituent Assembly on 11 August, 1947, already quoted earlier. He said: "*We are starting in the days* when there is no discrimination, no distinction between one community and another, no discrimination between one caste or creed or another. We are starting with this fundamental principle that we are all citizens and equal citizens of one state." No modern, 20th century nationalist could have defined the concept of a nation-state better.

The mention of the times-mid 20th century when Pakistan came into being—was a vital part of his address. Perhaps he was conscious of the phase of Islamic history when the Arabs and later the Ottoman Turks went about establishing Islamic states in the countries they conquered in Asia, North Africa and South Eastern Europe. But those were different times when the institution of nation-state had not emerged. The Quaid-i-Azam would have none of that, not only because he was a thoroughly modern political leader himself but also because Pakistan had come into existence in the modern era of advanced nationalism. If it had to grow to its full potential and prosper, it had to be religion-neutral in respect of its citizenry, which is the *sine quo non* of the nation-state system.

Addressing a public meeting in Dacca on 21 March, 1948, he said : "You belong to a nation now. You have carved out a territory, a vast territory, it is all yours. It does not belong to a Punjabi or a Sindhi or a Pathan or a Bengali, it is yours. *Make no mistake: Pakistan is not a theocracy or anything like that.*[2] "Even when he referred to Islam or teachings of the prophet in a general sort of way, it was to emphasise the basic principles of equality and social justice taught by Islam. For instance, in his broadcast to the people of Australia on 19 February, 1948, he said : "We follow the teachings of Muhammad—may peace be on him—in which all are equal in rights, dignity and self-respect."[3] But he clearly stated in his broadcast that Pakistan was not going to be a theocracy. He affirmed this in his broadcast to the United States also.

Incidentally, he was very alergic to one thing—the caste distinctions in Indian (Hindu) society—and he made no bones about his strong views on the matter. His repeated references to and emphasis on no distinction on the basis of 'caste' along with creed in all his important speeches about the basic tenets of his Pakistan bear testimony to his stout disapproval of the caste-system. Even while making out a case for separation before partition, he often referred to his total opposition to the invidious caste ideology gripping the Hindu society. Stanley Jones, an American writer who visited India and interviewed Jinnah just before partition was finally decided upon, writes : "In an interview with Mr. Jinnah, he began to say that there can be no cooperation with a society based on caste."

The Quaid-i-Azam had good reasons to bring home to his countrymen over and over again the religion—neutral character of the nation-state he had carved out for them in view of the background of Pakistan's creation. And more importantly, he had visualised a Pakistan inhabited by a very sizeable population of Hindus and Sikhs. And indeed, if there had been no large scale massacres and cross migrations and if Hindus and Sikhs had stayed in Pakistan, they would have accounted for about 30 per cent of the population of that country. In fact the partition of

Punjab had left the Sikh population divided almost equally between India and Pakistan. If the Sikhs had not migrated wholesale to India in the wake of the partition carnage, they along with Hindus would have constituted an important segment of Pak population. Like any modern nationalist leader—Jinnah would have most certainly welcomed that and wanted the message to go across in no uncertain terms.

Justice Muhammad Munir writes: "The Quaid-i-Azam had not even imagined that there would be communal carnage and cross-migration on such a large scale as actually took place. He was confident that the non-Muslims would willingly accept the citizenship of the new state, as it was to be founded on principles which nobody, whether a Muslim or non-Muslim, could deny."[4] And then in a remarkable ventilation of personal commitment to religion-neutrality or secularism, Justice Munir goes onto add: "In fact I was myself waiting for the day when I could demonstrate the Islamic principles of Justice that a Muslim Judge should do justice and not be influenced by the enemity of a party and acting on this injunction, I acquitted several Hindus who had been wrongly convicted by a Muslim special judge and confirmed the death sentence of several Muslim accused who had murdered a Hindu widow who had decided to stay in Pakistan."[5]

The Quaid-i-Azam did not live long enough after partition to cast his nation in the mould of modernism he had laid out for it. It is a measure of the dithering and incipient regressive trends of his followers that even the basic principles on which the new state was to be built up could not be formulated in course of a little over a year that the helmsman lived after independence. Apart from the broad Islamic principle of social justice and equality, which perfectly fitted with modernistic concept of a nation state, he was not prepared to accept any specific reference to Islam in the constitutional document. It was only after his passing away that Liaquat Ali Khan was able to produce the Objectives Resolution, which brought in the name of Islam without unduly compromising the basic equality of all citizens irrespective of their religion.

It was not possible in Jinnah's life-time because clauses like "sovereignty over the entire Universe belongs to Allah Almighty alone "or those implicitly making a distinction between the majority and minority would never have been acceptable to Jinnah. He had made it abundantly clear more than once that in the nation-state of his concept there was no question of any majority or minority on the basis of religion. In fact Liaquat had to wait for six months after Jinnah's death to move the compromise document called the 'Objectives Resolution' in the Constituent Assembly in March 1949. This Resolution was passed unanimously but by Muslim members only because the few Hindu members of the Constituent Assembly boycotted the session. The undoing of Jinnah and all that he stood for had begun in Pakistan.

But that was only a much too small, almost a harmless beginning, as it would appear in retrospect. What followed was inconceivable when Jinnah lived and rode like a colossus in the new state he had himself, more than anyone else, had done so much to bring into being. The anti-Ahmadi violence and disturbances that rocked Pakistan in early 50's were the first overt manifestations of the regression syndrome that started spreading its fangs in the country. The comprehensive 339-paged "Munir Report" on the anti-Ahmadi riots submitted in April 1954 is a highly revealing document on the backwards march of Pakistani polity reflected in the disturbances. The reaction of a Pakistani intellectual on going through the report, expressed in a letter to Justice Munir, is a telling account of the state of regression that had set in. It deserves to be quoted in extenso.

The letter goes on to say :

"Being very close to the Quaid-i-Azam since 1936, until his demise, I have learnt at his feet lessons which I shall never forget.........His utterances public and private, did not leave one with the slightest doubt that he was a progressive man and that he wanted a progressive Pakistan where people lived and worked in accordance with the highest and noblest principles of Islam, namely equality, fraternity and justice. I swear he did not at any time envisage the creation of a *backward theocratic state*, Islamic in name and totally un-Islamic otherwise. He did not create Pakistan to put on the map a state which should live in the clouds of pre-medievalism sliding backward instead of marching forward, and in indecent haste to slide in the neither depths of degradation and theocracy............I hold that those who are endeavouring to set the hands of the clock back a thousand years and are using the cloak of Islam to cover their own short-comings and sins are committing an unpardonable crime not only against society but against Islam."[5]

Thinking in retrospect again, that would perhaps appear to be an over-reaction at the time the letter was written. For what successive rulers of Pakistan have done to the country since then is a stunning commentary on the stage they have reached in their giant strides backwards. It was President Ayub Khan, a professional soldier and by no means a religious bigot, who by his First Amendment of 1963 declared Pakistan formally as an 'Islamic Republic'. It was surprising and yet not so surprising after all. By now Islam had become a political constituency, a matter of competitive populism among the politicians of Pakistan. Being a military ruler, Ayub perhaps wanted a more comprehensive political legitimacy that his hundred thousand odd 'Basic Democrats' could provide him. Islam came in handy and was gratefully made use of to legitimise his military regime.

The real surprise came when Zulfiquar Ali Bhutto, a charismatic leader in his own right who was popularly elected as the saviour of Pakistan after separation of Bangladesh, took another big stride towards theocracy in Pakistan. Ayub had been content with giving Pakistan the name of an 'Islamic Republic'. Z.A. Bhutto officially declared Islam as the state religion of Pakistan. He went further, adopting the Principles of Policy which talked of compulsory teaching of the Holy Quran, and giving encouragement to Islamiat, Islamic way of life, Islamic morals etc. He did not stop at that. When sectarian fanatics indulged in wide-scale violence against Ahmadis in 1974, Bhutto yielded to Muslim orthodoxy and declared Ahmadis a non-Muslim minority in Pakistan. Jinnah had been Zulfi Bhutto's idol in his younger days and yet when in power he undid Jinnah as no one else had done before.

But it was left to General Muhammad Zia-ul-Haq, the last military ruler of Pakistan, to take the process of regression to its logical end. He not only officially and legally made a distinction between Muslims and non-Muslims, putting them on different footings, by his provisional constitutional order of 1981, but also put severe restriction on the religious freedom of Ahmadis, opening the gate-way to their persecution by the state. He travelled backwards headlong on the path towards the Nizam-i-Mustafa of 1300 years ago. The first instalment of Nizam-i-Mustafa was introduced when General Zia promulgated five ordinances on Islamisation of criminal laws in 1979. These related to offences like drinking alcohol, adultery and offences against property for which punishments were sought to be provided on the lines of medieval times. For instance, unmarried persons indulging in sex were to be whipped in public, and the right hand and left foot of those committing offences against property were to be amputated. If a married person committed adultery, he was to be stoned to death.

Scenes of medieval savagery were repeated when there were public whippings and hangings in Pakistan during Zia's regime. The events were publicised in advance and thousands collected to watch the gruesome scenes. The idea evidently was to deter the large numbers who witnessed the horror from committing the crimes for which such punishments were meted out. There were also two cases of theft in which the hands of two thieves were ordered to be cut off but, mercifully, these sentences were not actually carried out. Similar practice of whipping thieves and robbers in public prevailed in parts of medieval Europe also. But criminologists and penologists came across several instances in which some of those who had witnessed such public whippings committed those crimes without any fear, perhaps for the thrill of it. General Zia and his cohorts, in their stride backwards in time, were of course immune to the advances made by criminological and penological sciences in modern times.

Perhaps General Zia was religious-minded personally which accounted for his extraordinary drive towards Islamisation of Pakistan. But only partly. In the main, he too used Islam as his political constituency to legitimise his grip over power. Others before him—Ayub Khan and Z.A. Bhutto—had other constituencies too as their power base. Apart from his 'Basic Democracy', Ayub Khan could take credit for providing a degree of ordered progress, stability with economic growth, to Pakistan as no other ruler before or after him. His declaration of Pakistan as an "Islamic Republic" was no more than just keeping in line with some other Muslim countries of the world. But he qualified his concept of Islam in a way which could appear sacriligious to the orthodox

Muslim clergy so much in ascendency during Zia's regime and even later. For instance, he once said an Islamic constitution did not mean reverting Pakistan to "backwardness". And went on to add that Islam was a progressive religion and a religion for all times and people. If being a Muslim meant going back to the system of 1300 years ago, then he was not for being a Muslim.

For General Zia, on the other hand, Islam was the only constituency he could count upon : With Bhutto's ghost haunting him as long as he lived, he needed the holy Islam to exorcise it. Just a month before Bhutto's execution, Zia had declared that all laws would be replaced by Shariat and "there will be nothing in Pakistan, which is repungnant to Islam."[6] In an article in *International Political Science Review*, 1981, Saleem Qureshi wrote: "In Pakistan, an extremely repressive and brutal regime has entrenched itself by championing Islamic reforms and by imposing fiscal and penal laws which, to the rest of the world, look barbaric and medieval, but which have aroused hardly any opposition within the country because they have been implemented in the name of Islam."[7]

By the time General Zia's regime came to an abrupt end, Pakistan had covered a long distance of around 1300 years back in time from the nation state of Jinnah's dream to Nizam-i-Mustafa of Zia. If there was to be a resurrection and the Quaid-i-Azam came alive in Pakistan of today, he would feel he was in Saudi Arabia or Sudan but not in the nation state he had so fondly created. For a leader who regarded even a distinction between majority and minority repugnant to his concept of nationhood, the present state of Pakistan would be completely alien and unrecognisable. Pakistanis have repudiated the Quaid-i-Azam as comprehensibly as Indians have undone the Mahatma, in less than 50 years since they led the two nations to independence.

In the process, they have sowed the seeds of unending sectarian strife and violence in their country. Once religion becomes the focal point of political mobilization, it opens the floodgates of inter-religion conflicts and violence. If it is a single religion country as Pakistan, it queers the pitch for inter-sect or sectarian disputes and strife. For no major religion in history has ever been such a complete monolith as not to admit of any divergence or difference in respect of dogma or ideology. Islam certainly has not been so from the beginning. It is not only Shias and Sunnis who have been dubbing each other as less than Muslims or even'Kafirs' since the beginning of Islamic history. There are numerous sectarian variations represented by the likes of Ahmadis, Ismailis, Bohras etc. Even in the interpretation of the scriptures, there are followers of divergent schools of thought like the Deobandis, Barelvis, Ahl-i-Hadith etc. who vitally differ from each other on religious dogma. By deviating from the course charted by its founding father, Pakistan has landed itself in a situation of perennial strife.

Even as these lines are being penned, news comes of strikes hitting some Pakistani towns in protest against sectarian killings. A news item with Multan date line reads : "A strike paralysed life in two Pakistani towns in Punjab province on Wednesday as residents staged protests against Muslim sectarian violence in the area, witnesses said. The shut-down hit Jhang, base of radical Sunni Muslim Sipah-i-Sahaba Pakistan (SSP), and another town Khairpur Tamewali where demonstrators blocked traffic for sometime by burning tyres on the roads, they said. Unidentified gunmen killed Shiete Muslims in Jhang on Tuesday and another in Khairpur Tamewali, while two people, including a lawyer for SSP were shot dead in Lahore. Meanwhile, lawyers in about a dozen towns in the southern part of Punjab stayed away from work on Wednesday to protest the killing of an advocate from the minority Ahmadi sect, a spokesman said. Mr Atiq Ahmad Bajwa, a member of Ahmadi sect was shot dead in the town of Kahror Pucca in southern Punjab this week."[8] Pakistan is fast developing into a full blown case of Regression Syndrome.

India: Denationalisation of the State

The real contribution of Mahatma Gandhi and his band of nationalists was not that they wrested freedom from the British. Imperialism exhausted its steam and came to an end on its own all over the world for reasons dealt with in the previous chapter. The Mahatma's biggest achievement was that he weilded such heterogeneous religious, regional, linguistic and political identities into a nation aspiring and struggling to assert its new identity. He transformed a patently Philistine society living on its decadent 'belly culture' for centuries, considering gratification of carnal desires as the be-all and end-all of life, into a vibrant political society straining at its leash for wresting freedom.

Charles Metcalfe, the eminent Raj civilian who studied Indian society in depth wrote about Indian village communities a long time back: "Dynasty after Dynasty tumbles down. Revolution succeeds to Revolution. Hindoo, Pathan, Mogul, Mahratha, Sikh, English are all masters in turn but the village communities remain the same. In times of trouble they arm and fortify themselves. A hostile army passes through the country. The village communities collect their little cattle within their walls, and let the enemy pass unprovoked." Dr Ambedkar was to tell the Indian Constituent Assembly later: "Such is the part village communities have played in the history of their country. Knowing this, what pride can one feel in them? ...... The question is on what plane they have survived, surely on a low, on a selfish level. I hold that these village republics have been the ruination of India". It was such a stagnant and decadent society that Gandhiji had to forge into a national society pulsating with life and vigour. He infused a new life into "a whole bunch of historical anachronisms," to use the derisive but true characterisation of the contemporary Indian society by Beverly Nichols, and brought them into the era of 20th century nationalism.

As observed by an Indian historian, Dr. S.N. Sen, "India in the first half of the nineteenth century was a geographical expression." In 1857, the Marathis, Punjabis, Bengalis, Hindustanis, Madrasis etc. never felt they belonged to one Indian nation. The much vaunted Rebellion of 1857 was no 'national' revolt as such against the British for the simple reason India was not a nation then. The leaders of the rebellion were no 'national' leaders nor was Bahadur Shah the 'national' king. According to Dr. R.C. Majumdar, the distinguished Indian historian, the sepoys who revolted were mostly inspired by desire of material gains rather than any political considerations. The sepoys at Delhi, Bareilly andAllahabad indulged in plunder and loot victimising the English and Indians alike. Dr. Majumdar concludes that "there is nothing in the conduct or behaviour of the sepoys which would justify us in the belief, or even assumption, that they were inspired by love for their country or fought against the British with the definite idea of freeing their motherland."[9]

Even more sympathetic historians of post-independence period, who have a tendency to ratify and romanticise the events of pre-British era in general, admit that it was not the revolt of the country as a whole. "Although the rebels received the sympathy of the people", write Bepin Chandra and his fellow historians, "the country as a whole was not behind them. The merchants, intelligentsia and Indian rulers not only kept aloof, but actively supported the British. Meetings were organised in Calcutta and Bombay by them to pray for the success of the British........Almost half the Indian soldiers not only did not revolt but fought against their own countrymen. The recapture of Delhi was effected by five columns consisting of 1700 British troops and 3200 Indians."[10]

It was the Mahatma's miracle that he metamorphosed and changed such a pre-national society into a modern national society by the time India achieved independence in 1947. The momentum of nationalism so assiduously built by him and his followers continued to hold the people under the nationalist sway for sometime even after his tragic departure from the scene soon after independence. But the momentum started slowing down as years rolled by and the process of denationalisation of the Indian state set in sooner than one would have thought.

1. Linguistic Splitting

As the freedom movement had started gaining momentum, every aspect of British administrative set-up in India had come to be an anathema to the nationalists. Any issue, which could excite people's imagination to want a change, even for the sake of change, was good enough for giving a philip to the national movement. It was in this context that the Indian National Congress, spearheading the freedom struggle, had adopted a resolution at its Nagpur session in 1920 in favour of a reorganisation of provinces on linguistic basis. The resolution-boomeranged on it when the Congress party came to rule India after 1947. When linguistic demands were raised in the South after independence, Nehru said in 1947: "First thing must come first, and the first thing is the security and stability of India." In any case, stirring the linguistic horneet's nest could certainly not be considered first, second or even third priority for India in face of the stupendous tasks on hand so soon after independence.

But Nehru was innocent of the process of regression that was slowly but surely setting in the country, as in the case of Pakistan. The opening of the language trap was the first symptom of the regression syndrome surfacing in India in the early post-independence years. It started with the demand for a separate Andhra state comprising Telugu-speaking population of the existing Madras province in the South. After the first Indian election of 1952, Potti Sriramulu, a Telugu Congressman died fasting for creating of a separate Telugu state. A violent protest followed resulting in the formation of a separate Andhra State out of the old Madras state. And that set in motion a chain reaction throughout the country. The door back to pre-nationalism was opened.

The reorganization of Indian states on linguistic basis that followed is well known. It may have been good, bad or indifferent but that is not the relevant issue here. The amount of acrimony, primordial passions, clashes and violence that linguistic reorganization ignited in India in its wake was a measure of the slide-back from modern nationalism beginning the early post-independence years. At its peak in 1956, the linguistic frenzy on the part of Maharashtrians and Gujratis over the issue of Bombay had reached demonic proportions. Jay Prakash Narayan, who had emerged as a latter-day nation-builder par excellence and a roving ambassador of peace within the country, burst forth: "The hooliganism shows to what depths we could descend in this country. It tore the veil off our much-vaunted culture and showed it in all its ugliness. This is not a question of democracy or non-violence but a simple question of culture and of ordinary human decency."[11]

For a while, the Maharashtrians and Gujratis, the two linguistic communities to whom Bombay had been home since its inception, fought for its incorporation in their respective linguistic states like Muslims and Christians had fought for possession of Jerusalem in medieval times. J.P. further lamented: "They are still talking in the language of war and do not seem to realise that even if Bombay is now given to them it is lost to them for ever, if they do not try to win back the affection and confidence of their countrymen who have made Bombay their home..........Maharashtrians and Gujratis are limbs of Mother India. How can India live if these wounds continue to bleed and how can Maharashtrians rejoice when India bleeds?"[12]

The linguistic cauldron kept boiling for long in Assam with occasional violent eruptions beginning 1959. There were serious anti-Bengali riots in Silchar in Assam which caused much loss of life and property. Reacting to the event J.P. said: "What gives serious cause for anxiety and throws the whole future of the country into doubt is that methods such as murder, loot, arson, and rape are being used for the solution of disputes. If these 'little civil wars', these barbaric methods are not abandoned, India cannot remain whole."[13]

Deeply disturbed by linguistic violence in Silchar, as well as communal riots in Jabalpur which took place near about the same time, J.P. went on to launch a "Citizen's Peace Pledge Campaign" proclaiming that " if we are to progress towards national integration and not disintegration, we all must renounce violence as a means of internal policy."[14] It was a classic example of treating the symptom rather than the disease—the regression syndrome—that had set in after independence and was leading the Indian society to violence and yet more violence. Anti-Bengali riots continued in Assam despite peace campaigns by pious souls like J.P. with intermittent eruptions in 1960, 1961, 1962, 1968, 1970 and 1972.

As early as 1st January, 1959, Durga Das wrote in *The Hindustan Times* on the state of the nation: under the caption 'Where and How We Go.' "India, having had the advantage of Gandhiji's leadership and the influence and authority of Nehru and the Congress Party, has fared better than Pakistan. However, this country too is showing historic tensions. *Tribalism, by whatever name it may be called—communalism, linguism, regionalism, clanism, casteism—is tryiung to assert itself against the forces of nationalism.*"[15] Compared to the stage, "tribalism" in all its manifestations has reached in India today, 1959 would appear to be a golden age. Only, the people of the country have simultaneously reached a stage of mental disorder or dementia which makes them go along merrily with it and stew in their own juice without any feeling or discomfort.

2. Casteisation of the Polity

The most corrosive, divisive, tearing and splintering anachronism that has come to occupy the centre stage of Indian polity and society today is caste. A horrendous throw-over from India's remote past, it has come to be the most accepted, recognised acknowledged and even hailed factor of political and social mobilisation in the country. Everyone swears by it openly, unabashedly as the most legitimate, valid Unit of the state. By its very nature it arouses primordial sentiments of the worst kind keeping the diverse caste groups in a perpetual state of war against one another. It has torn apart the entire nation not only in one set of majority and minority, as in case of Hindus and Muslims before independence, but numerous majorities and minorities in a situation of perennial conflict.

Based on occupationl division of society coming on since the time of the mythical Hindu law giver (Manu), or even before, caste is among the oldest relics of India's distant past. For thousands of years it functioned as a barrier to free social intercourse among people through its concept of 'purity' and 'pollution' and restricting matrimony within the caste. The inherent inequities of the system were exposed and severely challenged even in ancient times by Buddhism, but it survived the onslaught with the revival of Hinduism by Shankaracharya.

Apart from being hereditary, endogamous and occupational, the system implied a hierarchy of higher and lower castes. The system enjoined upon each individual to confine inter-personal relationship like marriage and exchange of food within the restricted circle of his own caste. Marriage was a slightly different proposition in which the hierarchy of high and low was not really involved. It was not as if the higher castes had any privilege of marrying outside their castes which the lower castes were denied. Each caste, so-called high or low, was a rigid endogamous group with no option allowed to its members of marrying outside its fold. Matrimonially, the castes represented horizontal rather than vertical structures.

The hierarchy of high and low was based on the concept of purity and pollution, probably coming on since the times the charioteering Central Asian tribes vaguely known as the Aryans came and settled in the Indian plains. It related mainly to exchange of food and water, which was not permitted between the so-called higher and lower caste groups. This invidious obscurantism—the purity concept—sometimes led to absurd occupational consequences. The poor and illiterate members of the highest among the castes often ended up as cooks in affluent house-holds of other castes, because food cooked by them was by hypothesis 'pure' enough for all castes to share.

But all this was a thing of the past long before the coming of independence, except for a lingering shadow in the back waters of backward rural areas. With the coming of the British and opening of India's windows to exogenous winds of modernity, the system came in for sustained attack from enlightened Indians. Under the liberating influence of modern ideas percolating through the western window, the tradition-bound Indian society steeped in ignorance and superstition was in for a big change. Raja Rammohun Roy, the great Indian social reformer, saw in western education, introduced in India by Macaulay after 1835 mercifully, "the key to the treasures of scientific and democratic thought of the modern west." In fact other Asian peoples like the Chinese and Japanese who were independent were also fervently falling for western knowledge of their own free will during the 19th and early 20th centuries. (Incidentally, many 'wise' men in India today often blame Macaulay for introducing western education through the medium of English as a colonial imposition. That is the surest symptom of their deep affliction with regression syndrome.)

The whiff of fresh air of western liberal ideas produced a gallaxy of such reformers and redeemers of Indian society as Raja Rammohun Roy, Keshav Chandra Sen, Swami Dayanand Saraswati and Swami Vivekananda, heralding what is somewhat debatably called the Indian 'Renaissance'. They all vehemently opposed the utterly outragious notion of 'purity' and 'pollution' and effectively contributed to the erosion of caste system. Caste was totally banished from the Brahmo Samaj founded by Raja Rammohun Roy in 1829, Arya Samaj founded by Dayanand Saraswati in 1875 and Ram Krishna Mission founded by Vivekananda in 1896. The nationalist movement for feeedom from colonial rule that started towards the end of the 19th century took off from where the socio-religious reformers had left. It was an organic continuum of the earlier reform movements which showed in social reform measures like abolition of caste and untouchability forming vital parts of the Mahatma's freedom movement.

Through such powerful social, religious and nationalist movements, the hierarchical aspect of caste, the higher and 'lower' syndrome based on 'purity' and 'pollution', was fast disappearing when independence came. It had almost disappeared in urban areas and was on retreat in rural areas too. Under the impact of economic changes, shackles of hereditary occupations were loosening, giving way to considerable occupational mobility. In the face of emerging socio-economic forces and modernising influences, caste was fast losing ground across the board, lurking only in corners of backward rural areas as a sour relic of a vanishing past.

It was at this stage that the slide-back started soon after independence, as in case of everything else. Caste came to be increasingly relied upon as an important factor of political mobilization. The tendency was held in check as long as the first generation political parties and leaders held sway. Their apprenticeship under Gandhi and Nehru in course of the freedom movement had cushioned them up to a point against succumbing to the temptation of caste mobilization. But only up to a point. As the Indian society as a whole started regressing, caste started asserting itself in politics as a potent factor. The cushion of nationalism started wearing thin as powerful caste lobbies started emerging to grab and corner benefits accruing out of a dispensing state. The trend remained subdued as long as Nehru was around. After him, his successors freely resorted to caste mobilization for retaining or capturing political power. In the bargain, caste, which was on way to dying a natural death, got a fresh lease of life and revived not only in the sphere of politics but in society on the whole. A century of great endeavours by India's foremost social reformers and nation-builders was set at naught in a few decades after independence.

A stage has been reached today when the political support base of a party or leader is calculated only in terms of caste numbers. It may be one caste against another or one combination of castes against another. Every relevant agenda, political, social, economic, administrative—has fallen by the wayside. There are political parties in states and even at the national level which are no more than caste organizations or 'Jati mahasabhas'. Even acknowledged national parties have caste complexions varying from state to state. A prominent political leader of a miscalled 'national' party is on record to proclaim that the future political set-up of the country would be a caste set-up. In course of his election campaigns, he unabashedly tells his castemen : "you must give your daughters in marriage and votes in elections to your own castemen."

Politics in India has gone down to such abysmal depths of degradation that people have become immune to the ravages caused by caste in the political sphere. It is the ominous shadow of caste revivalism on peace and order in society which causes real concern. For the perennial conflict situation created in society by casteisation of politics is taking a heavy toll of human lives. Political differences based on ideology conform to certain rules of the game. Ideology is something abstract, impersonal which does not arouse elemental passions among its adherents. Ideological differences are part of democratic polity and ideological battles are conducted at a rational, political level in any civilized society. But when politics is reduced to the level of a power game between and among rigid kinship groups like caste or tribe, it is no longer politics in the modern political sense. In that case, the miscalled 'political' battles assume the character of blood feuds between and among rival kinship groups like those between Hutu and Tutsi tribes in Rwanda and Burundi, resulting in unending blood-shed. That is exactly what casteisation of politics has done to India today, particularly to those parts of India which are highly casteised.

3. Bihar's Multiple Caste Wars

It was once the land of Buddha who had seriously challenged the rigid caste hierarchy of Hindu society in ancient times. It was a Buddhist 'Vihar' once upon a time, from which it has derived its present name. But today Bihar has become a metaphor for casteised politics, acknowledged as such by the whole country and accepted and acquisced in by Biharis themselves. Bihar's political parties and leaders swear in the name of caste, talk, hear, see and breathe in the name of caste and nothing but caste. Its longlasting leaders are those who have hailed and raised caste to the high pedestal of a cult. What casteisation can do and has been doing to India is best illustrated by what it has done to Bihar during the last two decades or so. Let the facts speak.

On 27 May, 1977, 11 persons, nine belonging to scheduled Caste and two others, were tied with a rope and taken to a field in village Belchi of central Bihar. Each one of them was then shot dead and tossed into flames which had already been kindled. When one of the victims tried to escape, his head was chopped off and the mutilated body thrown into the fire. *Belchi* drew national attention, not really because of the ghastly nature of the crime but because Indira Gandhi, then in political wilderness, made a token visit to the village a few months later on her first major public appearance after ouster from power in March that year. Since the village was inaccessible by any vehicle and rains had made it more so, Indira Gandhi had an elephant ride to the village on what was to be her comeback trail.

It was a horrific carnage by all standards, though not by Bihar standard of today, and yet the perpetrators of the crime enjoyed full support of their castemen. So much so that the principal accused of the case was duly elected to the Bihar Legislative Assembly, while still on trial in court, by his castemen who had a dominant majority in that constituency. He was subsequently convicted by the trial court also but retained his membership of the august Assembly simply by filing an appeal in a higher court, thanks to the permissive electoral laws of India. It was a telling case of caste loyalty washing off all sins of a caste leader, which has since become a characteristic feature of politics in India. That convicted member of Bihar Legislative Assembly, who died during the pendency of his appeal, has become a role model for many 'distinguished' political leaders today.

On 2nd February, 1980, 14 persons belonging to certain caste groups were roasted alive by armed gansters engaged by another caste group in village Parasbigha, again in central Bihar. The victims were taken unawares when on a moon-lit night the gangsters descended upon the village, bolted the doors of every house and set it on fire. The victims included seven women and two children.

In a repeat performance of the gory act three weeks later 14 persons belonging to Scheduled Castes were brutally massacred by another caste group on 25th February, 1980 in village Pipra in the same area. Striking again at night, a horde of marauders dragged the victims out of their houses, pumped them with bullets and torched their huts. Among the victims were two teenage girls, four women and three boys.

On 4th January, 1984, 14 teenage boys belonging to a particular caste were first kidnapped by members of another caste in broad daylight in village Piparia of Munger district. The victims were collecting fodder in the fields for their cattle when they were swooped upon, taken away and massacred.

At the crack of dawn on 8th November, 1985, a murderous mob on horseback belonging to a particular caste attacked the defenceless people of village Lakshmipur Diara of Munger district belonging to another caste. They ended up gunning down over 20 persons and setting over 400 huts ablaze. In this case also, one of the principal accused of the carnage was elected a member of the Bihar Assembly on the vote of his castemen while on trial in session court. He was subsequently convicted to life imprisonment but continued to be a member of the Assembly pending disposal of his appeal by the higher court.

On the night of 29th May, 1987, the biggest of the series of caste carnages till then took place in the twin villages of Dalelchak-Baghaura in Aurangabad district of central Bihar. The first to be attacked was the hamlet of Dalelchak inhabited by only a few members of the victim caste at about 9 p.m. The killer mob surrounded the hamlet, dragged out men, women and children from their houses, set the houses on fire, slit the throats of their captives and flung the dying into the raging flames. Sixteen innocent men, women and children were slaughtered and burnt in this little hamlet. Then the rampaging mob moved on to the main village Baghaura a few furlongs away and enacted the macabre drama of death and destruction with greater fury. Twenty-six persons belonging to the victim caste were butchered in this village in one swift operation. One family lost eight members, another seven and yet another five. The saddist act continued until every member of the victim caste in sight was eliminated.

An ultra left-wing outfit calling itself Maoist Communist Centre (MCC) claimed 'credit' for the action against the 'exploiters' who were actually no more than small or marginal farmers. Nor had they done anything personally to encur the wrath of this extremist outfit. Neither had they done anything themselves against any member or members of the killer caste group which had ravaged them under the garb of a left-wing militant outfit. The marauding castemen were taking revenge for the crimes committed by some other members of the 'victims' caste against some other members of the killer caste in another village a month and ten days earlier. It was a caste blood feud pure and simple between the two castes with all the brutal attributes of savage tribal warfare of by-gone ages. The Maoist tag was only a camouflage, as the same outfit has been committing similar brutalities on caste lines even more frequently in present day Bihar.

This outrage shared at least one aspect in common with the one committed at Belchi ten years earlier. Belchi had been visited by Indira Gandhi with great fanfare under full public gaze on her journey back to the Prime Ministership of India. Dalelchak-Baghoura was visited by another Prime Ministerial aspirant with the same fanfare and publicity on his maiden journey to that high office. After finally breaking up with Rajiv Gandhi in 1987, V.P. Singh the great 'redeemer', started his grand march to Delhi's throne with a visit to Dalelchak-Baghaura months after the tragic event. And the visit to proved as fruitful to him in due course as Belchi visit had proved for Indira Gandhi. But V.P. Singh had an additional reason for visiting the families of Dalelchak-Baghaura carnage victims. They belonged to his caste.

Bihar took another big stride back into medievalism when private armies of some dominant caste groups started mushrooming in the state. In course of the 80's, a number of such caste *senas* (armies), with tacit support and encouragement of caste leaders dominating the politics of Bihar, sprung up in many districts of central Bihar. The more notorious among them were 'Bhumi Sena', 'Kuer Sena', 'Lorik Sena', 'Brahmarshi Sena' and 'Sunlight Sena'. All these *senas* representing the landed classes came up ostensibly to fight against left-wing extremist or Naxalite groups active in their areas, but they were all basically militant caste organizations out to establish their caste supremacy in their respective areas. And three of the above named caste Senas derived their names from some old folk heroes of their caste. Retreat into the Middle Ages was complete.

The 90's heralded a new dark age in the recent history of caste carnages in Bihar. With a regime deeply sunk in the mire of caste, openly touting caste as its power base, using caste symbols and metaphors to assert its claim to power, massacres on caste lines touched a new peak. What is more, they have become routine happenings with sinister regularity as if perpetrated by a hidden machine running on its own steam. It would require a whole book to merely catalogue and describe all the caste massacres that have taken place in Bihar since the advent of this last decade of the 20th century till date. A few samples may perhaps be narrated here.

A front page story in *The Times of India* (Patna edition) dated 24th June, 1991 read: "At least 14 people were killed and nine others injured in the reign of terror let loose allegedly by the goons of an upper caste landlord......in the two villages of Deo and Sahiara last night apparently to avenge the murder of his three men a day earlier."

Analysing the event in a newspaper article at that time, the author wrote : "Bihar has done it again. When 14 people belonging to the weaker sections were gunned down on the night of June 22, many of them while asleep, in Deo and Sahiara villages of Bhojpur district, another bloodied link was added in the chain of mass murders which have pock-marked the bleak landscape of central Bihar. From Belchi (May 27, 1977) through Parasbigha (February 2, 1980).................and Deo-Sahiara now, the massacres have been happening with an ominous regularity investing them with the character of a macabre ritual. The story, written in blood, goes on unfolding itself chapter after one sordid chapter without, it seems, a concluding chapter."[16] One is waiting yet in vain for the "concluding chapter" to be written. In Bihar even the so-called Naxalite or left-wing extremist movement has got sucked up in the vortex of caste animosities getting more and more intense and bitter everyday.

Another gory killing setting up a new bench mark in brutality and saddism took place on 12th February, 1992 in village Bara of Gaya district in Bihar. In this case also, the killers belonged to the same Maoist Communist Centre (MCC) outfit which had committed the massacres at Dalelchak-Baghaura in May 1987. Here also, the victims belonged to one particular caste and were subjected to inhuman brutality only for the fault of belonging to that caste. In a well planned noctural operation, the killer castemen, with the tag of MCC to give them respectability and dubious legitimacy, slaughtered 35 persons belonging to the victims caste who could by no means be placed under the category of landlords or landed aristocracy. They were all small and marginal farmers leading the same kind of poor man's life as the people of rural Bihar.

But that is what the so-called left-wing extremist outfits in Bihar, with perhaps one exception, are doing in their killing operations. They are just playing the caste game, killing and counter killing people and sometimes even each other on caste lines. What marked out the Bara massacre of 12th February, 1992 as a case apart was the degree of saddism and brutality involved. The victims were dragged out of their houses and their throats were slit with knives. While 32 of the victims were literally butchered to death almost instantly, three of the unfortunate had their throats slit only partially. They were left to suffer the agony for sometime before succumbing to death slowly later. Such happenings occur only in stories of medieval barbarity and only primordial passions of caste and tribe could induce humans to indulge in such acts.

In course of the last three years, a more organised, well founded and aggressive caste 'army' known as 'Ranbir Sena' has come to the centre stage of caste warfare in Bihar. Claiming to fight for the land-owning class against growing left-wing extremist influence in central Bihar, it is led, funded and manned primarily by one particular land-owning caste in Bihar. On 11th July, 1996, 21 persons—15 women and the rest children—were massacred in village Bathani Tola of Bhojpur district in central Bihar by killer squads of 'Ranbir Sena'. Led by some well known do-gooders like Kuldip Nayyar, Nikhil Chakravarty, V.M. Tarakunde and Rajinder Sachar, some 200 prominent persons wrote to the Prime Minister angrily protesting this outrage and urging steps to disarm the 'Ranbir Sena'. But in the background of total casteization of politics and society in Bihar, theirs was a cry in the wilderness.

Meanwhile, this Frankestein of a caste army goes about its business of trading in blood without let or hindrance as the caste-oriented state progressively withers away. Early in 1997, the Sena released a pamphlet which morbidly proclaimed: "The earth is littered with corpses; identify which one is yours." The caste war goes on and on in Bihar without anybody being much concerned, except of course the hapless victims who are in any case no one's concern. *The Times of India* sums up: "There are no full stops, or indeed commas, in the killing fields of Bihar."[17]

4. North-East in Tribal Age

India's North-East presents a picture of wholesale transportation of a whole region from the nationalist era to the tribal age. And cutting of the Assamese melon, the steady and progressive dismemberment of what was the big province of Assam during British Raj, is its most telling exhibition. The picturesque, peaceful and sleepy province of Assam before independence comprised of areas parts of which now belong to two neighbouring countries and four provinces or states of India. At the time of independence/partition in 1947, the predominantly Muslim district of Sylhet, famous for its sweet oranges, was merged with East Pakistan, except for a tiny part. In 1951, a part of north Kamrup district named Devangiri was ceded to Bhutan. In 1948, North-East Frontier Agency (NEFA) was formally cut off from Assam and constituted into a separate administrative Unit. In 1963, Nagaland was separated and made a full-fledged state. The dismemberment of Assam did not stop at that. In January 1972, the beautiful Garo hill districts inhabited by Khasi, Garo and Jayantia tribes were detached to form another state somewhat meaningfully called Meghalaya (the abode of clouds), with its capital at Shillong which used to be the capital of united Assam. Simultaneously, the Mizo inhabitated areas were separated from Assam and converted into the Union territory of Mizoram. Cutting into pieces of the Assamese melon on the basis of tribal diversity of its people was complete.

The tribalisation of India's north-east started soon after independence with a virulent and violent Naga separatist movement. The Naga tribal people went on to establish their own so-called 'Federal Government' and a Parliament known as "Tetor Hoho" in their jungle hide-outs and held sway over sizeable areas of Naga inhabited territory. The Indian armed forces had a tough time trying to establish a semblance of national authority over the region for well over a decade after independence. The Naga separatists indulged in large scale violence including blasting of Railway tracks and trains causing considerable loss of life to press for secession. Their armed squads continued their operations even after the creation of the state of Nagaland within the Indian Union in 1963. At this stage Jay Prakash Narayan took upon himself to broker peace between the secessionist Nagas and the Government of India in association with Rev. Michael Scott.

In a note to the 'peace mission' negotiating for a settlement submitted in October 1964, J.P. observed that the significance of a preliminary agreement to hold talks "would be clear when the whole sad story of the past ten years in Nagaland is recalled to the mind. It has been a story of raids, ambushes, sniping, mutual killing, sabotage, burning of villages and innocent houses, regrouping of villages, nameless atrocities,........."[18] That almost set the tone for the orgy of tribal violence and bloodshed in the whole of North-East down to this day. Although Nagaland has since come of age as a viable and functioning state of the Indian Union and so have Mizoram, Arunachal (NEFA), Meghalaya, Manipur and Tripura, the whole of North-East has continued to reel under unceasing tribal violence. Some are indulging in violence against the Union government, some against the state government, some against each other, one tribe against the other and so on.

In Nagaland, a core of Naga tribal people who are still outside Kohima's charmed circle continue to live in jungles and hills bordering Burma and carry on a crusade for secession. Under the banner of National Socialist Council of Nagaland (NSCN), they keep indulging in terrorist acts in Nagaland and neighbouring Manipur. They attack not only the armed forces and other symbols of the established authority but also their rival tribesmen known and Kukis inhabiting the area. In fact terrorist violence against

Kukis has become the major part of underground Naga activities in the region. Naga tribesmen under the tag of NSCN or otherwise go about pillaging, burning and killing Kukis who in their turn indulge in retaliatary violence leading to a running tribal blood feud. In the state of Manipur, Kuki-Naga killings and counter-killings were estimated to have taken a toll of 280 lives in 1992 and 266 in 1993. About 50,000 Kukis were rendered homeless in the wake of Naga offensive in 1992-93.

Even as Nagaland, Mizoram, Manipur were going through their share of violence and terrorism, no one could imagine the cult of murder and arson spreading over to Meghalaya. One of the most peaceful and picturesque spots in the whole of India, this 'abode of the clouds' is inhabited by three ancient tribes—Khasis, Jayantias nad Garos—known for their peaceful, happy-go-lucky disposition. Christians by religion, adhering to matriarchical family structure, fond of good things of life like dancing, music, sports and drinks, the Meghalaya tribes are a class apart, least expected to fall a prey to the malady afflicting their counterparts in the rest of the region. But they could not remain immune to it for long. In less than eight years from the creation of Meghalaya, its peaceful fun-loving tribal people were up in arms against Bengalis and other outsiders inhabiting the land.

On 25th October, 1979, two Bengalis were murdered and 126 cases of vandalism, arson and assault against outsiders took place in Shillong. A Bengali professor was also murdered early in November 1979. And the peak was reached on 22nd December, 1979 when the normally peaceful, happy-go-lucky tribal boys indulged in large scale arson, looting and murder in Mawprem area of Shillong. The disturbances left at least 22 Bengalis killed and much property of outsiders destroyed in the sylvan habitat that Shillong once was. The tribal people of Meghalaya had caught up with the rest of them in Nagaland, Mizoram and Manipur.

Mizoram, which was the Lushai Hills district of Assam in British times, inhabited by Lushai and Hmar tribes, erupted into violence first in 1966. The tribal people organised under the banner of Mizo National Front (MNF) demanding independence started a terror campaign against non-Mizos, many of whom were killed in 1966. To assuage them, Lushai Hills district was separated from

Assam and formed into the Union Territory of Mizoram in 1972. But that did not stop the Mizo onlsaught against the non-Mizos inhabiting the area. It assumed alarming proportions after November 1974 when all non-Mizos were asked to leave Mizoram. A large number of non-Mizos were killed and about 10,000 outsiders left Mizoram after closing their business.

For a number of years, right up to the early 80's, the writ of the Union Government hardly ran in Mizoram. It was the MNF which called the shots and held sway. The governmental establishment was rudely shocked when in January 1975 the Police Chief of Mizoram, his D.I.G. and Superintendent of Police were shot dead in broad daylight right in their office by an armed gang of MNF. Peace talks with Government of India which followed were utilised by the MNF underground for regrouping and rearming themselves for another round. The next major bout of violence and terror erupted in March 1980 in course of which about 25 people were killed. At one stage, the situation was so bad that even the Lt. Governor and Chief Secretary did not move out of their houses. It was only later after a settlement with MNF based on power sharing that the situation improved.

Manipur, which was a Union Territory before 21 January 1972 and became a fully-fledged state of the Union after that has been the most disturbed area of the North-East since early 80's. Bordering Burma both in the south and the east, it is inhabited by 29 Scheduled tribes, of whom Nagas and Kukis are numerically most important. A majority of the tribal population is Christian. But the vast majority, about 60 per cent, of the population consists of Meitis of Manipur valley who are Hindus and are not entitled to the benefits meant for Scheduled tribes. Although the regime of violence in Manipur is multi-dimensional, Naga-Kuki clashes being one, it is the violence let loose by the Meitis which has made Manipur the most turbulent state of the North-East. In the pre-British era over a century back, they had ruled over the hill tribes and are not reconciled to their plight in the post-independence dispensation.

The Meity violence started in a mild way in 1978 and became quite intense by 1980. Hardly a week passed without killings and counter-killings involving the militants and security forces. They indulged in terrorist acts like looting of Banks, killing non-

Manipuris, attacking police stations and ambushing security forces. The fear of killings became so great that the capital city of Imphal turned into a ghost city after dusk and no one moved out except the security forces. Some of the more known militant outfits are People's Liberation Army (PLA). The People's Revolutionary Party of Kangleipak (PREPAK) and Revolutionary People's Front (RPF).

The spate of violence in Manipur shows no signs of abating. The situation has become more complex by intensification of tribalism reflected in frequent clashes between one tribe and another. Of these, Naga-Kuki strife has assumed more serious proportions. In many cases, it spills over from Nagaland to Manipur and vice versa. There have been a series of serious Naga-Kuki killings and counter-killings in the 90's in Manipur as well as Nagaland. In a recent spurt of violence in late June 1997, this time involving Kukis and another tribe Paites, 20 lives were lost in Churachandpur district of Manipur. In this latest clash, 15 Paites and 5 Kukis were killed. The multi-lateral inter-tribal warfare goes on, reverting Manipur back to the tribal age.

But with all the violence around, the real action, as the saying goes, is in Assam, the parent state of the North-East and the hub of all the goings-on in that region. The cannibalization of Assam territorially to create new tribal states not only failed to check the explosion of tribal paochialism in the North-East but has further ignited it in residual Assam itself. The scale, intensity, tenacity and ferocity of parochial and tribal violence in Assam surpass those in all the other smaller states of the region. Not because Assam remains still the most important of them all with regard to its population and resources, but for other reasons. In stead of bringing peace and stability, mutilation of Assam has accentuated the forces of parochialism and tribalism in that unfortunate state.

On the one hand, it has alienated the native Assamese people nursing a sense of grievous hurt inside their hearts. They remember with deep anguish and bitterness the continuous, serial truncation of their state just to cater to tribal sentiments of people who were part of it not very long ago. Many of them hark back to the times of the brave Ahom kings who had ruled Assam for centuries in the past. They remember with pride that unlike the rest of India, the Muslim invaders were never able to conquer Assam. The Ahom kings had six hundred years of uninterrupted rule over Assam until they lost to sturdier tribes from Burma in the 18th century. But the Burmese were driven out by the British who assumed control over Assam in 1826 after victory in the first Burmese war. The last Ahom king, Purandar Sinha, continued to rule over upper Assam till 1839, when that part was also annexed to British India. Conscious sections among the Assamese feel deeply hurt that six centuries of unifying work done by the brave Ahom kings had been destroyed in a span of about two decades or so.

The total alienation of the ethnic Assamese people led to the foundation of the United Liberation Front of Assam (ULFA) on 7th April, 1979. Its avowed objective is to secure the independence of Assam from India by armed revolutionary struggle. Since its formation right up to this date, ULFA has continued to be the foremost and most ruthless militant outfit in Assam spreading violence and terror all around. Its target groups are immigrants, mainly Bangladeshis or Bengali Muslims termed as 'foreigners', non-Assamese generally and of course government functionaries. Their intense hostility to the immigrants emanates from the fear of being reduced to a minority in their own home state. In a country in an advanced stage of de-nationalization like India, political majorities and minorities are measured not in terms of political ideology or platform but religious, ethnic, caste, regional and such other non-political criteria. In such a situation, the grave concern felt by Assamese people over influx of 'foreigners' or immigrants into their state becomes relevant. Because from 1951 to 1981, the Assamese majority in 60 per cent of Assembly constituencies has been reduced to about one-third.

Terrorist violence in Assam started in early 80's on a low key with a series of bomb explosions. There were 83 bomb explosions from 1980 to April 1981 which went largely unnoticed. When the 84th bomb explosion blew a senior government official of the rank of Divisional Commissioner to bits, everybody's attention was drawn towards growing terrorism in Assam.

By far the most gruesome anti-immigrants violence and manslaughter took place in Assam on the eve of February 1983 Assembly elections. For many hours, there was free-for all between the immigrant Bengali Muslims and Assamese anti-'foreign' agitationists and militants in Neilie, Mangaldoi and Gohpur. The Assamese naturally had the upper hand in the clashes which left about 5000 persons dead by the time the holocaust ended. The overwhelming majority of the casualties were from among the Bengali Muslim immigrants.

The ULFA militants also indulged in selected killings of important political personalities and government functionaries. Some of those assassinated were Tankeshwar Dhingia, Youth Congress (I) General Secretary and a former minister, Ranjit Barua, President of Jorhat Congress (I) unit and son of a former minister, Rajiv Rajkhowa, Chairman of the United Minorities Front, Saurav Bora, a student leader, Surendra Paul, Chairman Assam Frontier Tea Company and a brother of Lord Swaraj Paul of Britain, and Daulat Singh Negi, Superintendent of Police Dibrugarh. There have been numerous cases of kidnappings of tea garden managers, businessmen and industrialists for ransom and collection of 'protection money' from them by ULFA militants. Money so collected is utilized for buying arms and ammunitions and otherwise funding their activities.

Hide and seek attacks on security forces and ambushing of their vehicles by ULFA militants continues unabated. The latest of such attacks and killings of security forces took place in June 1997. On 17 June, 1997, the ULFA militants ambushed a bus in which Army personnel were travelling and killed five of them on the spot. Again on 23 June, 1997, they ambushed a Central Reserve Police Force patrol at Bokajan in Karbi Anglong killing four policemen. The war on the state goes on.

That is one side of the picture resulting from the alienation of Assamese people. On the other hand, the creation of tribal states out of the old United Assam of pre-independence days has given rise to demand for creation of yet another tribal state out of the much shrunken state of Assam. The tribal people inhabiting the plains of Assam collectively known as 'Bodos' have been trying to assert their separate identity for quite some time resulting in the demand for a separate state of Bodoland on the pattern of Nagaland, Mizoram and Meghalaya. The Bodos themselves are not a single tribe but comprise various tribes which go by the name 'Bodo'. Ethnologically, the Bodo race is spread from the areas near Purnea district of Bihar in the west to the far corners of Assam along the northern bank of Brahmaputra up to Sadia in Arunachal Pradesh. But the heaviest concentration of Bodos is in the Kokrajhar sub-division of Goalpara district of Assam. They have sizeable concentrations in 24 police station areas of Goalpara, Darrang and Lakhimpur districts of Assam.

Initially, they had organized themselves in the name of the Plains Tribes Council of Assam (PTCA) to assert their identity and articulate their demands. Their rising hope of having a separate state for themselves received a setback when in October 1973 the Prime Minister of India in a speech at Gauhati ruled out any further dismemberment of Assam. That drove the PTCA to desperation. With the growing cult of terrorism all over India, and often with support and encouragement from across the border, the Bodos embarked upon a bloody terrorist course in pursuit of their objectives. On the pattern of All Assam Students Union (AASU) spearheading the agitation against 'foreigners' in Assam during the 80's, they formed the All Bodo Students Union (ABSU) to spearhead their agitation for separation. The ABSU constituted a militant wing entitled the Bodo-Security Force (BSF) to carry on terrorist activities. Although the BSF was outlawed by the government, the ABSU continues to carry forward the agitation.

In course of their terrorist operations the Bodo militants blew up houses, buses, trains and road bridges in far off area of Assam. They kidnapped two tea garden managers and released them after 108 days of captivity in exchange for heavy ransom money believed to be to the tune of around Rs. 20 lacs. In one of their major operations in Gauhati, the capital of Assam, they set off two powerful remote-controlled explosive devices. One of these went off inside a bus killing 25 passers-by. The other exploded within the premises of the old Legislative Assembly hostel but fortunately there were no casualties.

Towards the end of December 1996, a splinter group of Bodo militants known as Bodoland Army Group blew off a concrete road bridge between Bijni and Bongaigaon in lower Assam through a powerful remote control bomb. While seven passengers of a bus which had just passed through the bridge were seriously injured the blasting of the bridge cut off road communication between the

North-East and the rest of the country. But the worst devastation was caused by Bodo terrorists the following evening when they triggered a high explosion on the main railway track connecting Assam with the rest of the country. The powerful bomb blast ripped through the Delhi-bound Brahmaputra Mail train near Sespani railway station in the Bodo stronghold of Kokrajhar district of lower Assam killing at least 300 persons. The deadly explosion took place after the ill-fated train left Kokrajhar railway station after a brief halt and had proceeded about ten kilometres away. This was actually the most inhuman and devastating terrorist act resorted to by Bodo militants in course of their violent campaign.

Through protracted tripartite negotiations involving the government of India, Assam state government and the Bodos, an agreement was reached about four years ago. Under it, the Bodo autonomous council broadly comprising the main Bodo inhabited areas was set-up within the state of Assam. But even after the lapse of four years, the government was not able to finalise the boundary of the area to be administered by the Bodo Autonomous Council (BAC). As a result the ABSU and its political ally, the Bodoland State Movement Council, have expressed their grave dissatisfaction over the functioning of the Autonomous Council. They seem to be veering round to the view that the council did not have enough financial powers and resources and could not function effectively. There is growing possibility of their launching a fresh movement with renewed vigour for a separate Bodoland state. That could mean fresh wave of Bodo violence and terrorism in the strife-torn state of Assam.

A fore-taste of what may be in store was had on 2 July, 1997 when two Army vehicles were blown to pieces by an explosive device placed on a narrow road in the Udalguri area of Darrang district. Six Army personnel were killed in the incident. Since Udalguri is a stronghold of Bodo militants, they are obvious suspects in this terrorist act.

Between ULFA and Bodo militancy and terrorism, which show no signs of abating, Assam continues to bleed. India's North-East as a whole is paying a heavy price in human blood for its journey backwards to the tribal age.

References

1. *Verdict on India*, Beverly Nichols, 1944.
2. *From Jinnah to Zia*, Muhammad Munir, Retd. Chief Justice of Pakistan, 1981.
3. Quoted in an article of Jinnah by Dr. Sachchidanand Sinha in *The Hindustan Review,* September 1949.
4. *From Jinnah to Zia*, Muhammad Munir, Retd. Chief Justice of Pakistan, 1981.
5. *Ibid.*
6. *Pakistan The Garrison State*, Dr. K.L. Kamal, 1982.
7. *Ibid.*
8. *The Times of India* (Patna Edition), dated 26 June, 1997.
9. *A New Look on Modern Indian History*, B.L. Grover.
10. *India's Struggle for Independence*, Bepin Chandra and others, 1989.
11. *Jay Prakash Narayan: Nation Building in India*, edited by Brahmananda.
12. *Ibid.*
13. *Ibid.*
14. *Ibid.*
15. *Ibid.*, emphasis ours.
16. An article entitled "Bhojpur Massacre: Another Endless Chain", by the author published in *The Times of India* (Patna Edition), dated 7 July, 1991.
17. *The Times of India* (Patna Edition), dated 24 April, 1997.

11

The Denouement

The Lost Horizon

In a study of India at the end of the First Five-Year Plan, partly funded by the US Carnegie Corporation and assisted by the Indian Planning Commission and Indian Commission for Economic Affairs in Washington, Barbara Ward wrote:"India today is engaged in a vast experiment to bring its giant economy into the main stream of modern life. Even if this effort of economic expansion concerned only the Indian people, the scale and vision of the attempt should still catch the imagination of the world. To create the conditions of modern living for over four hundred million people, to rescue from extreme poverty nearly half the inhabitants of the free yet underdeveloped world, to bring into the age of atomic energy and outer space one of the most ancient of the world's great civilisations—all these are stirring adventures of the human spirit in their own right. But the significance of India's plans extends beyond the frontiers of India. They are a vital, perhaps a decisive chapter in the wider history of modern man."[1]

That was the vision India evoked in the world when it launched upon its great endeavour to bring up the living conditions of its people to somewhere near the level of the modern world, through its Five-Year Plans. That was the vision of the pre-independence generation of the Indians too at the beginning of independence. Economists in India talked of virgin physical resources in abundance waiting to be tapped for improving the material well-being of the people. They talked of the largest iron ore reserves in the world, of abundant reserves of manganese, bauxite, coal and above all of vast untapped reservoir of hydro-electric power in the country. If only a part of these resources was developed with the help of necessary doses of capital and technology, one believed, the face of the land would change beyond recognition. Reference to large multi-purpose River Valley Projects, generating hydro-electric power, irrigating vast expanse of agricultural land and facilitating water transport, raised vista of unprecedented prosperity in their respective areas. Sky was the limit to the imagined economic betterment that the Five-Year Plans could usher in within the foreseeable future.

The scale of investment of capital and technology needed to give the economy a real boost was so enormous that it could not be left to the mercy of today's magic formula—'the market forces.' Planned effort on a gigantic scale was necessary if any meaningful change was to be thought of and brought about. Economic planning was not an unknown concept in India even before independence. Indian leaders with broad horizons like Jawaharlal Nehru were greatly impressed by the ostensible success of the Soviet economic plans. Before independence, in 1938, a National Planning Committee had been set-up by the Indian National Congress under the chairmanship of Nehru to pursue the idea. Later, as independence approached, some leading intellectuals and groups came out with some broad economic plans of their own for future development of the country. For instance, the great Marxist intellectual, M.N. Roy formulated what he called the 'People's Plan' and even a so-called 'Gandhian Plan' was floated by a Gandhian thinker S.N. Agrawala. A more serious planning effort was made by eight leading industrialists of the country who prepared what came to be called the "Bombay Plan". The idea behind all these endeavours was to promote swift economic development of the country after independence.

It was in this background that a Planning Commission was set-up by the Government of India in 1950 with Prime Minister Nehru as its first chairman. India embarked on the course of planned economic development—with the launching of the First Five-Year Plan in 1952. But, ironically, the beginning of the planning adventure also proved to be the beginning of the end of all euphoria about the miracles of planning. The First Five-Year Plan ending 1956 achieved an annual growth rate of about 3.6 per cent in national income largely offset by an annual population increase of 2.2 per cent. That meant a net increase of only 1.4 per cent per year in national income in course of the First Plan. And the pattern continued more or less right up to mid 70's when the Fifth Plan was launched. In between, the Third Five-Year Plan (1961-66) proved to be a disaster recording an annual income growth rate of only 2.2 per cent totally wiped out by the annual population increase of 2.2 per cent.

Overall, in course of the first 38 years of economic planning, all that India could achieve by way of economic betterment of its people was an average net per capita income growth rate of between one and two per cent. It was just peanut in relation to the magnitude of poverty and economic deprivation in India. A 2 to 3 per cent per capita income growth rate per year is considered quite good in case of developed countries which already have a very high level of per capita income. But for a country like India at the very bottom of the economic ladder, with its per capita income among the lowest in the world, an annual increase of between one and two per cent in its per capita income was a miserable pittance. It was a mockery of the objective "to create the conditions of modern living", as Barbara Ward put it, for the Indian masses, with which the planning endeavour started in India.

As far economic self-reliance proclaimed as a principal goal right from the beginning of planning till today, the less said the better. It evidently implies reduction in the dependence on foreign aid or concessional foreign capital to finance India's economic development. B.K. Nehru's recently published Memoirs throw some light on this widely touted sacred objective of planning. He had a long stint in USA as Executive Director of the World Bank, India's Commissioner General for economic affairs and ambassador. During his tenure in the US, he came to be known as India's biggest fund raiser. The foreign exchange funneled through his efforts went a long way towards financing India's Second and Third Five-Year Plans. J.K. Galbraith, who was US ambassador in India then, once remarked in a lighter vein that with the exception of Chengiz Khan, no single person had carried away more gold from one part of the world to another than Nehru.

One of the surest indicators of India's economic backwardness has been the preponderance of agricultural sector in the country's economy. In any developing economy, development process is reflected in the progressive shift of production pattern and employment from the primary sector like agriculture to secondary sector like industries and services. In Japan, for instance, the percentage of labour force employed in agriculture declined from 33 to 12 between 1960 and 1980. But in India, the planning effort could bring about only an insignificant decline from 74 to 69 per cent, which in the modern context can be considered an attribute of a primitive economy. In terms of production, agriculture contributes around 59 per cent of Gross Domestic Product (GDP) in India as compared to about 4 per cent in the US and 10 per cent in Japan.

What was true of India was equally true of Pakistan and Bangladesh and largely of Sri Lanka. And yet no one seemed to care. Any meaningful economic development reflected in improvement in the standard of living of the people was not the principal agenda of the South Asian people after gaining independence. It is not so even today. Instead they have been perennially embroiled in all manners of religious, sectarian, linguistic, ethnic, regional, casteist and clanish feuds right from the moment they became independent from colonial rule. Political debates in all these countries have remained centred round all kinds of anachronistic issues emanating from a not very glorious past. They are quite reconciled to living not only mentally and emotionally but also economically in the Middle Ages.

The issue of issues— improving their living conditions and raising their standards of living even remotely approaching the modern standards—has never really been anybody's agenda right through. If it was the dream or agenda of some like Nehru and Jinnah to start with, it was lost sight of early in the post-independence era. South Asia lost what should have been its prime agenda right at the start. On top of that, it lost its horizon also fairly early, leading to its ignominious retreat into the past.

They were the left-overs of history which had led to their subjugation at the hands of those who were centuries ahead of them on time scale at the point they came into contact with each other. When the march of history wiped out the Empire regime and made them masters of their own destiny, they had the historic opportunity to run fast and catch up with those ahead of them. But in stead of looking ahead, they started looking back. While those long ahead of them were moving further ahead towards greater and greater integration, the SouthAsians started moving backwards into more and more disintegration. While the front-runners were moving forward from nationalism to supra-nationalism or post-nationalism, South Asian were regressing into multiple divisive sub-nationalisms which were relics of pre-national times.

The result was further widening of the gap between the developed world and South Asia in terms of socio-economic and material well-being of their respective peoples.

It is reflected in their utterly low rating in every acknowledged index of human well-being. Admittedly, the annual per capita income is the most authentic index of the living conditions of a country's inhabitants. Judged by this vital yardstick, the South Asians rank among the poorest in the world. In 1992, their average per capita income stood at less than 350 dollars as against the world average of 4200 dollars. Individual countrywise, Bangladesh has less than 300 dollars, India less than 350 dollars, Pakistan a little above 350 dollars and Sri Lanka less than 400 dollars as their per capita income. Compare their income levels to Thailand's 2740 dollars, Korea's 9700 dollars and Taiwan's 13000 dollars, not to speak of Hong Kong's 23000 dollars and Singapore's 26730 dollars, and the wide gap between South Asians and some other forward looking Asian nations becomes pitiably evident.

Juxtaposed against the per capita income ranging from 10,000 dollars to 20,000 dollars per year of developed countries, the per person income levels of South Asian countries present a picture of abject poverty. In respect of literacy, only 35 per cent of the population over 15 years of age is literate in Pakistan and Bangladesh while the figure is around 49 per cent in India. Only Sri Lanka has a higher literacy rate of about 86 per cent, the highest in South Asia. Occupationally, about 69 per cent of the people in India, 65 per cent in Bangladesh and 55 per cent in Pakistan are employed in agriculture. In Sri Lanka about 80 per cent of the people work on small subsistance farms.

The other known indices of socio-economic status present the same miserable picture. In regard to the status of women, only 22 per cent females are literate in Bangladesh, 21 per cent in Pakistan and about 33 per cent in India. Child health care is a touch-stone to judge the efficacy of public health system in a country. In this regard also, South Asia fares very poorly. The infant mortality rate in Bangladesh is as high as 104.6 deaths per 1000 live births, in Pakistan 99.5 deaths per 1000 and in India 80 deaths per 1000 as against 40 in Thailand and 46 in Philippines, not to talk of the developed world. Only Sri Lanka has a much lower infant mortality rate at 38 per 1000. Similarly, India, Pakistan and Bangladesh have a maternal mortality rate of over 450 per one lac births as against 2 in Ireland, 4 in Israel, 41 in South Korea and 95 in China.

On the state of public health in India, Indranil Basu Roy writes: "There are 60 millions malnourished children in India. About 100,000 of them die due to malnutrition every *month*. Two and a half million children are threatened with blindness due to Vitamin A deficiency...... Despite all the rhetoric about progress and being the most developed of developing nations, India is literally a diseased nation. Its health statistics are worse than those of Ghana, Vietnam, the Philippines or Mexico."[2]

No wonder, in any international economic rating, India, Pakistan and Bangladesh find themselves placed very low. Two years back, the American Heritage foundation prepared a gradation list after scrutinising the actual performance of 140 countries in ten spheres of economic activities. It placed India at a lowly 117th position along with such tiny countries as Sierra Leone and Yemen. Pakistan and Bangladesh were placed lower down still. In its "Human Development Report" 1992, the United Nations Development Programme (UNDP) ranked India as 121st on the human development index on the basis of such indicators as income, health, education etc. Pakistan and Bangladesh figured lower still.

They have no dearth of excuses. They blame it on their high population growth rate which eats up much of what they achieve by way of increased output of goods and services or GDP. But that amounts to arguing in a circle. Because high population growth rate itself is a by-product and surest symptom of socio-economic backwardness and poverty. All the rich, developed countries of the world have almost static or marginally rising population growth rates.

The present overzealous protagonists of economic reforms, liberalization, open-doorism or globalization hold the so-called 'socialistic', controlled and close-doorist economic policies of South Asian countries responsible for all the deprivations and poverty of their peoples. But this too is wide off the marks or at any rate only partially explains the economic stagnation of South Asia. For those who have their visions right and sights correctly adjusted to right goals, ideology or any ideology-related shibboleths or vaguenesses do not come in the way of performing and achieving. Communist China under the stewardship of Deng Xio Ping, the 'paramount' leader of the Chinese communist party in post-Mao era, put ideology quietly aside when it came to achieving its goal of rapid economic advancement. Once a nation is seized with an intense urge to bring about a quantum jump in the living conditions of its people, no ideological hang-over can block its way.

An Indian corporate executive who visited China in June 1986 as a member of a delegation of Indian Merchants' Chamber recorded his impressions as follows: "No sooner you enter Kaitak airport of Beijing from the plane and thereafter enter the city..... You start disbelieving your eyes that you have entered a totalitarian country where Marxism rules supreme......The new slogans of 'walk away from Marxism Bookism' and 'Nothing wrong in embracing westernisation' have been given to the people by the Chinese Communist Party (CCP)".[3] In the name of his famous slogan of "four modernisations", Deng started leading his communist China away from the orthodox 'socialist' economy in order to keep pace with the world that mattered.

"Indeed", wrote an American columnist in 1992,"the joke making the rounds among Chinese intellectuals is this: under the leadership of the communist party, we are advancing from socialism to capitalism. It is true that one can spend days rummaging through the free markets of cities like Guangzhou or Shanghai and find little trace of communism."[4] "Evidently", concluded the columnist, "Deng's China seemed to have taken the four super capitalist `dragons' of Asia— Singapore, Taiwan, South Korea and Hong Kong — as partial model for its economic development." Deng's line was officially confirmed by the Chinese Communist Party Congress in October 1992.

In case of South Asia, it would be wrong to hold ideology or anything remotely connected with that responsible for the region's miserable plight. Nor would it be right to blame it on constraints like population growth rate, resource crunch etc. It is not so much a case of performance failure on the part of South Asian leaders, political parties and peoples as of their *aspirational* failure. They have failed to catch up with others in the race for human development because of the lack of right aspirations, goals and visions. While others, including the East Asian countries, have been forging ahead, the South Asians have remained bogged down in sorting out their internecine, historical conflicts and divergences based on religion, tribe, caste, language etc. They have no mental space left for imagining and aspiring for any meaningful upliftment of their living conditions. With their flawed vision, clouded by all kinds of anachronisms, they have wasted 50 years of their freedom from colonial rule stewing in their own juice.

21st Century Beckons

They are both parts of the same continent. South Asia and East Asia are geographical neighbours and yet socially and economically they are as wide apart as 17th or 18th century from 21st century. While South Asians are still glued to the socio-economic mores of the 17th or 18th century, the East Asians are hurtling fast into the 21st century. In fact, even as the eventful 20th century is about to be consigned to the dust-bin of history, the East Asians have already arrived in the 21st century.

Japan had caught up with the march of time about a century back and has since kept pace with it in spite of ups and downs in its political destiny. During the Middle Ages right up to late 19th century, Japan was under feudal dispensation socially, politically and economically. Towards the end of the 12th century, political power in Japan passed from the hands of the Emperor to the most successful feudal community Chief with the title "Shogun" which literally means "barbarian— quelling generalissimo". Since early 17th century, a long line of 'Shoguns' belonging to one particular clan ruled over Japan—until the end of the institution of 'Shogunate'. It was during the 'Shogunate' that the western imperial powers appeared in Japan during the 19th century. By 1860, Japan, like China earlier, had to sign unequal treaties with America, Britain, France and Russia placing Japan in an inferior or even subservient position in relation to these powers. The treaties, for instance, provided for opening of Japanese ports for trade by western powers, stationing of their consuls in Japan, grant of extra-territorial rights to them etc. The Japanese people held the Shogun regime responsible for these humiliating unequal treaties and there was a sudden outburst of loyalty to the Emperor of Japan who for centuries had only "reigned without governing." This resulted in the Restoration of the Meiji Emperor of Japan to full sovereign power in 1867. And Meiji Restoration did to Japan in about 20 years what the independent republics of South Asia have failed to do in 50 years. That is, it brought about the modernization of Japan.

In fact, Meiji Restoration not only freed Japan from the shackles of the feudal Shogun regime politically but also heralded the beginning of economic and, to some extent, social revolution of great importance. In the economic sphere, Japan set upon a course of rapid industrialization which in due course was to bring it at par with the already industrialized west. Since private capital was shy of investing in modern industries, the Meiji government developed modern industries, particularly basic heavy industries, through government enterprise. (That, incidentally could have inspired Nehru to undertake the development of heavy industries through public sector during the initial planning years in India.) Western technicians were employed on a large scale to train the Japanese. The Government also helped the growth of private industries through incentives and subsidies and encouraged Japanese students to go to the west for education in science and technology. As a result of all this conscious and concerted drive, Japan emerged as a developed modern nation to challenge the western powers by the beginning of the 20th century.

It continued to develop fast through the First and Second World Wars until its defeat at the hands of the Allied Powers in 1945. At the end of Second World War, Japan lay totally shattered politically and economically. But the Japanese people picked up the thread from where they had left and started on their new course of economic progress and prosperity after 1945, almost simultaneously with the newly independent South Asian nations. Starting almost from scratch, they have scaled new heights and reached the top of the world in the sphere of economic progress and prosperity.

But it is not the Japanese miracle that the South Asians have particularly to take note of. For Japan was already a developed nation before the Second World War and had only to rebuild its economy on the ruins of the war. It is the example of the other, relatively unknown and insignificant little miracle-makers of East Asia which represents a real challenge to the stagnating, squabbling peoples of South Asia. The true miracle makers of East Asia today are South Korea, Taiwan, Hong Kong and Singapore, all minor players in the Asian drama till the other day. Like South Asian nations, they were all colonies of imperial powers before the end of the Second World War. Like the South Asians again, they all started on their own course of progress and development after getting freedom from colonial powers after the end of the war.

To recapitulate, Taiwan (Formosa) was conquered by Japan in the First Sino-Japanese war of 1894-95 from China which ceded it to Japan in 1895. Since then it continued to be a Japanese colony until the Japanese defeat in World War II. When China was finally taken over by the communists in 1949, Chiang Kai Shek, the defeated Kuo Min Tang leader, fled to Taiwan and established the little republic which is still claimed by China as a part of it.

Korea was annexed by Japan in 1910 and remained its colony until the Second World War. After Japan's defeat in 1945, the US and Soviet Union divided Korea into two zones— the North and the South— for accepting the Japanese surrender. Thus North Korea came under Soviet and South Korea under American military occupation immediately at the end of the war. This was followed by the bitter Korean war beginning June 1950 ending in armistice in July 1953. It was only after the end of hostilities that South Korea embarked on its path of economic recovery and development.

The remaining two—Hong Kong and Singapore— were British colonies, like South Asia. Singapore which was a crown colony became independent along with British Malaya only in 1957, a decade after the independence of South Asia. After remaining a part of Malaysian Federation for some time, Singapore separated from Malaysia amicably and emerged as a fully independent state on its own. And Hong Kong remained a British colony till June 1997 when it reverted back to China where it belonged.

To think these tiny ex-colonial Asian countries would make it so big in the arena of economic development and material prosperity is the real wonder of the post-war world economic scenario. Since the beginning of World War II, living standards have trippled in Europe and America. But in the miracle making countries of Asia Pacific region, living standards have risen *thirty-fold* or more. Singapore and Hong Kong now have a higher per capita income than Britain, their former colonial master. Taiwan and South Korea are richer than ex-imperial countries like Spain and Portugal. Ten years ago in 1987, as much as 20 per cent of America's huge foreign trade deficit was accounted for by trade with these four economic giants of East Asia— South Korea, Taiwan, Hong Kong and Singapore. These countries have been among the achievers of the highest economic growth rate in the world.

If East Asia, with identical colonial background, has done it, why has South Asia lagged so miserably behind? The entire book, which is a factual record of the 50 wasted years of South Asia's independence from colonial regime, provides the answer. A more relevant form of the same question can be: If Asia Pacific or East Asia has made it, why South Asia cannot make it? Or better still, can South Asia also make it?

The question can be answered by referring to the contemporary economic and commercial developments in the world. On the one hand, a pervasive Technological Revolution is sweeping across the world in this last quarter of the 20th century, which is going to spill over to and accelerate in the 21st century. If the Industrial Revolution based on fossil fuels like coal, oil and other minerals determined the fate of the world during the last two centuries, it is the progressively unfolding technological revolution which is going to shape the world during the next century or centuries. The physical resources of coal, oil or metals stored underneath the earth's surface, are limited and exhaustible, but technology is not. For technology is not a product of matter or muscle but of mind, and human mind is an inexhaustible source of technological innovations. Technological Revolution has made it possible for a nation or group of nations to produce goods and services which can out-sell others in quality and price and thereby enrich their people.

On the other hand, the world as a whole is opening up as a gigantic market in which to sell your products and increase your wealth. How a quantum leap in sale of a country's products in markets abroad brings about a quantum leap in prosperity of the country and its people has been well brought in a newspaper column by Swaminathan S. Aiyar, editor of *The Economic Times*. He writes: "Through most of history, living standards were stagnant. Prof. Colis Clark estimates that living standards in the Roman empire in the third century were comparable with those in England in 1850, France and Germany in 1870, and Japan in 1950. But subsequently incomes sky rocketed. In 16 developed countries in the century after 1870, per capita income rose 700 per cent and labour productivity 1200 per cent. There were many reasons for this, of which one stands out—their exports increased 96,500 per cent. That mind-boggling figure underlines how trade revolutionised living standards, how inter-dependence provided infinitely more prosperity than the earlier self-sufficiency."[5]

Malcolm Rifkind, the former British Foreign Secretary, wrote in November 1996: "we have a vision of global free trade by 2020—our 2020 vision for the world. This is achievable. All around the world, countries are entering into commitments to free up trade flows. There is now a window of opportunity to spread the benefits of free trade and open markets on a truly global scale..... Prosperity, based on closer trade and economic ties with other countries, acts as a powerful force for world peace and stability..... Growing prosperity provides the resources for raising standards.....There is no more effective means of promoting higher standards than by allowing countries to make the most of the opportunities of free trade."[6]

With such wide open opportunities afforded by technological revolution on the one hand and opening up of a vast world market on the other, it is for the South Asian countries themselves to set their visions right and go for the big leap forward rather than standing still or regressing into the past. Even their immediate South-East Asian neighbours, leaving aside the North-East Asian giants like South Korea, Taiwan and Hong Kong have been doing it and are well set on their course to progress. The ASEAN is another success story, if not a miracle, which South Asians can look up to as a model for their own salvation.

Four years ago in July 1993, Malaysia, Thailand and Indonesia launched a growth triangle comprising parts of their territories fully integrated for purposes of economic development. The triangle covered five provinces in southern Thailand, four northern states in Malaysia and two Indonesian provinces in Sumatra, across the Straits of Malacca. The aim was to ease the flow of goods, capital and labour within a 200,000 square kilometre region with 20 million people to improve the lot of poorer, neglected corners in the three countries. Malaysia, with greater per capita income than the other two countries, hoped to shift its simple electronic assembly work to southern Thailand or northern Sumatra where labour is cheaper while retaining high tech research and testing in its own territory. Rejecting some muted criticism that by this arrangement Malaysia stood to gain more than its partners, the Malaysian finance minister said: "We must get rid of the *old mind-set* that the cooperative arrangement will create relative disadvantages for some members."[7]

That would show how national boundaries become irrelevant when it comes to achieving significant economic growth and bettering the lot of the people. West Europeans have shown the way and now South-East Asians are showing it. Both the European Union and ASEAN have shown that for making good in the world market, countries of a geographical region have to come together, establish closer economic ties among themselves first. Nations geographically placed together can set about conquering the world commercially only after establishing close economic and commercial linkages among themselves. They can reap tremendous economic benefits and become commercially competitive worldwide by dovetailing their available resources and inputs like labour, capital, raw materials, technologies etc. as well as availing of their combined market potential.

It is to reap these benefits that Thailand, Malaysia and Indonesia embarked upon the growth triangle idea which amounted to virtual abolition of national frontiers in regard to economic activities. It is a measure of the economic and commercial success of ASEAN that in 1987, at least 5 per cent of the total foreign trade deficit of America was on account of the ASEAN countries. They are making their presence felt in the American market because they have first integrated their own economies successfully. Even developed countries like the US and Canada have established a free trade area between themselves and with the less developed Mexico, because they are geographically placed together. No group or combination of countries can develop their full economic potential and compete in the world market by ignoring their geographical togetherness.

South Asians have yet to learn their lessons in this regard. A simple comparison between the mind-set of the fast developing Asia Pacific Rim countries and South Asians would confirm that. At the Osaka Summit of Asia Pacific Economic Cooperation (APEC) in 1995, the member countries offered tariff cuts on trade in large number of items among themselves. China reduced tariffs on 4000 items, Malaysia on 1300 items and Australia on 1500 items. In sharp contract, at the SAARC summit in 1997, India offered tariff cuts on 106 items, Pakistan on 35 items and Sri Lanka on 31 items only. That goes to show how far behind South Asian countries are in regional economic cooperation in comparison to the APEC countries.

No doubt, they formed the SAARC about a decade back in a bid to emulate others. But apart from the ritual of annual summitry, which is gone into routinely from year to year, with leaders mouthing homilies of togetherness and cooperation, all that SAARC has done so far is nothing more than an exercise in tokenism. For what to talk of cooperation in trade and commerce, it is not easy even to travel from one SAARC country to another, the only exception being travel between India and Nepal. There are cumbersome formalities of passport, visa, foreign exchange etc. to comply with, besides walls of suspicions and prejudices which hinder free travel from one country to another.

As for cooperation in trade, a telling example is provided by the Indo-Pak wheat deal of 1996. Pakistan agreed to import 10,000 tons of wheat from India through a third country by paying 30 dollars more per ton. India faced a similar situation during the sugar shortage crisis two years earlier. This happening in the 8th year of SAARC's creation was a comment enough on the seriousness which the member countries attached to it. According to one estimate, trade within the South Asian countries is a measly 3.5 per cent of their trade with the rest of the world. A newspaper columnist covering the 9th SAARC Summit at Male in May 1997 reports that "the Maldivian capital, where SAARC summit is taking place now, is literally chocked with imported Japanese or American cars. Nobody here seems to have heard of India— built Maruti."[8]

In such a situation of cool and frozen economic interaction, it was an achievement of sorts when the 9th SAARC summit at Male held in May, 1997 decided to implement South Asia Free Trade Area (SAFTA) economic regime by the year 2001. If actually achieved, SAFTA can turn out to be the engine of rapid economic growth for each of the SAARC countries. Through bilateral and multilateral economic cooperation the SAARC nations cannot only enrich themselves but also count for more in the global trade. Provided of course SAFTA really comes through by 2001. That is, if in the meanwhile, Indo-Pak relations do not deteriorate sharply over Kashmir or Indo-Sri Lanka relations do not slump over Sri Lankan Tamilians question or Bangladesh does not switch over to a political regime based on anti-Indianism. All these are variables which are very much within the realm of possibility. One can only keep one's fingers crossed.

But however stiff they may stand with their backs to each other, India, Pakistan, Bangladesh and Sri Lanka cannot escape the logic of geography. India may make forays into the Indian ocean rim countries to look for cooperation in trade and commerce. In fact 14 Indian ocean rim countries have already moved in the direction of forging strategic alliance and close economic ties by forming the Indian Ocean RimAssociation for Regional Cooperation (IORARC). Not to be left behind, Pakistan and Bangladesh are looking up to Muslim countries physically as wide apart from each other and from South Asia as Turkey on the north-western fringe of Asia touching southern Europe, Egypt on the northern tip of Africa and Indonesia and Malaysia in South-EastAsia. At a Summit held at Istanbul, Turkey, in June 1997, the Prime Ministers of Turkey, Iran, Nigeria, Egypt, Pakistan, Bangladesh, Malaysia and Indonesia agreed to set up the so-called D-8 group of nations. It aims at implementing socio-economic development based on the principles of peace, justice, equality and democracy.

As far as economic integration is concerned, there is little to integrate between Pakistan and Bangladesh on the one side and the rest of the D-8 countries on the other. In the same way, there is not much to integrate between India and the other Indian Ocean rim countries. If Pakistan, Bangladesh and India are interested in forming international political groupings, that is another matter. But if they are serious about bettering the lot of their people through meaningful economic cooperation and integration with others, they cannot ignore geography. They have to look for partners where they are, that is, in their neighbourhood and not go about hunting for economic cooperators in distant corners of the globe. All viable and successful regional economic entities or unions in Europe, America, and Asia are based on geographical proximity among the nations of a region. South Asia cannot be an exception.

India, Pakistan, Bangladesh and Sri Lanka are natural allies. They cannot wish away geography even if they wanted to. They have already wasted 50 precious years beating about the bush, seeing enemies in friends, fighting phantoms and ghosts. In the process, they have turned one of the most peaceful regions of the world during the colonial regime into one of the most dangerous and violent ones. At the end of the most turbulent half-century of their recent history, the incoming century beckons them to make a new start, to embark on a new course based on peace not conflict, dialogue not confrontation, and whole-hearted economic cooperation to bring up their people in the modern age.

With all the opportunities at their door, the 21st century throws a challenge at them. The question is: "Will South Asia take it?"

References

1. *India and the West*, Barbara Ward, Indian edition published in 1961.
2. Article entitled "Still on the Sick Bed", by Indranil Basu Roy, published in *The Times of India* (Patna edition), dated 8 September, 1996.
3. Letter of the Corporate Executive, Mr. Wazirani, written to the author in 1986.
4. "China's Secret Farewell to Communism", Nicholas D. Ekristof, *New York Times Service*.
5. *The Times of India* (Lucknow edition), dated 23 December, 1996.
6. *Britain's Vision 2020*, Macolm Rifkind, then British Foreign Secretary, published in *The Times of India*, dated 30 November, 1996.
7. *The Times of India*, dated 28 October, 1993.
8. *The Times of India*, dated 12 May, 1997.

Selected Book References

A short list of books and documents referred to, consulted or relied upon in writing of this book is given below. Many books from which notes had been taken in course of my studies during the past several years which came in handy at the time of writing have also been included in the list. For the sake of convenience the books have been listed under a few broad groupings subject-wise, although many deal with more than a single topic.

Multi-National History

Hellenism: The history of a civilisation, Arnold J. Toynbee.

A Study of History, Arnold J. Toynbee, Abridgement of Volumes I to VI by D.C. Somervell.

The Hellenistic World, F.W. Walbank.

Glimpses of World History, Jawaharlal Nehru.

A History of the Far East in Modern Times, Harold M. Vinacke.

History of Japan, R.K. Majumdar and A.N. Shrivastava.

A Concise History of China, Jian Bozan, Shao Xunzheng and Hu Hua.

Modern Europe to 1870, C.J.H. Hayes.

Europe Since Nepolean, David Thompson.

Modern Europe up to 1945, C.D. Hazen.

Roman Britain, R.G. Collingwood and J.N.L. Myres.

Visions of the Past, Christopher Taylor and Richard Muir.

An Unfinished History of the World, Hugh Thomas.

The Global Conflict (The international rivalry of the great powers 1880-1970), C.J. Bartlett.

Studies in the Development of Capitalism, Maurice Dobb.

Indian History

The Wonder that was India, A.L. Basham.

A History of India, Romila Thapar.

A Short History of the Muslim Rule in India, Ishwari Prasad.

A History of South India, Nilkanta Shastri.

A New Look on Modern India History, B.L. Grover.

The Writings and Speeches of Edmund Burke, Volume V: India and Bengal 1774-1785 edited by P.J. Marshall, 1981.

The Oxford History of India, Vincent A. Smith Edited by Percival Spear, 1958.

Modern India 1885-1947, Sumit Sarkar.

Social Background of Indian Nationalism, A.R. Desai.
History of Ancient India, Arun Bhattacharjee.
History of Political Thought, Ancient and Medieval Volumes I and II, J.P. Suda.

India: Pre- and Post-Independence

Verdict on India, Bexerly Nichols, 1944.
Reflections No. 1: The Bihar Tragedy (25th Oct.-31st Dec., 1946), Sayed Abdul Aziz, Barrister-at-Law, December 1946.
India's Struggle for Independence, Bipin Chandra, Mridula Mukherji, Aditya Mukherji, K.N. Pannikar and Sucheta Mahajan.
Freedom Struggle, Bipin Chandra, Amles Tripathi and Barun De, 1971.
Mission with Mountbatten, Alan Campbell, Johnson, 1951.
Operation Rescue, Lt. General S.K. Sinha PVSM (retd.)
Freedom at Midnight, Larry Collins and Dominique Lappierre, 1976.
Last Days of the British Raj, Michael Edwards.
Freedom Movement in Bihar, Volume III, Dr. K.K. Datta.
Constitutional Government in India, M.V. Pylee.
Introduction to the Constitution of India, Durga Das Basu.
Constituent Assembly Debates, Volume VII.
Jawaharlal Nehru, M. Chalapati Rao, 1979.
Speeches and Writings of Jawaharlal Nehru, (Four Volumes) (Selected Parts).
The Nehrus and the Gandhis— An Indian Dynasty, Tariq Ali, 1985.
Nation Building in India: Jay Prakash Narain (Collection of Speeches and Writings), edited by Brahmananda, 1975.
J.P.: His Biography, Allan and Wendy Scarfe, 1975.
India and the West, Barbara Ward, 1961.
India Today, Frank Moraes, 1960.
India From Curzon to Nehru and After, Durga Das, 1971.
The Government and Politics of India, W.H. Morris-Jones, 1964.
The Crisis of India, Ronald Seagal.
Indo-Pak War, V.P. Juneja, December 1971.
India: The Siege Within (Challenges to Nation's Unity), M. J. Akbar, 1985.
India: A Million Mutinies Now, V.S. Naipaul, 1990.
India: A People Betrayed, A.S. Dasan and Bhamy V. Shenoy.
Change in India, Robert W. Stern, 1993.
A Heart Full of Burden, T.N. Seshan, 1995.
India Wins Freedom, Moulana Abul Kalam Azad.

South Asia—Post-Independence

Governments and Politics of South Asia, J.C. Johari, M. Nazrul Islam, W.A. Wiswa-Warnapala, Lok Raj Baral and Prakash Chander, 1991.
The Nature of the Non-Western World, Vera Micheles Dean, 1957.

Old Societies and New States: The Quest for Modernity in Asia and Africa, edited by Clifford Geertz, Indian edition 1971.

Empire and Islam (Punjab and the Making of Pakistan), David Gilmartin, 1989.

Report of the Court of Enquiry into Punjab (Pakistan) Disturbances of 1953, Justice Muhammad Munir and Justice M.R. Kayani, 1954.

Friends Not Masters, President Mohammad Ayub Khan of Pakistan.

Pakistan Crisis, David Loshak, 1971.

From Jinnah to Zia, Mohammad Munir Khan, Retd. Chief Justice of Pakistan, 1981.

Politics in Pakistan: The Nature and Direction of Change, Khalid B. Sayeed, 1980.

Pakistan: The Garrison State, Dr. K.L. Kamal, 1982.

Jinnah as I knew him, an article by Dr. Sachchidananda Sinha Published in *The Hindustan Review*, September, 1949.

Inside Pakistan, Jamal Naqvi, Shaukat Ali and Farz Ali, 1986.

The Sole Spokesman: Jinnah, the Muslim League and the Demand for Pakistan, Ayesha Jalal, 1985.

Pakistan: Birth and Early Days, Sri Prakash, India's First High Commissioner to Pakistan, 1965.

Report of the Independent South Asian Commission on Poverty Alleviation: Meeting The Challange, November 1992.

From SARC to SAARC: Mile stones in the Evolution of Regional Cooperation in South Asia, vol. I (1980-1988).

Internet-factual information about Pakistan, Bangladesh and Sri Lanka.

Violence and Terrorism

Communal Riots in India, S.K. Ghosh, 1987.

Communal Violence: Psycho-social, Political and Economic Dimensions, an article by Dildar Khan Published in *Denouement* magazine in March 1990.

Street Fighting Years, Tariq Ali, 1987.

Denouement (Magazine) : The Roots of Violence, March 1990.

Terrorism and Crimes in India, S.H. Subba Rao.

Terrorism, article by Dr. Krishna Mohan Mathur published in *National Police Academy Journal*, January-June 1986.

Terrorism in India, edited by S.C. Tiwari, 1990.

The Terrorism Reader, Walter Laqueur.

Terrorism: History and Facets in the World and in India, N.S. Saxena, 1985.

The Naxalite Movement, Biplab Das Gupta.

Naxalism in the Plains of Bihar, Kalyan Mukherji and Rajendra Singh Yadav.

International Terrorism, edited by Charles W. Kegley Jr., 1990.
Terrorism: World under Siege, S.K. Ghosh, 1995.
Beyond Terrorism, Salman Khurshid, 1994.
Lajja (Shame), a fiction on Post-Ayodhya communal riots in Bangladesh, Taslima Nasrin, English edition 1994.
Mizoram: Dynamics of Change, Dr. Animesh Ray, IAS, 1982.

Contemporaneous World Affairs

New Dimensions of Peace, Chester Bowles, a former US Ambassador in India.
The Abolition of War (The Peace Movement in Britain 1914-1919), Keith Robbins.
The Achieving Society, David C. Meelelland, 1961.
Inside Europe Today, John Gunther, 1961.
Communist China Today, S. Chandrasekhar, 1962.
Khrushchev's Russia, Edward Crankshaw, 1959.
Religion and Peace, edited by Home A. Jack, 1966.
The Anarchical Society (A study of Order in World Politics), Hedley Bull, Second edition, 1995.
Preparing For the Twenty-first Century, Paul Kennedy, 1993.
The Third Wave, Alvin Toffler, 1980.
Power Shift, Alvin Toffler, 1990.

Index